THE DEEP SELF

The aim of CONSCIOUSNESS CLASSICS is to bring to life significant publications in the consciousness field, which have no longer been available, and showcase new books, which are destined to become classics.

CONSCIOUSNESS CLASSICS conserve these texts as the authors originally intended them, in a carefully re-designed contemporary format for new generations of readers. These books are an important legacy of some of the groundbreaking consciousness explorers of our times.

THE DEEP SELF

CONSCIOUSNESS EXPLORATION
IN THE ISOLATION TANK

JOHN C. LILLY, M.D.

Published by:
Gateways Books and Tapes / IDHHB, Inc.
P.O. Box 370
Nevada City, CA 95959
http://www.gatewaysbooksandtapes.com
Layout and cover design by Matthias Schossig, iTRANSmedia

Library of Congress Cataloging-in-Publication Data

Lilly, John Cunningham, 1915
  The deep self : consciousness exploration in the isolation tank / John
C. Lilly.
      p. cm. -- (Consciousness classics)
Previously published: New York : Simon and Schuster, 1977.
Includes bibliographical references and index.
  ISBN 0-89556-116-6
  1. Sensory deprivation. 2. Consciousness. I. Title. II. Gateways
consciousness classics.
  RC489.S44 L53 2002

Preface to the Consciousness Classics Edition of *The Deep Self*

Since this book was first published in 1977, it affected the lives of hundreds of thousands of readers. *The Deep Self* has been a profound inspiration for people to explore unchartered domains of consciousness. The testimonials in this book document the maiden inner space voyages of many people who have become household names of pioneering consciousness: Gregory Bateson, Werner Erhard, Richard Feynman, E.J. Gold, Stanislav Grof, Alejandro Jodorowsky, Jerry Rubin, Andrew Weil, Robert Anton Wilson, to name a few.

Change is in the nature of consciousness, as well as in many external things which have gone through transitions since this book first appeared. However, the original text of the book is as poignant and significant today as it was thirty years ago. We included the entire text of the first edition, carefully redesigning the layout and adding a few updates. Only the chapter on tank design, written by Steve Conger for the original edition of *The Deep Self,* is not included in this edition since it has become obsolete through the developments in tank design over the past thirty years. The seeds that were planted with this Consciousness Classic over thirty years ago, have fruited in time. The Samadhi Tank Company is alive and well, perfecting the floatation tank design and making the technology available to thousands of users of this highly efficient exploration tool worldwide—from their headquarters, now in Northern California (www.samadhitank.com). Other floatation tank manufacturers have followed their example; experimentation, inner exploration and scientific studies using the floatation technique are being conducted globally.

John C. Lilly, M.D. died in the fall of 2001 in Los Angeles. It was his wish that this book be re-published.

The Editors

Prologue to the Gateways edition
by John C. Lilly

In everyday life one's human biocomputer is busy programming, being programmed, looking for future programs, thinking about past programs, and
carrying out the actions made necessary in the course of these activities.
One's only real respite is going to bed and sleep at night. Here one can leave
this behind and sometimes enter alternate domains of thought, experience,
and emotion not necessarily in the day's consensus reality programmed for
the most part by our society and our immersion in it. If one knows how one
can meditate, use auto-hypnosis, daydream, night dream, or practice lucent
dreaming as if one were awake and fully functioning in the strange and
wonderful dream domain.

For these latter pursuits one uses the ordinary bedroom in one's home,
usually only at night, the time at which fellow human beings agree to let
you be alone to do what you will without interruptions. There is now at
least one other place where you can have this freedom to think, feel, and do
internally that which you and no one else chooses. This place I found,
invented, discovered, was led to, guided in such a way that I hunted for the
first one of these places, or I needed such a place for my own research on
myself, the Universe, the Divine, the New and Unexpected never before
seen or programmed by any known persons.

This place or places is called by different names: the Isolation Tank,
Floatation Tank, the Solitude Tank, the Womb-to-Tomb Wet Box, the
Place one can rent for Money to Seek Nothingness, etc. In 1954 when I was
floating in the silence, darkness, wetness, alone, after the 1st ten hours, I
called it the Isolation-Solitude-Confinement-Happiness-Freedom-Domain.
I realized that noone at that time would believe me if I used that name: they
were still caught in belief systems in which what I was doing was to be

feared and avoided because one was in Sensory Deprivation. I knew nothing of Sensory Deprivation: I found the tank was and is a vast and rich source of new experience or 'inperience' as Franklyn-Merrell Wolff calls it. One is not deprived; one is rewarded.

Some of my 'inperiences' were so far from consensus opinion and reality, that I avoided relating them to my colleagues in the National Institute of Mental Health. I expected that they would make quick judgements: "those are psychopathological experiences: he must be mentally ill." So for the first 2 years I enjoyed my findings alone and without outside judgements, happy with the basic discoveries – insights and alien friends I found not by seeking them. At times I was so overwhelmed with the happiness I found that I was tempted to share it with others. I learned several years before this not to share my psychoanalytic work with anyone: the ideas and new insights lost power in the telling.

I was very lucky and privileged to be the first human to enter the tank domains. There was no literature to program my inperiences; no one more knowledgeable than myself to advise or teach me. I was really free!

I made no reports to anyone on either the activity or the results until some years later. In the meantime I was free to integrate and investigate as I felt necessary. In the first 2 years I was offered LSD-25 from my colleagues in NIMH. I refused it without explanation. My reasons were connected with the tank work and what I called "my brain and mind baseline" unmodified by chemicals or the basic belief systems of others. I spent 10 years developing this baseline which read, "my basic beliefs are unbelievable and incredible."

1964 ended the 10 years. I felt ready to try LSD-25 in the tank of sea water in the Lab of the Communication Research Institute in St. Thomas in the U.S. Virgin Islands.

I suggest that if you would like to find out what happened, read the books, *The Center of The Cyclone. Programming and Metaprogramming in the Human Biocomputer,* and *The Scientist.* Of course if you do this you are no longer free the way I was: free to be unusually happy, unusually frightened and quite free to be anything I wanted or the suprahuman intelligences wanted at unexpected times. If you disbelieve me, try it your own way: it's a vast universe and I am only a human being as I write this for you, another human being on the planet Earth. Have fun. I do and did. Good luck.

John C. Lilly

Acknowledgments

This edition of *The Deep Self,* is respectfully dedicated to Dr. Albert Hofmann on the occasion of his 100th Birthday in 2006, and in honor of the long friendship he shared with Dr. Lilly, both pioneers in modern human consciousness research. It is also dedicated to Lee and Glenn Perry at Samadhi Tank, Grass Valley, California, www.samadhitank.com, for designing and producing state of the art Isolation Tanks based on Dr. Lilly's research, and their long enduring presence in his life, including their efforts to republish this edition. Faustin Bray at, www.soundphotosynthesis.com, for her steadfast support of Dr. Lilly through her extensive video and audio archives, chronicling Dr. Lilly's work, and her unwavering dedicated friendship to him in time of need. Brian Wallace for his music, poetry, art, and many contributions to Dr. Lilly in California and Maui, Hawaii. Ann and Jerry Moss for providing a safe haven for John to land in Hawaii during his retirement and all their many kind blessings. Craig and Aliya Inglis for their contributions to Isolation Research and Tanking technology. Dr. Larry and Char Raithaus, Roberta Goodman, Paradise Newland, Dr. Michael Hyson for providing a family and support to Dr. Lilly in Hawaii. Barbara Clarke Lilly, daughter and long-time travel and research companion.

Lisa Lyon Lilly, John's confidant, daughter, and muse. Heartfelt thanks also to Cynthia Lilly Cantwell, as well as John and Colette Lilly. John Allen, Institute of Eco-Technics, London, Biosphere II Founder and trusted colleague. Napier Marten and Ian Middleton for continuing Dr. Lilly's efforts in Cetacean conservation, www.cetaceaproject.org. Rudi Vogt for covering the cosmic waterfront in Switzerland. Thomas Welch, Esq. for his wise counsel. Dr.

Beverly Potter at Ronin Books, Berkeley, California, www.ronin-pub.com, for her continued championing and publication of Dr. Lilly's literary works in the United States, including *The Scientist*, *Programming The Human Bio-Computer*, *The Quiet Center*, and *The Steersman*. Dr. Lilly's World Wide Web site, www.johnclilly.com was designed by James Suhre, also known as BigTwin, who along with Patricia Sims, serves as a director for the John C. Lilly Research Institute, Inc. Both Jim and Patricia cared greatly for John, his love of the sea, dolphins, whales, and continue his work through their efforts. Finally, to the joyous memory of John's family and friends that have gone on before us: Charles Richard Lilly, Dr. Timothy Francis Leary, Dr. Oscar Janiger, Allen Ginsberg, and Caroline Bentley Ely.

Philip Hansen Bailey
Executive Director, John C. Lilly Research Institute

Dedication

To Craig Enright, M.D., for his courage, understanding, compassion and his personal explorations of the Deep Self.

Craig Enright died in 1975 from damage sustained in an automobile accident in Big Sur, California, at age thirty-three years. He was a medical doctor of a new sort: one fully aware of the vast range of the states of being of the human mind. He had many personal experiences of the far-reaching range of his own mind, and deeply appreciated such experiences in his friends and in his patients. He was an explorer of the inner domains; he used any available means of exploration. He was a scuba diver, guitar player, motorcyclist, a raconteur, an enthusiast for a full life in many inner/outer domains. He was an excellent therapist of the body, of the mind and of the spirit.
We miss him.

The Deep Self

Contents

APPENDICES

Laws as such do not make people better, they must practise certain things, in order to become attuned to inner truth. This form of truth resembles apparent truth only slightly.

The Tales of Nasrudin
Idries Shah

To become impartial, dispassionate, and *general purpose*, objective, and open-ended, one must test and adjust the level of credence in each of his sets of beliefs. If ever Man is to be faced with real organisms with greater wisdom, greater intellect, greater minds than any single man has, then we must be open, unbiased, sensitive, general purpose, and dispassionate. Our needs for fantasies must have been analyzed and seen for what they are and are not or we will be in even graver troubles than we are today.

Our search for mentally healthy paths to human progress in the innermost realities depends upon progress in this area. Many men have floundered in this area of belief. I hope this work can help to find a way through one of our stickiest intellectual-emotional regions.

Programming and Metaprogramming in the Human Biocomputer

Introduction

It is a rare event when an author-researcher has the clear opportunity to present to a new generation of researchers and searchers an original contribution based on twenty-three years of research. This book and the technique and the theory expressed here have slowly developed over that interval of time. There has been adequate time to carry out several hundreds of personal observations and experiences, and to allow several hundred other persons to make their own observations and have their experiences under adequately controlled conditions (Chapter Twelve). There has been enough time to integrate these data sufficiently to furnish a current theoretical position with which this researcher is relatively satisfied (Chapters Seven, Eight, and Appendices). This book summarizes the method developed (Chapter Two); some personal observations and experiments (Chapter Thirteen); the work of others (Chapter Three); and the current development of the theory.

Over the years, since its first development in 1954 (see Chapters Nine and Ten), the original method of tank isolation and solitude has been simplified and made safer. A clear and necessary set for tank manufacture and use has been developed (Chapter Eleven). The resulting technique is now made available in a relatively perfected form for the use of others not directly under the supervision of this researcher.

Other researchers with other bases of knowledge, other aims and goals, can utilize this method in pursuit of their own research. Those with interests in research on the physiological/psychological effects of isolation, on meditative methods and processes, on educational and therapeutic applications, on medical amelioration of physical traumatic damage, on psychopharmacologic applications, will now have a tested, developed method to apply to their own domains of research.

Over the years, this method to this author has been a research tool, applied to the philosophical as well as scientific questions of the nature of reality, in its inner as well as outer aspects (Chapter Four). For the first ten years (1954-1964), the tank method was used primarily for self-analysis, continuing the author's psychoanalysis under Dr. Robert Waelder (1949-1953). During these years a self-discipline was developed in the tank: the author learned to be tolerant of his own inner realities. He learned to expect the unexpected in the inner domains. He learned to allow that which would occur spontaneously to develop to his current limit of tolerance. He also learned not to carry these inner realities into his outer consensus reality beyond what he conceived to be the tolerance of his professional colleagues and his professional milieu. His first scientific paper (on the isolation tank) of 1956 (reproduced here as Chapter Nine) reflected the care with which he edited his reports of his experiences and placed them in an acceptable context for his colleagues of that time. With a psychiatrically oriented colleague Jay T. Shurley, he published a second cautiously worded article on the tank method in 1961 (see Chapter Ten).

In 1964, multiple opportunities arose to extend his researches with the tank isolation to include the aid of psychopharmacologically active substances. Through the help of several professional colleagues (Dr. Sydney Cohen, Dr. Charles Savage, Mrs. Constance D. Tors, Mr. Ivan Tors), the National Institute of Mental Health, and the Sandoz Company of Basel, Switzerland, he was able to pursue his researches into the deeper recesses of the internal realities. These research results (1964-1966) were reported in a carefully edited book: *Programming and Metaprogramming in the Human Biocomputer*. Further results were published in *The Center of the Cyclone* 1972. Excerpts pertinent to this book from both these titles are given in Chapter Thirteen.

In 1973, an opportunity arose to expand the tank isolation work in Malibu, California. A home with outlying facilities housing five tanks was established. From 1973 to the present (at the time of the first edition of *The Deep Self* in 1977), in addition to personal research, additional persons used the tanks and reported their experiences in personal logs (Chapter Twelve, this book). In 1974 the number of tanks was reduced to two, in a small isolation building. Only a few carefully chosen persons currently use this facility; the personal work is once again dominant for this researcher.

Currently, the method of tank isolation is being researched for applications to everyday problems for rest and problem-solving for nonresearch purposes. The safety is now such that relatively untrained persons can use the tank for these purposes. The floatation is a solution of Epsom salts and water in a density of 1.30 gms./cc. allows all of the body to float supine, with head, arms, legs and trunk at the surface (Chapter Eleven).

Foreword

Craig S. Enright, M.D.

Solitude. To me the word has always brought forth images of hiking alone through forested mountains that were filled with clear, bubbling streams and grassy meadows; a sense of detaching from my usual daily involvements with people and things, immersing and refreshing myself in the untainted world of nature; however, during the summer of 1973, these associations suddenly began to shift as the logical extension of the idea of solitude manifested itself in the form of a sensory isolation tank, inside of which there was, in effect, nothingness; over 99 percent attenuation of all external stimulus input; a black hole in psychophysical space; psychological free-fall.

Naturally I jumped right in and promptly left my body, owing perhaps to having just read Robert A. Monroe's book, *Journeys Out of the Body*. Little unexpected things like this separation from my body, which I experienced, kept happening to me during my tank sessions, and I came to admire the instant-karmalike ability of a session to bring forth items lying around in the recesses of mind and body.

Entering an isolation tank is much easier than getting into most other spaceships. I would simply climb in, stretch out and float off on a buoyant solution of $MgSO_4$ $(7H_2O)$ (Epsom salts) and water, kept at neutral temperature, neither warm nor cool. Inside the tank there is absolutely no light and virtually no sound (low-frequency vibrations from airplanes do come through and that can really flash you out— there you are suspended in embryonic silence one hundred million miles out in deep space, and suddenly the Logos, the Universal Vibration, begins to pervade the fabric of awareness, coming at once from inside and from all directions). Usually the first minutes of the session go to the monitoring of body sensations. In a very short time the minimal sensation of the water meniscus rising and falling with respiration will fall below the threshold of awareness. Initially in the rather corrosively yang medium of sodium chloride (NaCl), minor skin nicks and abrasions could delay this stage indefinitely, but with the substitution of $MgSO_4$ the supporting fluid becomes very soft and yin. The skin actually feels slippery. With full relaxation of the body, the small waves produced in the liquid die away. Automatically the body assumes a position in which all sets of agonist/antagonist muscles are precisely balanced, with knees and elbows flexed. With the external forces and stimuli reduced to virtually zero, the only forces left are internal ones—those energies stored in the muscles, tendons and ligaments of the body, the physical record of our life in a gravity field—and those energies forming a continuously varying stream of awareness, quite detached from the outside stimuli to which we continuously and unconsciously orient ourselves. I learned a good deal about my habitual physical tension-patterns and tightness from old injuries from the asymmetry of my body in this relaxed state.

Here we have come to the brink of the experience and I will leave you there. There is quite a variety of possible experiences available to any given subject, and elsewhere in this manual you can read some firsthand reports from voyagers just freshly emerged from the tank. These reports were collected right from the beginning of operational capabilities at the Decker Canyon ranch, John and Toni Lilly's home in Malibu, California. The facilities there began in 1973 and eventually included five tanks running simultaneously. For obvious reasons we soon began referring to the ranch as the Lilly Pond, although the official mailing name is Human Software Inc. These tanks were the result of collaboration between John, who had been tripping in a long and varied series of tanks since the 1950s, and Glenn Perry, a computer programmer and engineer who developed and is president of the Samadhi Tank Company (P. O. Box 2119, Nevada City, CA 95959, www.samadhitank.com). Steve Conger has developed tanks in the shape of rectangular boxes measuring about forty inches wide, ninety inches long and fifty inches high. They are constructed of plywood, lined with plastic sheeting (vinyl) and provided with large counterbalanced lids for ease of entry and exit. The support equipment included an air pump, water pump and bacterial filter, and a thermoregulatory system, which maintained the temperature in the tank water at about 93°F. A fourth tank was added, which was constructed of Fiberglas. It was larger, shaped like a symmetrical bivalve rectangular prism and affectionately dubbed the White Whale. Still later, a fifth tank was built of concrete blocks in a circular design, with an inside diameter of about seven and a half feet. This was the joint effort of John, Joe Hart and Will Curtis. Inside this round tank the water rotates counterclockwise at about one revolution per five minutes. I mention these different tank shapes because each had a definite influence on the nature of the experience; a good example of the unexpected preprogram. The round tank was especially far-out because although you had no sensory clues to that slow rotary motion—unless you touched the side or bottom—on some other level you still *knew* you were spinning very slowly at the air-liquid interface, in a roomy lotuslike container—a real, live Experiential Mandala—and this produced some uniquely cosmic experiences.

There were also some intriguing psychological phenomena that occurred among the daily users of the tanks, but I'll leave those tales to others contributing to this manual.

Right now I want to move to another perspective on this business of sensory isolation tanks and awareness and consider it from the point of view of my past training in Western technical science.

In the time since I graduated from medical school, my ideas of disease and its origins have undergone some drastic alterations. Living the past three years at Esalen Institute in Big Sur, California, and experiencing daily an incredible community of people interested in exploring consciousness have been profoundly enriching. For me a most important lesson of the past several years of my life has been the realization of the viewpoint that each one of us is totally responsible for whatever is going on in our lives. I don't know how many times and in how many ways I have got this message, but each time I do it is like: "Oh, yeah, when am I going to remember that?" For me and for many people it is a big message and I am content to go on nibbling at it until I really assimilate it. I'll restate it for myself as much as anyone reading this. Wherever I am and whatever is occurring in my life, *I* am responsible for being there and *I* am responsible for changing it if it isn't satisfactory. I have gone through a lot of changes with this, and one big change was in my old concepts of preventive medicine and how most people get sick— get "dis-eased."

Much of Western medicine is symptom- and disease-oriented and it thus forever treats effects rather than keeping the whole organism balanced, tuned, functioning and high, or in other words, maintaining health in the first place. In areas amenable to technological methods, Western-style preventive medicine is fantastically effective—e.g., in the prevention of smallpox by vaccination or of cholera and typhoid by sewage disposal systems and chlorinated water, but of course the precursors, the predilections, the origins of "dis-ease" are not only external and objective but internal and subjective. *IN THIS LATER AREA THE NAME OF THE GAME IS AWARENESS.*

To illustrate: In the case of an alcoholic with accompanying liver disease we would concur that he is *choosing* the process that is occurring; at least we would feel that he is potentially capable of not injuring his health by ingesting so many molecules of ethyl alcohol. Without justifying or condemning, we can say that at some level he is totally responsible for his situation. This is a very clearcut example, but many disorders of health are not so clear-cut. There are many medical syndromes the causes of which are completely unknown or are only partially understood. Are disease entities such as cancer, schizophrenia, leukemia, multiple sclerosis, and rheumatoid arthritis and the other collagen disorders, to name a few, simply examples

14

of cosmic bad luck that just happens to befall the victims of these illnesses? Even if researchers discover some external culprit such as a virus that causes cancer, does it "cause" cancer any more than C_2H_5OH "causes" cirrhosis? For me it is a fascinating speculation to consider that the ultimate treatment is prevention and that the ultimate preventive medicine may be the development of the inner awareness of what allows these negative processes to develop. To restate it: How much hardware malfunction is the sequela of software bugs?

The successful surgical removal of an abdominal malignancy or a brain tumor is still pretty late-stage therapy; treatment of effect, not cause. (This is in no way a put-down, it is only the state-of-the-art. We need every recourse available.) "Early detection" is an excellent concept but must someday merge with the more encompassing one of primary prevention.

Is there some more ultimate cause of "dis-ease" than that which we hope to find at the small end of the microscope tube? What if we should peer in the other direction through the microscope, letting it become a telescope presenting us with a holistic rather than an atomistic or particulate picture?

Now we have reversed our perspective on this problem of what gets us sick. The problem is how we get ourselves sick (actively), or allow ourselves to become sick (passively). To what extent is disease a state of mind or a result of one's attitudes... a breach not in the defense of the body mechanisms but beyond that some maladjustment in the relationship of ourselves to ourselves and to our environment? This is scarcely a new idea, but we Westerners have been slow to grasp it.

There is already a large and growing body of evidence that leads immediately to such a hypothesis, and conventional medicine already acknowledges the correlation between psychological states and hypertension and coronary artery disease, peptic ulcer disease, ulcerative colitis, asthma, various skin disorders, and a host of other illnesses. Even poison oak dermatitis can be viewed as a temporary but self-correcting lapse of awareness.

Gestalt, psychoanalysis, LSD work, yoga, meditation, dietetics and other techniques are mediums for process, leading to a more developed awareness. In all fairness to disease-oriented technical medicine, I wish to point out that in the long view it also leads to the same development of awareness. It begins with the manifested syndrome, the disease, and uncovers more and more detail about that disease, about the evolution of the disease process, gradually progressing from describing and isolating the condition (i.e., we learn to distinguish it) to defining its origin and ultimately how to avoid it. This may take decades, generations or centuries of combined observations, inductions and experiments.

Hippocrates described the clinical syndrome of hypertension. In the past few decades, medicines have been developed to treat it and in the past few years some therapists are closing the circle at its source and using biofeedback methods to allow the patient to distinguish and avoid the psychophysical states that elevate his blood pressure, or alternately to choose those states of being in which his blood pressure remains normal. Incidentally, do you find it slightly humorous, as I do, that technically oriented Western man devises machines to help him get into himself? From Hippocrates to now is a long time coming, so in a way, technical medicine is like justice. It grinds slowly but exceedingly fine.

The scientific development of awareness of the external vehicles of the black death, syphilis, and tuberculosis has changed our beliefs of their origins from that of God-sent plagues to their being quite avoidable situations. What science, which is itself just a point of view, is beginning to acknowledge in the experiential wisdom of the East is that the entirety of the central nervous system, both "voluntary" and "involuntary," is potentially under the *direct* influence of the conscious mind and vice versa, and furthermore, that mind and body are themselves a unitary whole and in total feedback relationship to the environment.

16

The tank is a tool for process, like meditation, like Gestalt, like psychosynthesis, like psychotherapy, like a hammer or a saw, and like any of the above tools I found tank work to be effective to the extent that I familiarized myself and practiced with it. I would say that it is Gestalt/psychosynthesis, except that there is no longer a middle-man—you become your own therapist or guide or explorer or whatever. (Of course, a good middleman can be of enormous value: it depends on how you like to fly.) Here I wish to express special thanks to Shakespeare, for in the tank one is the playwright, the director, the stage, the actor, the background scenery, the script, the audience and the critics; the inner theater.

I don't mean to imply that tank work is only problem-solving active process. It is as easily passive—a sort of ZaZen and Tai Chi of the inner world, in which one eliminates all distinctions of Self and other and merges with his own deeper Self.

The tank assists in a very simple function; it allows us to expand our awareness of our internal state of being, of our internal flow. This augmented sensitivity to the ranges and varieties of the inner world enriches not only that realm but of course the everyday world where we do most of our living. It is a chance to quite literally unplug from the karmic merry-go-round and recenter ourselves, or to begin the voyage to that center. In a way, tank work bears a relationship to the present-day proliferation of human potential trips as does the concept of a control group to modern scientific experimentation; it is useful in isolating the variables, in finding who is doing what to whom, that who and whom are the same person—yourself. In the tank there is nothing happening but what you are doing, or not doing.

In the terminology of Gestalt psychology I can describe my flow of consciousness as a continual interplay of foreground and background, or as G. Spencer Brown pointed out in *Laws of Form*, a fundamental operation of the psyche is that of the making and unmaking of distinctions. This is taking place continuously on all sorts of levels of consciousness and unconsciousness.

Living on the surface of this planet we are continuously immersed without interruption and throughout every second of our entire lives in a wide range of input stimuli through the receptors of our nervous system. There are literally millions of bits of information arriving every second at the central nervous system. Usually we respond to only a tiny percentage of the stimuli presented to us and our responses to many of these are unconscious, i.e., preprogrammed or habitual.

I remember an LSD trip once when I looked into the face of a three-month-old baby. He had no habit patterns filtering out input—everything was just going directly into his system like it was going directly into mine. He hadn't yet learned to selectively choose and ignore any input and so he hadn't learned any particular description of the world. It took don Juan almost fifteen years to undo Carlos Castaneda's internalized descriptions, in *Teachings of Don Juan*; *A Separate Reality*; and *Tales of Power*. The world we live in we continually create by what we choose or allow ourselves to observe and in the way we respond to and experience it. In a way, we are all musical instruments, each with our own fundamental tone but the same underlying frequencies, infinitely interlocked in the orchestration of the Tao, free to vibrate on as many levels as we desire with one another and within ourselves, changing, exchanging and expanding, finding new and different rhythms and vibrations, resonating and learning to resonate more. In the midst of this a bit of free-fall in silent, dark solitude can be enlightening.

No promises, you understand. People in the tanks have experienced (their own) fear, love, exhilaration, profound peace, and assorted other spaces. Personally, I have had a lot of fun, met some fine people, and learned some things as well. It comes with something of a start for me to see my tank experiences, paradoxically, as actual *interruptions* of my patterns. I kept coming face to face with myself and found therein some of my habitual thought-feeling-movement programs. Some left and some remain, but all in all I did succeed in "stopping the world" from time to time and feel the more fluid for the experience.

One last thing: I also found that the "I" that "I" have used so liber-
ally in this essay is only a construct, a program, a point of view, even
though "I" still identify with it most of the time. "I" am "me" im-
persona-ting mySelf. Do "you" see what "I" mean?

CHAPTER ONE

Physical Isolation Experience in the Tank

In the original concept, the solitude, isolation and confinement tank was devised as a research instrument in 1954. In the ensuing twenty-three years of working with tanks, I have found various ways of making the apparatus simpler and safer.

In the original tanks, we were required to wear rather complicated head masks in order to breathe underwater. These have been eliminated completely.

In the latest models of tanks, we use a saturated solution of Epsom salts ($MgSO_4 \ 7H_2O$) at a solution density of 1.30 grams per cubic centimeter. It was discovered that this density of solution allows one to float supine and have the whole body at or near the surface of the liquid. One's hands float, one's arms, legs, feet and, most important, one's head, float. We have found that even the thinnest person with the least amount of fat floats in this way in the tank.

With these simplifications of the technique it has turned out that we have devised a method of attaining the deepest rest that we have ever experienced. The research instrument has become a practical possibility for use by those untrained in research. We have records of over five hundred cases of persons who have used the tank for one or more hours and several cases of much more intensive use, up to several hundred hours. The safety of the method for use by the average person is demonstrated by the fact that these persons range from housewives, businessmen, scientists and mystics, to children.

Some preprogramming of many of our tank users has gone on because of my personal research using the tank and the publications of the work.* Such preprograms generate expectations in various people's minds about what they will experience when they go into the tank.

It is not necessary for one to have any expectations upon entering the tank. One may go there for a rest, to get away from the busyness of one's life for an hour or two; one may have a problem in the middle of the night in which case the tank, rather than a bed, is more suited to relax one's muscles, provide the rest that one needs physically, and at the same time allow mental operations to continue toward solving the problem.

I have not made it clear in my previous publications that this "rest" is my primary personal use of the tank. Whenever possible I have furnished my environment with a tank, no matter where I was. I first had one at the National Institute of Mental Health (Bethesda, Maryland); I made one in the Virgin Islands (Saint Thomas, U.S.V.I.) and one in Miami in the dolphin laboratories. In our present location (Malibu, California), over the last two years, we have had as many as five tanks operating simultaneously.

I find it essential to be able to relax completely irrespective of anything that is going on in the environment at certain times. Sometimes I wake up in the middle of the night with an idea that I want to work out, so rather than disturb my wife, I float in the tank and work out the idea at great length and in fine detail. I am then able to put it down on paper or to dictate it in the morning. For a businessperson, a scientist, a professional of any sort, this is a boon: to be able to think, free of physical fatigue of the body. The method allows one to become free within a few minutes.

In certain cases the gravitational-field-countergravity forces in the body cause pain because of arthritis, broken bones, or some sort of disease. The tank is specifically beneficial to these people in that it relieves these pains in a way that nothing else can.

* John C. Lilly, *Programming and Metaprogramming in the Human Biocomputer; The Center of the Cyclone; Simulations of God: The Science of Belief; The Dyadic Cyclone.*

Recently I had an accident with a bicycle and broke several bones. As soon as I returned home from the hospital I arranged to have the tank changed in such a way that even though still convalescing, I could get into it. I had not slept for a period of three nights in a row. As soon as I found that the pain disappeared while I floated at the surface of the Epsom salts solution, I slept soundly for an hour and a half, the deepest sleep that I have ever had. In this particular case I came out amazingly refreshed. (For sleeping in the tank we have a special float for people who need it, to feel safe: the head won't turn sidewise while they are asleep.)

For those who do meditation, it is also a definite aid. It turns out that the tank and its isolated environment do for one what one must do inside one's own mind-body when meditating in the usual environment. While meditating, sitting cross-legged or on a chair, or lying in a bed, one examines the environment, the sounds coming from the environment and whatever light patterns are shifting around in that environment. Slowly but surely during the meditation, one can inhibit the responses of these patterns of stimulation and get deep down inside one's mind.

The tank eliminates the presence of these shifting physical input patterns and their changes and reduces the intensity of stimulation down to the most minimum level possible; this "reduced" environment allows one to start the meditation at the point only achievable outside the tank after some inhibitory work and some time spent doing that work. In the tank one need not do that work. Undistracted, one starts concentrating immediately upon one's inner perceptions and dives deep into one's mind (when one is trained on how to do this transform).

Some people come to a tank expecting certain things to happen. All we can say to these people is—nothing will happen that you don't already know about; *nothing can happen that you will not allow to happen*, i.e.: *"What is forbidden is not allowed."* Some people expect to be able to program "visual displays" (hallucinations), acoustic displays, various kinds of bodily sensations or movement into spaces other than the accustomed ones within their body-mind. All we can tell these persons is that one must develop the discipline in order to do what one wants to do. Self-metaprogramming is exactly that, a discipline. It is not a given set in a particular biocomputer. It is part of the metabelief operator.*

The metabelief operator is a system of beliefs that applies and controls sets of one's beliefs, i.e., beliefs about beliefs. One such metabelief operator that we have found in our own work in the tank is as follows:

"In the province of the mind, in the inside reality, what one believes to be true, either is true or becomes true within certain limits. These limits are to be discovered experientially and experimentally. When so determined these limits are found to be further beliefs to be transcended."**

To this particular metabelief operator that controls the expansion of one's belief systems, we always add the caution: "The body imposes definite limits." We are not sure that the bodily limits can be transcended; however, one may have beliefs about one's bodily limits that *can* be transcended in the tank in a safe environment, leaving the body, as it were, to do its own thing.***

The tank is designed to take care of the bodily limits. The temperature is held at between 93° and 94°F. We have found that certain people prefer 93° and others prefer 94°. Once the temperature is set, however, it is held within a tenth of a degree Fahrenheit. The air that one breathes is renewed over the water of the tank by a very small and quiet pump. When no one is in the tank, the water is pumped through a filter to clear it of whatever the previous subjects have left in the tank. The water and the Epsom salts are renewed after several tens of hours of use.

---

* John C. Lilly, *The Dyadic Cyclone*; and *The Deep Self* (Chapter Six).
** John C. Lilly, *Programming and Metaprogramming in the Human Biocomputer; The Center of the Cyclone; Simulations of God; The Dyadic Cyclone.*
*** John C. Lilly, *Programming and Metaprogramming in the Human Biocomputer.*

The tank is an asset to anyone who leads a very busy life. It allows one to attain rest faster than one can in a bed in a darkened room. It allows one to experiment with states that one could not otherwise experiment with safely: states of being, states of consciousness. For example, one can ask the question: "If I am fatigued from a long day's work, what can the tank do for me?"

Floating in the tank after a busy day's work brings a great relief. Suddenly all of the stimulation of holding one upright against gravity disappears. One realizes that a good deal of the fatigue accumulated during the day is caused by keeping one's body upright in a gravitational field. From a neurophysiological standpoint, one has immediately freed up very large masses of neurons from the necessity of constant computations (as to the direction of gravity, the programming by visual and acoustic inputs, by temperature changes, etcetera). For example, one's cerebellum is now freed for uses other than balancing the body.

In summary, then, the tank experience is a very refreshing one, a resting one. If one wants to push further than this, one can do so to the limits of one's mental discipline and to the limits of one's imagination.

CHAPTER TWO

The Application of the Sciences to Floatation and Physical Isolation

The system of physical isolation (water tank) being used has been described briefly in two of my previous publications (*The Human Biocomputer* and *The Center of the Cyclone*). This is a system devised in 1954 to free the body from the necessities of the external reality programming and metaprogramming. First let us describe how we eliminate (or attenuate) each kind of stimulation that is present in everyday life.

1. *Other persons*

The most active, attaching, and demanding source(s) of stimulation for a given person is another person or a group of persons. To free one from this source one goes into solitude.

Our definition of solitude includes all of the preprogramming and postprogramming of contacts with other people, individuals and/or groups. In a sense, there is no way to achieve the full effects of solitude without allowing sufficient time to pass (in solitude) between one's last contact with a person or persons and one's current aloneness in a solitudinous situation. The leftover programming from contacts with others can be considered as a continuing invasion of one's solitude. This can easily be seen by going into solitude for an extended period of time.

In the accounts by various people who have been in solitude in the Arctic or on small boats sailing across the ocean (see Chapter Nine,

The Deep Self), one finds that there is a period of many days in which the effects of the contacts with humans still persist and gradually die out. In a sense, one must devise programs or metaprograms to help attenuate these effects (the leftover programming and metaprogramming of other persons).

There is also a preprogramming or "expectation" effect. If one sets a definite time for leaving the tank or desert or cave, or one makes an arrangement with another person who is expected to come and interrupt exposure to the solitude situation (whether tank, desert or cave), one tends to be programmed into expecting that person to make that interruption. For the expectant interval of time, this will determine to some extent the phenomena that one experiences under these conditions.

Therefore it is recommended that one go into solitude with a freely floating program, a freely floating schedule, and avoid overscheduling, either in terms of immersion or emersion into and from the alone situation.

2. *Light and patterns of light stimulation*

We are sighted animals. A very large fraction of our cerebral cortex is given over to visual processing, in terms of perception, central data processing and outputs from this region. Our memory and our language are closely allied to our visual experience.

We say, for example, "I visualize your face when you are not here." We do not say, "I hear your face when you are not here." (A dolphin might communicate, "I hear your face," but a human says, "I visualize your face.") We also use words such as "I picture," "I see," which have to do with visual operations and their analogues in thinking processes.

We are not restricting our analysis of light and light patterns to the immediate psychophysical perception here and now. We are also including all of those activities having to do with visualization itself as a central activity of our biocomputer. In this region we call such activities "visual displays" to be created by the Self-metaprogrammer (in line with the information set out in *The Human Biocomputer*).

To be free of all light stimulation, including nonpatterned light stimulation, one goes into a completely blacked-out space, a dark room, in which there are no sources of light whatsoever. When one does this, the isolation of the observer from the "light" is not complete. There are persisting central process visual activities: all one has to do is open one's eyes in the dark and look. Immediately one sees peculiar cloudlike phenomena, or one may see points of light, flashes of lightning, etcetera, depending upon one's present state. One can see that the visual system, isolated, maintains its activity in a "visual display" manner.

These visual displays are not necessarily those produced directly by the Self-metaprogrammer. One can see that levels of the biocomputer below one's level of awareness generate visual displays, some of which are random in appearance or "noisy" and some of which are well organized.

In special states of being, when in a completely black room, one can begin to see light levels comparable to a well-lighted room. This is commonly called "hallucination." Here we do not use such terms, we continue to use the more useful and operational term "visual display."

For certain neurophysiological and philosophic reasons, one can see that visual displays are what one actually sees when in a well-lighted room; one is not used to one's biocomputer producing visual displays in a black room, even though it is a very natural process for that biocomputer to do so. We can dream, for instance, in full Technicolor in complete darkness with eyes closed. It has been found in the previous isolation work that one can, as it were, have "waking dreams" in the dark and see fully lighted threedimensional colored objects without benefit of light. These are visual displays presumably produced from the storage mechanisms of the human biocomputer.

Light is one of the easiest of the stimulation modes of energy for one to eliminate from the environment; sound is not so easily eliminated.

3. *Sound*

Sound is transmitted through solids, through liquids, and through gases. One can eliminate (or attenuate) airborne sounds most easily by interposing a solid or liquid barrier between the ears and the sound sources. The mass per unit area and the sound velocity in the material interposed between the sound source and the ears determine how effectively the barrier will attenuate sound.

An air-water interface is excellent for turning most of the sound around and not allowing it to penetrate into the water from the air. The acoustic mismatch here is 5000:1 (this is a better barrier than, say, a steel plate underwater, which is only 500:1). If one is immersed in water, airborne sounds hitting the water will be reflected in the ratio of 5000:1. Only 1 part in 5000 of the energy of the sound that hits the water will be transmitted to the water.

For the significant attenuation of sound, immersion with the water loading the eardrums is very effective. The loaded eardrum has a sharply reduced (by 30 to 40 decibels) sensitivity to airborne sound. If, in addition, surrounding the water, one has dense walls, one can further attenuate the sound that can be transmitted into the water. (Lead or steel or some metal in air is extremely effective in reflecting sound, as are concrete, rock, and similar heavy materials.) For maximum reflection away from the isolated person, "sound mirrors" rather than sound absorbers are used.

In lieu of sound mirrors one can use absorber "sound-black" materials such as acoustic tile and similar materials. These operate in a very different way and are less effective. They operate by setting up interference patterns among the sound waves so that they destroy one another when the sound enters into the fibrous structure. The friction of the sound traveling within very narrow passageways absorbs the energy. This absorption process is never complete and the transmitted component of the residual reflected component can be considerably higher than the reflected component itself. There is a saying in physics: "an open window absorbs 100 percent of the sound"—this is used as the standard of absorption, i.e., it is an instance where there is no reflected component; the sound escapes rather than being merely partially absorbed.

Other sources of sound are those coming through the solids and the liquids, i.e., through rigid piping (if any) that leads into a tank. These sources can be extremely powerful within the tank. Liquid or solid conducted sound is difficult to attenuate before it gets into the tank. In general, we use flexible tubing in the water or air supplies leading to tanks so that the tubing will not transmit much sound through its solid structure. Using baffling and absorbing materials in the acoustic pathways can also attenuate sound from the liquid and air sources.

Other sound transmitted from outside sources to the tank through, say, a concrete floor, has to be attenuated also. This can be done by suspending the tank on the top of materials that give an acoustic mismatch between the tank and the floor. In other words, if the tank is built of plywood and it rests directly on a concrete floor, there will be almost 100 percent sound transmission. To attenuate these sounds, one inserts an acoustic filter between tank bottom and the floor. One puts a steel plate on top of a thick rubber sheet, and then rubber on top of that and the tank on top of the rubber sheet. One other way of attenuating these floor-borne sounds is to use a garden hose and wind it back and forth in a spiral or a sine-wave fashion and support the tank on this. This arrangement has the advantage of giving thermal as well as acoustic insulation, and can be used as a heat source (or sink) for warming (or cooling) the tank when necessary by passing hot (or cold) water through the hose.

Even as in the visual sphere, in isolation, the acoustic sphere is found to be filled with information from one's own biocomputer. There is an inherent noise level within the central nervous system and within the end organs for hearing. In isolation, some people hear very high-pitched whistles, others hear popping sounds like bacon frying, or rumblings, hissings, and so on.

There is a very rich internal set of sounds, which we call *sonic displays* (analogous to the visual displays, see Light and Patterns of Light, above), which the biocomputer and its end organs create *de novo*.

There are intrabody sources of sound, such as the respiration and the heart. These can be somewhat attenuated by careful body position and careful breathing. As more time and more tank sessions are experienced, these sounds tend to disappear from the awareness domain. Sometimes one can hear gut sounds; they may be projected "as if" coming from outside the tank.

In general, isolation tanks are not designed to take care of subsonic and very low-frequency sonic vibration. For example, with the sound of some kinds of airplane engines, the low-frequency component will come through even though one won't hear the higher frequencies. Earthquakes and similar sources of subsonic vibrations of course are of such high amplitude that they are going to come through in spite of any insulation. Some kinds of building vibrations owing to highway traffic in the distance, etcetera, cannot be taken out of the tank. In general, it is best to put the tank on a ground floor so that one is free of the low-frequency after-oscillations within a building structure.

4. *Gravitation*

In ordinary, everyday activity, below our levels of awareness, we are constantly computing the direction of gravity. These computations are carried out within our biocomputer, mainly through the cerebellar mechanisms and the inner ear. Under gravitation we are also presuming that computations having to do with inertia, rotational accelerations and linear accelerations are included. As Albert Einstein made clear many years ago, there is no way that we can distinguish between the effects of gravity itself and an acceleration of 1 g. in a space that is free of gravity. The end organs in our ears and our body in general would recognize the 1 g. acceleration as if it were a 1 g. gravitational field.

For example, if one starts a simulation of a rotary movement in the tank (Appendix II) without knowing that this is taking place, one can mistake this for an outside force coming into the tank. In other words, it is very easy to project accelerations as if they are gravitational forces.

In ordinary, everyday life we must continuously compute the direction of gravity, in the presence of acceleratory movements of various sorts, in order to avoid falling down. We must be sure that our center of gravity is securely lined up with a support before we lower our weight onto that support. We must constantly make adjustments in our visual field for the varying direction of gravity as we move our head. Some of these effects can be shown to be incredibly powerful, for example, in the human centrifuge.

The changing accelerations of three to four to five times gravity in the human centrifuge can crossprogram the visual field (generate synesthesias) to such a considerable extent that one is sure that gravity is changing its direction continuously, for example. The preeminence of the acceleratory and gravity programs over visual and body sense programs can be demonstrated in this way. These effects can also be detected when one is floating in water in the darkness and silence.

In everyday life, the body exerts counterforces against that of gravity through the muscular-skeletal system. Correct here and now body position is automatically computed through cerebellar and other mechanisms. For example, these computations place the feet in just the right position to keep the center of gravity supported at a given height when walking or running. One doesn't have to pay much attention to these mechanisms; they are automatic.

As we walk, stand or run, we can see that there is a very small area of contact between our feet and the earth. All of the effect of gravitational pressure is now exerted in this area of the foot; this is maximal *antigravitational stimulation* in the periphery. If one can increase the area of contact for the antigravity forces, such as by lying down flat on a comfortable bed, one reduces the amount of stimulation (the local pressure) by gravity on the periphery of the body. One does not reduce it in regard to the inner ear.

The only way stimulation can be reduced on the inner ear is to move out into a field free of gravity in far-out spaces beyond the solar system, or to go into orbit around the planet, so that the centrifugal force balances the gravitational force. Then the inner ear is free of gravity.

All we can correct by floatation techniques is the peripheral countergravity stimulation exerted by the force of the accelerated mass, i.e., the weight of the body. Floating in water, one distributes this countergravity pressure over the maximum possible area and hence attenuates this source of stimulation to the minimum possible value while still on this planet.

5. *Heat flow and temperature*

In ordinary, everyday life our skin (our periphery) is stimulated by differences in temperature from the feet to the top of the head. The amount of temperature difference at the skin is determined by the amount and kind of clothing, the humidity and the temperature of the medium (air, water, snow or other) in which the body is immersed.

The humidity of the air determines the amount of cooling by evaporation of perspiration from the skin and hence is a powerful determinant of skin temperature.

The temperature gradients across the face, the head and the rest of the body are very powerful programmers of our states of being. All one has to do is take off all one's clothes and move around in the nude for a bit to realize the sudden change in the programming.

In order to eliminate such sources of stimulation and reduce temperature gradients, partial immersion in a liquid, such as water, with a high heat capacity and a high mobility reduces these gradients to a minimum possible value. Saturating the air with water vapor above the solution prevents evaporative cooling of the body surfaces that are above the surface of the water. The air above the water in the isolation tank is kept near 100 percent humidity, full saturation.

Gentle convective stirring of the water prevents shells of different temperatures (gradients) building up between the skin and the water. These movements of the water are to be minimal, below threshold for skin detection of movement. To create these convection currents, the heaters are located in the right places in the walls and bottom of the tank. If one is lying perfectly still in water, with no convection taking place in the water, one can warm up a very thin layer of water over the surface of the skin and feel warm in spite of the cool water. When one moves a part, such as a hand, through the water, this part immediately feels cooler than when it was still.

One's subjective appreciation of temperature over the surface of one's body is varied (within certain physiological limits) by biocomputer programming. Inside the body are many sources of heat, one hundred billion cells, each one of which produces a little bit of heat while it is living. All of these one hundred billion cells add up to a total body basal metabolism of about eighty watts, in a resting state. That which seems to determine the subjective appreciation of either cold or of heat is the temperature gradient between the inside of the body and the surrounds; thus skin temperature determines to a certain extent the subjective appreciation of heat or cold.

The normal deep body (brain) temperature is 98.6° F (37°C). The brain, through the body, regulates its own temperature. The skin temperature must be lower than 98.6°F (37°C) or the body and brain temperature itself will rise; in other words, the body itself is a heat source that needs a "downhill" temperature gradient to dump its heat into the surrounds. If one is immersed in water at 93°F (approximately 34.5°C) and one's metabolism is at a very low resting value, then one feels neither hot nor cold. However, if one raises one's metabolism, either by muscular activity or by certain kinds of internal programming of the metabolic control centers in the brain, one can begin to feel hot with an environmental skin temperature of 93°F.

If one comes into the tank after an active outside set of muscular activities so that one's metabolism is high, and one's muscle tone is high, one can feel that the water is very "hot" at 93°F and that the saturated atmosphere above the water is extremely muggy and uncomfortable. As one stays in the water, however, the metabolism can drop, one's skin is cooled by the water and one gradually approaches a steady state in which one feels the temperature is neutral (neither hot nor cold).

Or, if one is particularly good at the internal programming of one's metabolism and can relax the musculature totally, one finds that 93°F is "cold."

The internal control of the heat production over a certain limited range is extremely important in these experiences. It is very important to move the control of these systems into the conscious programming of the individual. This conscious awareness and conscious control can avoid projecting causes that are actually inside oneself, "as if" outside.

It is very possible to say that the tank is entirely too hot for you and leave it, when actually all that has happened is that your metabolism has gone up for some reason or other. The interlock with the tank must always be remembered in such situations. *Objective measurement of the temperature of the water is an absolute must in order to know whether it is the water that is too hot or too cold, or whether it is the body that is producing too much or too little heat, or whether one is metaprogramming "as if warm" or "as if cool."*

There is a caution to be observed here in regard to water temperature. One must remember constantly that in order to survive, the body must be in environs at a lower temperature than that of the brain. The brain temperature is approximately 98.6°F (37°C); it is an isothermal "heat engine." It produces heat that somehow must be dissipated to the environment. Even as there is a cooling system in one's car to dissipate the heat of the engine, so must the brain be cooled.

(The brain at rest produces about 40 watts.)

The body operates in such a way that the temperature of the brain is maintained at a constant value. The rest of the body is sacrificed for this purpose under a hierarchy of programs. In other words, the brain is the most important organ of the body and must be kept isothermal at 98.6°F (37°C). If due to extreme environmental temperatures the brain temperature is either lowered or raised, the quality of our thinking is decreased until it ceases in the coma of overheating or of over-cooling ("going to sleep" while freezing is a danger recognized in northern climates).

If the water temperature goes too high in the tank because of inadequate control, one is in danger of raising the body temperature and hence the brain temperature to dangerous levels. *The first sign of such overheating is usually muscle spasms in the legs.* One can very easily become feverish while immersed in water by allowing that water to become too hot. (In one experiment by accident and in a situation in which we did not have adequate control of the water temperature, I went into coma, apparently with a body temperature of 105°F, as a consequence of letting the temperature in the tank get too high. Various emergency mechanisms in the body took over, including an activation of the mesencephalic vocalization center [midbrain], which produces "moans," which were heard outside and my "safety-man" [observer] introduced cold water quickly enough to lower the body temperature and restore me to consciousness and adequate thinking about the situation.)

One additional danger of overheating the body is peripheral vasodilation leading to hypostatic draining of blood from the brain. This can occur immediately after standing up from a horizontal position. For example, arising too rapidly from a hot bath, one can lose consciousness ("white out") and fall to the floor. This effect has not been found to happen in tanks at 93°F, but has been experienced at 95°F to 96°F.

Since then, we have introduced overall feedback for temperature control on every tank so that the temperature cannot run away. There is a thermostat and a temperature sensor in the tank controlling the heating system so that the temperature is maintained at a constant value (within 0.1°F).

If the tank temperature changes rapidly enough the changes are easily detected by the subject; if it changes too slowly it cannot be detected. For falling tank temperature there is a critical temperature for shivering phenomena: the first evidence that it has dropped is tremors. Shivering is a physiological mechanism for creating new heat by rapid fine muscular contractions so as to warm up the body to compensate for the drop in the external temperature. If the shivering warning is ignored, one can get cold enough to cause nerve conduction to stop in the periphery so that one is unable to move. This is a very low temperature (45°F) and has not been experienced in these tanks. One can demonstrate this mechanism by swimming in water at 40°F long enough so that one's arms and legs totally fail. Neuromuscular conduction in the periphery is cut off by too low a temperature, ending in "cold paralysis." This is an extreme of temperature, not likely to be experienced in this tank; but it is wise to know about this other limit of temperature functioning of the human body.

6. *Tactile and pressure stimulation of skin and subcutaneous tissue*

In the discussion of gravitation in this chapter, I talked about gravity-resisting forces on the surface of the body. These are expressed (insofar as their detection by the central nervous system and by the Self-metaprogrammer) through tactile, proprioceptive and other pressure-type detectors within the substance of the body itself (in the skin and subcutaneous tissues). These detectors are in addition to those devoted to the detection of temperature gradients, which are present in the skin.

Floatation in water minimizes these effects; however, slow body movements in water can stimulate these tactile endings—one can feel the flow of water across the skin.

One can also feel the peculiar boundary which is called "the meniscus," between the skin, the air and the water. The angle that water makes between any solid perpendicular surface and its own surface is determined by the surface tension of that water and by the nature of the surface on which the water impinges. (If one uses a clean glass tube, of 2 or 3 millimeters inside diameter, and puts it in water, at the lower end one can see that the water tends to climb the walls of the glass tube, leaving the center of the column depressed, forming a concave-upward meniscus. If one now greases the inside of this glass tube, one can see that the meniscus forms in the opposite direction, convex upward, moves downward at the sides rather than climbing, and that the center of the column of water is higher than that which is close to the glass. These are called "hydrophilic" and "hydrophobic" effects, and depend upon the wetting properties of the water and the surface. Grease cannot be wetted and clean glass can be wetted. One interesting substance that has a 90° angle of contact neither depressing nor raising the meniscus is Teflon.)

The interfacial angle between human skin and water varies with the amount of oil on the skin. If there is a lot of oil, the meniscus is depressed; if there is very little oil and the skin is very dry, the meniscus rises. With just the right amount of oil it can be at 90°. In each case there is a different stimulation at the boundary between the air, the water and the skin. (Detergents in the water lower the surface tension of the water so that one can possibly get a lesser tendency for this edge to be stimulating.)

With an Epsom salts-water saturated solution in the tank, the air-water-skin interface can be detected. There is something more here than just the contrast between the stimulation of the air impinging on the skin and the water on the skin. It may be possible with detergents or some other agents to change this degree of stimulation. The problem of this stimulation is not as great as others considered above. Some very interesting psychophysics could be done here. Conscious awareness of the meniscus tends to disappear with time of exposure and with repeated exposures.

7. *Miscellaneous sources of stimulation*

The electromagnetic spectrum and its ability to stimulate has not been investigated thoroughly, except for the visible light region. In the vicinity of powerful radio stations some people's teeth fillings, for example, can rectify the electromagnetic energy and convert it into sonic energy so that they can hear broadcasts through the fillings in their teeth. It is wise to avoid this effect by not putting a tank up in the vicinity of a powerful transmitter.

Some people can see radiation at the ultraviolet end of the electromagnetic spectrum owing to the fluorescence of the media of the eye, i.e., the eye emits electromagnetic radiation. It is wise not to have ultraviolet radiation in the tank.

At very high intensities of X-radiation (X rays), some people can also see various phenomena. It is wise not to put the tank anywhere near an X-ray machine—Gamma radiation, even though nonstimulating, is incredibly dangerous, so it is wise not to put the tank anywhere near a radium storage vault, or a cyclotron, or other gamma-ray source.

Radio waves of long wavelengths of sufficient intensity can raise body temperature. This process is called diathermy. One should not place the tank anywhere near a radio source, either of a diathermy or a radar type. Some people can pick up the extremely powerful beamed radiation from radar transmitters. It is wise not to have the tank in such a field. One can detect whether or not there is such a field present by hooking up a hi-fi amplifier and having an open input with a small antenna. Every time the radar beam sweeps through the area, one can hear the pulsing of the beam through the hi-fi set.

The various elementary particles of physics, ranging from neutrinos to mesons, pions, protons, etcetera, have not been studied with regard to their psychobiophysical effects on either the brain or the body in sufficient detail to be useful to us here. In this regard, for example, we apparently can detect secondary cosmic-ray showers hitting a particular part of the nervous system in such a way as to stimulate it. To date this is pure speculation (we would like to hear more from others about this).

There is no record at all, as yet, of a human being able to detect gravity waves from distant sources in the universe. As interest in gravity waves is increasing, and the methods of detecting them are being worked out in physics, we may hear more from this region in regard to the humans detecting these waves, possibly directly without instruments.

Detection of thoughts, images, feelings, etcetera, transmitted by others is currently under research. No one yet securely knows either how to shield against or how to produce such effects reliably.

There may be other sources of stimulation beyond our present scientific understanding for transmitting information to a person in an isolation tank. One of the points of devising the tank was to work on ways of detecting such influences. This area is open for future research.

THE PHYSIOLOGY OF ISOLATION IN THE TANK

In the tank, the respiratory and the cardiovascular systems continue to operate as they do when one is lying on a bed at rest; however, one is more conscious in the tank of these two functions since they produce the main residual noises. There are important points to remember in regard to each of these systems.

As was said in *The Human Biocomputer*, Belief System No. 1 for tank work is that one can allow respiration and heart activity to "go on automatic." No matter where one is in one's simulation spaces, these two automatic functions will continue to operate on their own. Park the body and allow it to do its own respiring and its own blood pumping.

"Assume that the subject's body and brain can operate comfortably isolated without him paying any attention to it. This belief expresses the faith that one has in one's experience in the isolation situation, that one can consciously ignore the necessities of breathing and other bodily functions, and that they will take care of themselves automatically without detailed attention on the part of one's self."*

(In the early tank work, there was a special respiratory mask and apparatus to allow one to be totally submerged underwater. Later, in the 1964 to 1966 experiments, this was found to be unnecessary when using a saline solution, which allowed one to float at the surface with one's mouth and nose safely out of the water.)

Floatation

In the original tank experiments, water at a constant temperature (93°F) was made up through a thermostatic hot-and-cold water-mixing valve. This water flowed through the tank and out to the sewer. In this particular situation the fresh-water buoyancy was not so great as later experiments showed one could achieve with seawater (3 percent salinity) or with 15 percent salinity or a saturated solution of Epsom salts (53 percent). One advantage of the continuous flow system was that any urine that was produced was carried through the system and out. From the standpoint of personal hygiene and personal preferences, this was a desirable result.

However, the advantages of the high magnesium sulfate content have led to a closed system using a filtering system; urine is undesirable in this system (our subjects are asked to empty the bladder before entering the tank).

The antigravity value of a high-density liquid is obvious once

* John C. Lilly, *Programming and Metaprogramming in the Human Biocomputer.*

one tries it. The antigravity forces can be neutralized over the leg and the arm areas with a saturated solution of Epsom salts (53 percent by weight) for most people. For those who have less fat on their bodies than the average person, this density is high enough so that they can float at the surface. (Great Salt Lake in Utah is a near-saturated solution of sodium chloride and other salts so that everyone who goes in the lake floats.) In a saline solution of sufficient density, the feet and arms do not sink the way they do in fresh water.

Table 1 gives the solution densities for magnesium sulfate in various concentrations by weight. We use 53 percent by weight of commercial (hydrated) $MgSO_4 \cdot 7H_2O$, which results in a specific gravity (density) of solution of 1.30 gms./100 gms. of water (see Table 1). This is the amount of the hydrated salt that results in a saturated solution of $MgSO_4$ with visible undissolved crystals in the solution in the bottom of the tank.

Body position

When free-floating in deep water with the proper mask equipment for breathing, one can realize that there is a complex network of reflexes that determines body position. If one moves one's head toward the back, one's feet tend to assume an arc that continues down the back and the body forms a bow. This is similar to the body position seen in a type of seizure in epileptics called opisthotonos. In cat experiments in which the cerebral cortex was removed, one can see a total release of these reflexes of the body.

If one relaxes in the tank, one can see these reflex patterns carrying out control that one can counter by the proper programming of one's own control. For example, as one tilts one's head back and the feet tend to sink, one just raises the feet by voluntary effort and retrains the system. Rotating the head to the right will bring the corresponding arm and leg up; rotating the head to the left will do the opposite.

TABLE 1.   28 Magnesium Sulfate, $MgSO_4 \cdot 7H_2O$*

Molecular Weight = 120.37
Formula Weight, Hydrate = 246.48
Relative Specific Refractivity = 0.572

A% by wt.	H% by wt.	P D_4^{20}	D_{20}^{20}	Cs g/l
0.50	1.02	1.0033	1.0051	5.0
1.00	2.05	1.0084	1.0102	10.1
2.00	4.10	1.0186	1.0204	20.4
3.00	6.15	1.0289	1.0307	30.9
4.00	8.19	1.0392	1.0411	41.6
5.00	10.24	1.0497	1.0515	52.5
6.00	12.29	1.0602	1.0621	63.6
7.00	14.34	1.0708	1.0727	75.0
8.00	16.39	1.0816	1.0835	86.5
9.00	18.44	1.0924	1.0944	98.3
10.00	20.48	1.1034	1.1053	110.3
12.00	24.57	1.1257	1.1276	135.1
14.00	28.67	1.1484	1.1504	160.8
16.00	32.76	1.1717	1.1737	187.5
18.00	36.86	1.1955	1.1976	215.2
20.00	40.95	1.2198	1.2220	244.0
22.00	45.05	1.2447	1.2469	273.8
24.00	49.14	1.2701	1.2724	304.8
26.00	53.24	1.2961	1.2984	337.0

A% = anhydrous solute weight percent, gms. solute/100 gms. solution.
H% = hydrated solute weight percent, gms. solute/100 gms. solution.
p or D_4^{20} = relative density at 20° C, kg/l.
D_{20}^{20} = specific gravity at 20° C.
Cs = anhydrous solute concentration, g/l.

* *Handbook of Physics and Chemistry,* Chemical Rubber Co., 1974.

It is wise to experiment with these as each individual has different patterns of expression of these reflexes because of previous training and control. The ideal is to relax totally near the surface; neither sinking nor coming out of the water.

One "safe" position (to avoid turning over) is to grasp one hand with the other hand with the fingers interlaced in the hair underneath the back of the head in order to support the head; the elbows are immersed in the solution.

The necessity for this maneuver is lessened in an Epsom salts solution at a density of 1.30 gms./cc. of solution (see Floatation, above).

Respiratory system

If, standing with the feet down, the chest up and the head just barely out of the water, one is immersed in deep water, there is a pressure gradient running from the feet through the chest to the neck. This pressure gradient facilitates venous return from the lower periphery to the heart, and impedes respiration. It is more difficult to expand the lungs under the pressure that is brought to bear upon the submerged chest.

To avoid this pressure-gradient effect, the position chosen for isolation in the tank is horizontal on the back with the feet and legs floating straight out at the surface, the hips and thorax at the surface, and the face sticking out of the water. The arms can either be at the sides or behind the head. In the latter position, the fingers should be interlocked underwater.

This position allows the pressure in the lungs and in the venous system to be relatively uniform and constant (as in the case of one lying on a bed). There is a very small pressure gradient from the back to the front of the body; only a few inches of water are involved here. Thus we are not impeding respiration by the waterpressure effect, nor are we particularly facilitating or impeding venous return.

The first fear that many people have in regard to tank use is involuntarily inhaling the water, with the possibility of drowning. This fear can be eliminated easily by an experiment in the tank. Saturated Epsom salts are irritating to the nasal mucous, to the eyes and to the mouth. If one lies on one's back and turns one's head so that the saline gets into one eye and nostril, one will find that very quickly one comes up out of the water—in a reflex activation of a survival program. One or two such "negatively reinforcing" experiences train the subject to allow activation of these primitive systems only under careful control.

These survival systems have an amazingly high priority in the hierarchy of programs within one's biocomputer. One merely has to experiment with these systems to find this out. Lying on one's back in the tank and allowing the solution to run into the nose or the eyes is one of the first training experiences that one can do to avoid further repetitions of this rather unpleasant experience. It is wise to try this and see that the body can handle the salt in the water and that it is not so dangerous as one presumed it to be.

One's buoyancy in solutions is linked up with the amount of air in one's chest and one's fat deposits. The main buoyancy of the body is the result of the air in the chest. With fully inflated lungs one floats higher than one does with empty lungs. In a 1.30 density solution (even with empty lungs), one's body floats high. Only fat people will float with empty lungs in fresh water (density 1.00). Even the leanest persons (density 1.1) float in the 1.30 density solution.

One source of stimulation is the change in water level as one breathes, filling and emptying the lungs. The body tends to go up and down, moving the meniscus on the sides of the chest up and down while the buoyancy is changing. This effect can be minimized by a method we call "dolphin breathing."

In doing the dolphin-breathing maneuver, one fills one's lungs as full as possible, holds the air in the lungs as long as possible without any movement. When one needs to breathe, one blows all of the air out as far as one can, very rapidly, and then very rapidly inspires again to fill the lungs.

If one does it rapidly enough, the body does not sink even in fresh water during the brief period the lungs are empty. With practice one can hold the air in the lungs for a minute between each respiration. With this system one prolongs the period with full lungs between respirations. During this period carbon dioxide is being produced in the body and being dumped into the lungs, and oxygen is being absorbed from the inspired air now in the lungs, so that the lungs are collapsing somewhat, though not very much. The amount of carbon dioxide produced is almost equal to the amount of oxygen absorbed, depending upon one's diet.

If one prolongs this period beyond a certain interval, two possible things happen; either:

a. The carbon dioxide accumulates in the blood to the point where the respiratory center is excited and respiration begins automatically. This is subjectively experienced as an overwhelming desire to breathe, if one is still in the body domain. If one is not in the body domain, the body will start breathing automatically at this point. (There are a few rare individuals who do not have this carbon dioxide respiratory activation reflex; it is wise to find out if you are one of those people or not);

or: b. One may absorb all of the oxygen in the lungs without the respiratory reflex taking place. This leads to anoxia and a dissociation of the Self from the body. Clinically, this would be called "coma": subjectively it may or may not be a "passing out." One may end up just in some other domain, which may be very interesting to oneself. The automatic breathing may or may not start at this point.

The clinical diagnosis of coma is a judgment made by medical personnel who are not tuned-in to the subjective domain that one may be in. One may look as though one were unconscious, but have a very active conscious life somewhere else than in the body, which one can remember when one comes back. It is wise to have a person trained in

47

this area, one who knows his/her own systems well enough to be a safety-man/-woman, while doing experimentation in this region.

The correlation between consciousness and the external behavior of the body is very poor. Some people have a talent of being able to apparently go into "coma," move out of their bodies, explore various domains that they're interested in, and stay away for quite some time while the body looks as if it is totally unconscious and/or headed for death. Here we do not wish to minimize the dangers, we merely wish to point out the phenomena that are involved. Once one gets into these rather far-out domains, the choice is up to oneself, unless somebody from the outside interferes. One can choose to stay in the domain or choose to come back to the body.

In the new models of tanks there is a small air pump, a very quiet one, which pumps fresh air from the room through the tank to eliminate carbon dioxide and keep the oxygen level up; thus, the environment of the nose and mouth has adequate oxygen and a minimum of carbon dioxide.

Cardiovascular system

In the tank, one can have an enhanced awareness of one's body in many ways. For example, one may become very conscious of one's heart action. If one studies the situation, one finds that one can speed up the heart or slow it down, within certain limits that one finds through experimentation. If one speeds up the heart, there can be a rise in metabolism concomitantly with the increased heart action; one may become overheated. If one slows the heart too much, the opposite metabolic effect may take place; one may become cooled off as a result of this action. Remember, there is controllable variable feedback between all of these systems and the observer/operator.

The respiratory system and the cardiovascular system respond to Self-metaprogramming in the tank; the Self also responds to changes in respiration and changes in heart rate. There are no absolutes: it's all relative to where you are at the time you do the experiment.

Remember that advanced yogis, studying for years, can slow their heart rates to extremely small values (something of the order of 30/minute down to 5 or 6/minute); they have done this in situations of isolation similar to but not identical with the tank. They have also become adept at controlling their respiration so they can go for long periods without breathing. Very few of them report the trips they take under such circumstances.

A few cautions

If you are in good health, proceed cautiously in experimentation in this region. If you have had a heart lesion, or if you have had heart murmurs or any cardiovascular disease in the past, be sure you check out with your medical doctor as to the advisability of doing this kind of work. The same applies to respiratory diseases such as emphysema and other severe lung problems.

When one perfects one's technique in the tank, one will find that it is an extremely restful situation, so that if one is fatigued and there is a lot of heart and respiratory action, this will calm down with continuation of exposure to the floating environment.

Hyperventilation

For changing states of consciousness there is a maneuver, a type of *pranayama*, from Hatha Yoga. In Western terms this stage is called hyperventilation. In this maneuver, one breathes as fast and as deeply as one can in order to blow off carbon dioxide from the lungs. When one blows it off to a sufficient extent, one finds that respiration can be held in abeyance for a long period of time, something of the order of two-and-a-half minutes. Associated with the hyperventilation state there is a change in the body state so that one feels tingling in the hands and feet and possibly has carpopedal spasms, in which the hands and feet turn inward. This is due to the pH change consequent upon the lowering of the carbon dioxide content of the blood.

At the same time, one can experience a change in consciousness as a consequence of the lack of carbon dioxide circulating through the brain. This maneuver is sometimes used by children in order to swim a long distance underwater. This is dangerous to do because one does not then have the protective mechanism of the accumulating carbon dioxide as a signal forcing one to the surface. One may become unconscious under the water and die; I have seen two such cases (one in the Virgin Islands and one in Tahiti): each became unconscious, the automatic mechanisms took over underwater and each breathed water and hence drowned.

It is wise to know about these facts of respiration, not to fear them. If you are going to do hyperventilation experiences, lie down on the floor out of the water of the tank. Ask someone whom you trust to monitor your respiration and heart (feeling your pulse); that way, if you get into trouble during the hyperventilation, he will be there to stop you and make you breathe normally so that you can come back. If you do not have any trouble and go through the phases described above, you will gain some confidence in terms of your own ability to do this without someone there to help you. (Some esoteric schools use this maneuver for changing consciousness for certain purposes of their own.)

Until you are a sophisticated landborne hyperventilator, do not do it in the tank. Later, after you have become more aware of your own respiratory processes and what they do to you when hyperventilated, you can cautiously try experiments in this region.

Hyperventilation causes waves in the tank; it is a very active process, as you will find out.

It is wise to become aware of your own respiration and heart action, but not attempt to control them. The reason for the awareness is so you will know when you are excited or frightened or in a high-energy state. Most people when they are frightened do one of two things with their respiration: they either stop breathing, hold their breath and hence accumulate carbon dioxide and use up their oxygen; or, they start to hyperventilate, blowing off carbon dioxide and increasing their oxygen. In either case, their state of consciousness changes and reinforces their anxiety, which then feeds back and causes more of the effects on respiration and the heart. One can avoid such feedback processes by being aware that when frightened, one tends to do something of this sort. In order to know it is occurring, an outside observer should be present because the subject tends to hide this from himself. This feedback is studiable in the tank also. If you are frightened in the tank, sort of step aside, watch your fright, watch your respiration, watch your heart, and see what is happening.

Gastrointestinal system

In terms of consideration of the gastrointestinal tract, there is the question of the length of time involved. If one intends to stay in the tank, isolated, for many hours, one has several problems not present when the subject is exposed to the tank for only short periods (say two or three hours). The first problem is hunger.

The tank is a beautiful place to study one's hunger and one's reactions to hunger. If one has fasted, say for twelve hours, and goes into the tank early in the morning, it will be noticed that one is not hungry at the beginning. Hunger may or may not develop at some point during the subsequent hour or two. If this happens, stay in the tank and monitor the hunger. It has been found in the past that hunger comes and goes. At about the point that one feels an almost overwhelming urge to go out of the tank and eat, suddenly the hunger will disappear. Try the experiment and see if this applies to you.

Another problem to be considered in studying the gastrointestinal tract is that of feces. In an enclosed circulating system with a filter in it, feces are a problem. It is wise to make a bowel movement before entering the tank; how soon an urgency for it develops is a function of one's own physiology and one's own psychology. One will find if there is an urgency developing in this region that, like hunger, it can be programmed out and made to disappear; unless, of course, there is some irritation of the gastrointestinal tract causing diarrhea, in which case it is wise not to be undergoing the tank experiment.

In two of our tanks constructed in the past, we made full allowances for the disposal of feces so that one could stay in for two or three days at a time. This requires very special plumbing. Feces tend to be of two types; those that float, and those that sink. If one's diet is primarily carbohydrate-sugars, green vegetables and starches, the feces produced tend to float—there is a lot of gas in them. If the diet is primarily protein, very little feces are produced and those produced tend to sink. The plumbing was designed to handle both types of feces, disposing them down the sewer as the new water flowed into the tank.

In the current closed-cycle tanks, we do not provide facilities to handle feces. It is wise to control diet and times of exposure to the tank, so that it is not necessary to worry. Preoccupation with this matter can absorb hours if one wishes to do so. The gut tract, the gastrointestinal tract, is another part of the body that is best left alone to do its automatic thing (except for the production of feces at its extremity). In the tank one can start concentrating upon one's gut actions, listening to the noises that it produces, worrying about the duodenum, the ileum, the colon and so forth, hours upon end, and cause disturbances in this automatic system.

Urinary system

In the older tanks with a continuous flow through the tank, urine was not a problem. In the new closed-circuit systems, it can accumulate if allowed to be released. It is better to empty the bladder before going into the tank and not worry about it when in the tank. Again, the impulse to urinate can be encountered and it will subside (after it has built up to a peak) without urination. This is also studiable in the tank.

In some people, just being in water causes a reflex to urinate. If you are one of these people, be sure you empty your bladder and then take a bath/shower before you get into the tank.

In the flow-through tanks it was found that there was an automatic bladder effect in which the bladder would void itself every fifteen minutes. In the closed-system tanks, this is to be suppressed. If one puts in a negative program against urinating and it works, one can "leave the body" safely and it will not urinate in one's absence.

Genital system

One problem for females is whether or not to go into the tank during their menstrual period. The use of Tampax or similar materials will, of course, minimize the amount of blood that goes into the water during a period. It may be found that the high Epsom salts content may be irritating during this time, depending on the sensitivity of the region involved. The genital region may be sensitive to the solution to the point where something should be done about it. There are various kinds of oil-containing creams that can be used to protect the sensitive tissues; the best are those which contain a silicone, which will not dissolve in water and will not mix with the water. Short of that, lanolin will work, but some of this will go into the water and have to be taken out by the filter. In the closed systems it is probably advisable not to go into the tank during the time of maximum flow during the menstrual period.

For the male, if one has an orgasm and an ejaculation in a closed-circuit system, the semen will remain in the tank. One can learn to control orgasm so that one does not have an ejaculation.

Skeletal system

Those of you who are acquainted with information from NASA realize that there is a problem with the skeletal system when the body is not exposed to the usual countergravity forces that one experiences in everyday life. If one is in a prolonged bed rest situation, or floating in a tank situation, or in orbit without exercise, the skeletal system tends to lose calcium and become weak. This takes several days or weeks to occur; for the usual exposures to physical isolation in the tank this is not a problem.

Most people when in the tank have found that if they lie still for a very prolonged period (several hours) they develop impulses to stretch. Some do isometric exercises.

In the tank, special states of being (leaving the body, etcetera) are facilitated by keeping the body in good physical shape. To be in good physical shape, there may be periods in which it is necessary to move, in order to circulate the lymph and venous blood in the body and to tone up various organs such as the liver, kidneys, etcetera. We are a walking, running, climbing animal, whether we like it or not.

Periods of violent physical exercise before going into the tank give interesting results when in the tank. After such a bout, one can relax in a supine position for many hours.

Before immersion in the tank, it is wise to do either yoga or gymnastics, or some other form of exercise to attenuate the need for movement.

Bacteriological considerations

The diatomaceous earth filters used in the closed-tank systems are bacteriological filters that will filter out any organisms left in the water by one's self or others. The solutions we use will not support most organisms that are pathogenic, i.e., the solutions are bacteriostatic.

If one has influenza or a bad cold, it may not be a good idea to go into the tank. However, once again, experimentation by sophisticated individuals is not prohibited. In my own experience, where there is no danger of infecting anyone else, I have found a great relief from most of the symptoms of the common cold and influenza by staying in the tank. The well-known relaxing effects of a warm bath are accentuated under these circumstances.

Skin

If one has a severe skin problem it is wise to consult a dermatologist as to whether or not one should go into a saturated Epsom salts solution. If one has ichthyosis or a similar skin disease, it may be an

54

uncomfortable experience.

It is wise to have some sort of an ointment with silicone to use to cover any lesions that one may have on one's body such as bug bites, scratches, and similar sources of irritation. The initial irritation of these lesions disappears after about fifteen minutes in the tank, if one can stand the initial stinging.

In general, we have found that normal persons, without skin disease, exposed to the solutions for periods of a few hours every day for many months did not suffer any ill effects. Some find that their palms and their soles wrinkle; this wrinkling goes to a certain point and then goes no farther. There is no pain associated with the wrinkling at all. The hypertonic saline removes water from the palms and soles (where there are few oil-producing glands). The outer layers of the skin are "drying out" from the hypertonic solution so that the wrinkles appear. If for some reason one wants to avoid this, one can coat the palms and soles with a suitable ointment to avoid it (preferably containing silicone).

Hair

From a public-health standpoint, before going into the tank it is wise to shampoo. This will insure that whatever oils, loose hair, bacteria or dirt one has in one's hair is removed, so as not to overload the tank system. The Epsom salts solution may or may not affect one's hair. Immediately after exposure to the tank a freshwater shower removes the Epsom salts.

Eyes

If you wear contact lenses, take them out before getting into the tank. There are conditions under which one could lose them. One should be cautious with regard to allowing saltwater in one's eyes. Tears will wash salt out for a brief exposure; for total immersion it may be very difficult to clean the eyes without getting out of the tank and taking a fresh-water shower.

Heavy metals

Some systems containing copper pipe should not be exposed to a high Epsom salts concentration; this tends to dissolve the copper, which then goes into the solution. Copper may rise to levels at which it is possible to get a chronic poisoning through the mucosa or skin. In a similar way, mercury salts should be kept away, and paints that have cadmium, mercury, copper or arsenic in them should not be allowed anywhere near the tank or its containing room. In our systems there are no metals in contact with the saline solution; it is a system manufactured totally out of plastics, including the pump. (In the 1960s I attempted to use a bronze pump for pumping the seawater used in the tank and found that the copper content of the tank water went up very rapidly.)

Pregnancy

Pregnant women will find the tank to be of aid in the last few months of their pregnancy. It relieves a good deal of the problems that they have in walking around under the pressures of a gravitational field. Medical advice should be sought as to when to stop using the tank during pregnancy.

Children

We have had very little experience with children in the tank, and suggest that if experiments are going to be done in this direction, the parents take full responsibility.

PSYCHOPHARMACOLOGY

Tobacco

The use of tobacco has several disadvantages for tank work. The urgency of the habit may force one out of the tank. However, if one can overcome the impulse, one can examine one's addiction to this particular plant. In some people the urgency does not arise in the tank.

56

In the early experiments using total immersion and a face mask, one rebreathed a small amount of one's own expired air. It was found that if one smoked, the smell of the products of smoke from one's own lungs became rather unpleasant.

Nicotine tends to cause vasoconstriction in the periphery (beyond one's reprogrammatic abilities) that results in body cooling in the tank.

Frequent exposure to the tank can be a surprisingly effective way of dealing with tobacco withdrawal symptoms.

Caffeine

In some people, drinking coffee causes restlessness, which may militate against relaxing comfortably in the tank. Caffeine is primarily a stimulant of the spinal cord, a part of the central nervous system, whose activities are below one's levels of awareness. The restlessness arises from this hyperstimulation of the neurons of the spinal cord. If one can do without the coffee it will lead to more extensive experiences than one can have with caffeine present. Caffeine prevents total relaxation of the central nervous system.

Alcohol

One of the most interesting results for those who imbibe sizable quantities of alcohol is that the tank is a very specific environment for hangover-avoidance. If one has drunk too much alcohol, has a very bad hangover and goes into the tank, most of the symptoms disappear. However, if one gets out of the tank too soon, the symptoms will reappear. Most of the symptoms of alcohol poisoning apparently are due to the gravitational effects on the body. No one that I know of has experimented with the drunken state in the tank. One possible danger is that common to all anesthetics—an attenuation of survival programs to a dangerously low level.

The toxic effects of alcohol can be quite adequately shown in the quiet environment of the tank. One can very quickly see the effects of alcohol on systems within one's body and within one's thinking.

Cannabis

Because of the laws against cannabis, very little study has been done on the effects of the isolation tank on someone who has been smoking or otherwise absorbing cannabis or the compounds derived from this plant. Once again, this is an area for new research. Those who are interested in finding out what happens to them in the tank when they are stoned had best do their own experiments.

Those who have used the tank for many hours find that they get quite as stoned (without benefit of any chemical) as they can get with cannabis. We will discuss this later in this chapter under the section "Self-metaprogramming in the Tank."

Tranquilizers

Very little work has been done in the tank with tranquilizers. The reasons for which one takes tranquilizers are probably better treated by exposures to the tank without the tranquilizer. If one allows it to be such, the isolation tank is a physical tranquilizer of itself.

Barbiturates

Because of the depression of cerebral processes, of respiratory and of heart action, it is not wise to take large doses of barbiturates and go into the tank. One's access to control over automatic systems is very much depleted under barbiturates in any sizable dose; therefore it is not advisable to take them and go into the tank, nor to go into the tank while under their influence. The Self-metaprogrammer is very much simplified on barbiturates. He/she cannot carry out the necessary complicated computations that he/she usually does.

Morphine, heroin, etcetera

Once again, these substances cause depletion in the Self-metaprogrammer, and it is not advisable to use them while being exposed to tank work.

Cocaine

No experience with this substance. Research is needed before recommendations can be made.

Corticosteroids

There are no contraindications to tank work while one is under medication of the corticosteroid variety. Some people have reported that they can "trip out" on corticosteroids quite as well as they can on psychedelics. This effect might be useful if one is working in this region. However, it can be dangerous; too fast a withdrawal leads to "psychosis" and depression.

Other hormones

The effects of other powerful hormones such as birth-control pills are studiable in the tank. This has not been done as yet but would be helpful and well worth the investigation. Thyroid, thyroxin and similar chemical substances also can be studied, though here one will have to be aware that the action extends over a very long period of time so it may not be so visible to the observer as some of the other pharmacologic agents mentioned.

Psychedelic chemicals

Among all of the pharmacologic agents, these are of the greater interest in terms of tank work. A caution here is that currently, except under very special research grant auspices, such work is illegal and the illegal chemicals are not pure. If one wishes to do some work in the tank with pure LSD-25 for example, the Maryland State Psychiatric Research Center has had an isolation tank and they have been running professional subjects in a program of training and research on the effects of psychedelics. (The current status of this program is not known.)

For those interested, two of my books (*Programming and Metaprogramming in the Human Biocomputer* and *The Center of the Cyclone*) give details of my own past experiences (1964-1966) in the tank with pure LSD-25 in various doses. This is not an area of psychopharmacologic research to be undertaken by naive subjects without training and professional experience.

LSD-25 is the major United States psychedelic, mescaline is a close second and psylocybin and psylocin are in about third place. The series known as MDA, MMDA, TMA-2, etcetera, are not recommended. They have side effects very much like the amphetamines in addition to their psychedelic effects.

Amyl nitrite, nitrous oxide

No experience, no recommendations. Various dangers are associated with the use of each of these substances. Hypostatic anemia is common with amyl nitrite. Loss of conscious control is common with nitrous oxide.

Amphetamines

These are extremely dangerous drugs. They include dextroamphetamine, Benzedrine, methamphetamine and amphetamine-like compounds such as Ritalin. In general, in high doses, these drugs cause a "body trip" and cessation of thinking activity. In the early days when Dexedrine was first synthesized by Smith, Kline and French in Philadelphia, I did some psychopharmacologic experiments on myself with it. In doses of 150 mgm. there is a spectacular increase in bodily energy and a spectacular decrease in one's critical faculties in regard to this bodily energy. There is a hedonistic overvaluation of one's own bodily activity so that repeating tapeloops of bodily movement, for example, can occur for hours at a time. With amphetamines, tank work can become rather repetitious and simple-minded.

For three or four days after such a trip, there is total exhaustion of the organism. This state can lead to negative things such as trying to get "back to normal" by taking more of the amphetamines. This drives one further into the exhaustion cycle and finally one becomes quite paranoid, quite frightened, and may "freak out" totally. In an attempt to escape the penalty of such tripping, certain persons have taken to barbiturates to calm down the system after the trip. This leads to a cyclical effect in which one gets so depressed by the barbiturates that one takes amphetamines to come up again; one gets so excited by the amphetamines that one takes the barbiturates to go down again. This cyclical "tapeloop" of two drugs can be extremely dangerous—one can end up dead in a hurry. We recommend that amphetamines not be used in tank research.

SELF-METAPROGRAMMING IN THE TANK

Self-metaprogramming has been presented in some detail in *Programming and Metaprogramming in the Human Biocomputer,* in *The Center of the Cyclone* and in *The Dyadic Cyclone.* As I suggested earlier, the basic lesson of these books is stated as follows:

> In the province of the mind, what one believes to be true, either is true or becomes true within certain limits. These limits are to be found experientially and experimentally. When the limits are determined, it is found that they are further beliefs to be transcended. In the province of the mind, there are no limits. The body imposes definite limits.

This is an operational statement and a point of view from over twenty years' work in the tank with and without chemical aids. It is a statement that lays the responsibility for what happens directly on you, the person in the tank. In isolation you cannot escape this responsibility by projecting onto others. As I stated in a paper written in 1958 on tank work:

> Alone with one's God, there are no alibis. There is no goat on which to project the negative, nor a lover on which to project the positive.

You may try your usual evasions of penetration of Self, you may carry out multiple tapeloop dances of all sorts, but you cannot escape the fact that you are alone. (I am not there, even though you may project a simulation of me. As I write this I am projecting my simulation of you. Please don't take it personally.)

My book *Simulations of God: The Science of Belief* * deals in much greater detail with these matters.

THE USE OF TANK EXPERIENCES
OUTSIDE THE TANK

Certain people take any method, tank or drugs or whatever, and become addicted to it as a "crutch." In our work we call these "crutch programs." If one allows the tank to become a crutch program, one can change one's state of consciousness in the tank quite readily and easily to anything that one desires, but cannot do this under any other circumstances. This is a sure sign of a crutch program operating. An exclusive necessity of any outside aid for a given state of consciousness is defined as a crutch program. As one can deduce from the above statement, in our experience this is not necessary.

One can learn, by means of the tank as an aid, to do things with one's state of being, one's consciousness. One can practice what one learns in the tank *outside* the tank under other circumstances, say, lying on a bed in isolation and solitude, or under whatever other circumstances one wishes to work with. For this point of view a good training is to go into a cave, or into the desert, and be alone in pure solitude without the tank, and examine some of these things. Under these other circumstances one has an interlock with the environment, but without the interlock with the demanding, attaching "people effect." Thus one can separate this from the tank and its effects.

* John C. Lilly, *Simulations of God: The Science of Belief*

Finally one learns to be able to close one's eyes in the middle of a conference for a period of a minute or two and change one's state of being, of consciousness, as one desires.

By integrating/organizing/meditating on tank versus nontank experience, one discovers for oneself the use and the usefulness of this restful tool in one's own planetside trip.

CHAPTER THREE

Peace in Physical Isolation vs "Sensory Deprivation"

In the 1950s, several research projects were started that were called "sensory deprivation." In our experience in the tank ("physical isolation"), there has been no psychological state that can be termed "sensory deprivation." In the absence of sensory input (and physical output), we have found no "deprived" states except those created by Self-metaprogramming. The latter are reprogrammable into richly elaborate states of inner experience.

Apparently the term "sensory deprivation" was invented by those psychologists who did not do self-investigation and who did experiments on subjects, expecting a "deprivation state" in the isolated circumstances. In a series of over three hundred subjects we have found no such states of "deprivation," nor the predicated "stress" of physical isolation.

In Peter Suedfeld's review of "sensory deprivation,"* the author begins to understand that such isolation work does not necessarily lead to unpleasant consequences. This field of research has been very slow to take up "physical isolation" as a tool rather than a state of mind preprogrammed by negative expectations ("stress"). Our 1961 paper (J. C. Lilly and J. T. Shurley, reproduced in this book) was omitted from the Harvard Press (1961) Symposium on Sensory Deprivation, apparently because our point of view was not consensus preprogrammed. We disagreed with the then consensus opin-

* Peter Suedfeld, *The Benefits of Boredom: Sensory Deprivation Reconsidered.*

ion that the phenomena experienced were "psychopathological." We found most of the phenomena experienced to be quite within an expanded view of "normal mind-processes."

In my first paper on physical isolation, written in 1956 (reproduced in this book), I examined the literature on the effects of extended periods (weeks to months) of solitude (in small boats on oceans, in the polar night), and came to the conclusion that physical dangers combined with solitude are very stressful. This does not say that physical isolation and solitude without danger are stressful. This confusion between factors responsible has been perpetuated in the "sensory deprivation" literature.

Our current work bears out our early findings that if one eliminates external sources of low-level pain and sources of danger, the inner experience ("inperience," if you wish) can be anything that one can allow oneself to experience.

With our high-density solution (H_2O saturated with $MgSO_4$), the last remaining low-level physical danger ("a sinking head") was removed. The subjects report mostly "self-programmed" or "spontaneous" experiences rather than fear-filled/stressful/deprived ones. The complete comfort of the isothermal supportive bath in the dark and the silence affords a complete physical/mental/spiritual resting place, which can contain a great peace for those ready for it.

CHAPTER FOUR
The Search for Reality*

Starting very young (seven years and younger) up through the present, I have been concerned with the problem (usually enunciated as a question): *What Is Reality?* Almost as soon as I could read, I pursued the writings of Immanuel Kant, Sir James Jeans, Bishop George Berkeley, and any other authors I could find who had something to say about Reality. At age sixteen, I wrote my first article on the subject ("Reality", published in 1931, and reproduced in full in Appendix One, pages 281-290, *Simulations of God: The Science of Belief*).

By 1931 I realized ("made real") an intuitive feeling, which I articulated at that time, that reality has a dual aspect, an outer ("objective") and an inner ("subjective") aspect. I quote:

Today reality may be said (in its less involved meanings) to possess the same attributes as the original meaning of the [Latin word] res ["a lawcourt"]. First it expresses that which is completely objective as opposed to anything subjective. By objective we mean existing without the mind, outside it, and wholly independent of it. Subjective, on the other hand, takes the meaning of that which is in the mind...

How can the mind render itself sufficiently objective to study itself? In other words, how are we able to use the mind to ponder on the mind? It is perfectly feasible for the intellect to grasp the fact that the *physiological changes of the brain occur simultaneously with thought, but it cannot conceive of the connection between its own thoughts and these changes.* The difficulties of the precise relation between the two have caused many controversies as to which is the more real, the objective or the subjective reality [italics inserted].

* Reprinted from J. C. Lilly, *The Dyadic Cyclone*.

I then quoted Bishop Berkeley's dictum that there is no existence without the mind, either in ours and/or in "the mind of some Eternal Spirit." This article guided my search for answers. I am still in the search, forty-six years later.

From Kant's *Critique of Pure Reason,* I began to understand that word, language, logic and mathematical descriptions were not adequate expressers of either the inner or outer aspects of reality. Somehow, all *descriptions of reality* were sterile: they tended to play word games, to cleverly juggle with ideas in intricate patterns as if meaningful. My search for the answer to the question *"What Is Reality?"* continued in the study of mathematics, of logics, of semantics ("metalanguages," for example). I found them, each in turn, sterile in the deeper search and helpful in widening my representational capacities, my abilities to see relations internally in myself, my own mind. I was not satisfied that skill in manipulating concepts, no matter how precise, no matter how inclusive, could answer my question.

Consequently, I went into the experimental sciences. I pursued experimental (and theoretical) physics. Cosmogony (the study of the origins of the cosmos, the universe) raised her lovely head: for a time I was entranced ("in trance") with her seductions (astrophysics, astronomy, etcetera). The study of submicroscopic realms of matter seduced me (quantum mechanics) as did the study of known physical energy (light, photons, thermodynamics, etcetera).

Finally I realized that the study of my own brain and its "contained-restrained" mind was needed in this lifelong search. I took a new direction into new domains: I turned to my program for the search, given above in "Reality": *"the physiological changes of the brain occur simultaneously with thought, but it cannot conceive of the connection between its own thoughts and these changes."* How can one make these connections? How can one record in objective records (1) these changes in the brain and (2) the corresponding thoughts and their fast changes?

As a dedicated young experimental scientist I saw, in a course in neurophysiology at Cal Tech in 1937, a possible means of recording "the physiological changes of the brain." I inquired of Dr. van Hareveld how to do this desired recording: he gave me (Lord) Edgar Adrian's paper "The Spread of Electrical Activity in the Cerebral Cortex." I read it and determined to devise a better method of recording the electrical activity. I wanted a more complete picture (recorded, of course!) of the electrical activity throughout the brain, not just in small areas of the cortex. I also needed to learn more of the mind in the brain (its thoughts, their changes, their "sources and sinks") in order to find/devise/create a method of recording its activities in parallel simultaneously with the changes in the brain. In short, I was seeking methods of objective fast recording of the activities of the brain, and, simultaneously, objective fast recording of the activities of the mind in that brain.

In this search I went into medical school, seeking more knowledge of these two domains of parallel process. (At Cal Tech, Henry Borsook, M.D., Ph.D., professor of biochemistry, said to the young seeker: "All of the current knowledge you are looking for is in medical school: you will need that medical degree to be free to search further. A Ph.D. degree is not sufficient.")

In medical school, I continued the search, in neuroanatomy, neurology, neurosurgery, psychiatry. I found more data but no new methods. I saw the limitations of the methods used: spoken and written language and questions (in the mind domain), EEG and fast electrical recordings (in the brain domain). *Literally, there was no method (yet) of recording the mind activities and the brain activities simultaneously.* I also learned that most medical researchers did not feel that there was any hope of ever accomplishing this difficult task.

Upon graduation from medical school, the search was interrupted by a period of devising means of measuring fast physiological changes in high altitude aircraft personnel: oxygen and nitrogen in the gas breathed, in explosive decompression, in conditions of anoxia and bends. I learned about states of my own mind engendered by too-low oxygen in the brain, about states of my mind in the excruciating pain of decompression sickness (bends), and states of my mind excited by fear during explosive decompression of a pressure cabin. My knowledge increased, but I felt diverted from the search.

Soon after the war, the search resumed. I devised new methods of recording the electrical activity of the brain in many places simultaneously, recorded and reproduced on a two-dimensional array.* I worked out new safer ways of placing small electrodes within the brain.** This work lasted eleven years and was terminated when I realized that, as yet, there is no way of picking up/recording the activities of the brain without injuring/altering the structure of the brain itself, and changing the capacities of its contained mind.

Also soon after the war, in my "spare time," I pursued the study and development of the mind, my own. I studied semantics, logic, mathematics, means of modeling the brain's and the mind's activities. Warren McCulloch and Heinz Von Foerster were working in the area of representation of the brain's activities and I studied their work. For the mind studies, I needed more "new data." I pursued psychoanalysis in depth—I found a psychoanalyst's psychoanalyst: Robert Waelder, who had a Ph.D. (Vienna) in Physics and was trained with Anna and Sigmund Freud in Vienna, Austria. I worked with Dr. Waelder for three years, five to seven days a week, one hour a day. I found much that was pertinent to the search: the question "What Is Reality?" was researched within my mind intensively.

I confirmed (as I had earlier suspected) that wholly complex domains of thought/feeling/doing/memory below my levels of awareness acted so as to program my current beliefs about "what is real." Inner reality had its own laws, distinct from (and many times counter to) the laws of outer reality. I struggled with the theories—belief sys-

* "A Method of Recording the Moving Electrical Potential Gradients in the Brain: the 25-channel savatron (brain activity visualization device) and Electro-Iconograms (electrical image records)," Institute of Electrical Engineers, 1949.
** John C. Lilly, "Electrode and Cannulae Implantation in the Brain by a Simple Percutaneous Method," *Science*, May 16, 1958, vol. 127, no. 3307, pp. 1181-1182.

70

tems—of others in regard to inner reality. I revised my own belief systems in regard to my own inner reality ("realities" would now be more accurate: "the inner reality" of 1931 had acquired a plural label "inner realities"). With Waelder's help and quiet acceptance, I was able to enter new inner domains of feeling/thinking/emoting, emerge, and represent the experiences verbally—vocally—in writing. My modeling of inner reality became more open: my respect for the Unknown in my own mind increased greatly. I realized, finally, that the depths of mind are as great as the depths of cosmic outer space. There are inner universes as well as outer ones. My concept of metabeliefs (beliefs about beliefs) as the limiting beliefs restraining-confining-limiting the processes-operations of my mind originated in the work with Robert Waelder.

In parallel with the brain-activity studies, the mind studies continued with the solitude-isolation-tank work and its origins at the National Institute of Mental Health (1954). Why is isolation necessary for the study of mind? My reasoning was founded on a basic tenet of certain experimental sciences (physics, biology, etcetera): in order to adequately study a system, all known influences to and from that system must either be attenuated below threshold for excitation, reliably accounted for, or eliminated to avoid *unplanned disturbances* of that system. Disturbances from unknown sources may then be found and dealt with more adequately.

Using this injunction from experimental science, I decided to isolate my body-brain-mind, insofar as this is currently possible (without damage-"trance"-chemicals) in the external reality. I saw that to study my own mind, it must be isolated from all known "sources" of stimulation and from "sinks" of reaction, in the here-and-now external reality. I devised the isolation tank method for the study of my own mind, an isolated mind studying its own processes, free of feedback with the external world. Quite quickly I found this method gave a new source of data of great richness.

During such studies over the last 21 years (1954-1975) I have found that which began to open during the years with Robert Waelder: a newness, a uniqueness, a penetration deep into new (for me) domains of the mind. (Some of these experiences and domains are recounted in limited-by-consensus-articles-books-lectures: see republished papers in appendices to *Simulations of God: The Science of Belief;* in References and Categorized Bibliography in *Programming and Metaprogramming in the Human Biocomputer* and in Recommended Reading in *The Center of the Cyclone,* and other portions of *The Dyadic Cyclone.*)

The limitations placed upon communication of these new domains of the mind to other minds were also found: once one has been deep in one's deeper and deeper Self (it deepens at every exposure to isolation), one's ability to transmit the data must also be increased. I found that most (not all) other minds are not prepared to hear-understand-grasp what it means to explore-experiment-be-immersed-in such researches. Certain domains of the mind, certain states of being, certain states of one's own consciousness, are so foreign-alien-weird-strange-unfamiliar to most other minds that they cannot listen to or read what one says or writes without becoming upset, or without using ready labels for the explorer, rendering one's efforts to communicate either negative or null and void.

I have found a few others who do not do this. I hesitate to give their names here; they, in turn, do not want, nor are they yet ready to want, to face the onerous burden of open communication in an unreceptive, possibly hostile or coercive consensus world. Among these others are those who went too far: the consensus world of the (numerically superior) persons who fear these domains exerted powerful external reality means to reduce the communications of those they fear to near zero.

Over the years of this search, I have carried out several experiments in public communication about these domains of the mind. I experimented with means of reaching those who in the privacy of their own minds were in or entering into new domains. I wrote books, gave workshops, lectured—in this experimental mode. I openly pushed my own accounts to dangerously unaccepted edges of credibility. I purposely held back accounts that in my judgment and/or my publisher's judgment would break the consensus thread of communication, with possible disastrous results for me.

Many of my former colleagues disavowed me and my researches: I understand their belief systems and the power such systems have over our minds. I do not recriminate them, nor do I blame former friends for not maintaining contact with me. In my search (for "What Is Reality?"), I have driven myself (and hence, close associates-relatives-friends) to the brink of the loss of all communicational contacts for months at a time, by means totally alien to the previously accepted belief systems (what is appropriate?) in our culture. I have explored and have voluntarily entered into domains forbidden by a large fraction of those in our culture who are not curious, are not explorative and are not mentally equipped to enter these domains.

I find rebels quite disturbing to research unless restrained, disciplined and limited in their actions to effective realms; consensus external reality furnishes a platform for exploration, as long as it is stable enough for the researches. Such research as I have done/do has required, over the years, stability in support (financial, emotional, intellectual, political), or I could not do the work required. There have been numerous difficulties in maintaining the necessary support, but no insurmountable difficulties, yet. So far, there has been a peculiar concatenation of the right events to support one or another aspect of the search. A person, here or there, suddenly comes over the horizon of my mind to facilitate either the new ideas, the new money, the new emotional-intellectual-environment, or the new political means needed for the continuance of the work. Somehow, by at times apparently mysterious means, the social consensus reality provides that which is needed at the right time. For this support I am profoundly thankful and grateful.

My own mind provides its own difficulties in this search: there are times in which I feel the search must stop; it is too much to ask of my biology as a human; it is too much to ask of my functioning as a social being in the world of humankind with its neglected suffering millions of humans. I take time for the search away from other activities. It may be that I should not continue the search and should turn to politics, to more direct expressions of helping others to help one another. This dilemma has always been a distraction, a seduction enticing me away from the search as I now know it. Over these years of work I have sidestepped, or once in it, I have desisted from, leading/participating/belonging to various groups in a responsible position: scientific societies of many sorts, local town/city politics, fraternities, and even dedicated family life. Because of the search for the bases of reality I minimized participation in the social reality, limited it, insofar as this was possible, to communication of the results of the search.

In the search there have been many times of great joy, of breakthroughs into new domains, of a new grasp of the previously ungraspable. Internally, in the privacy of my own mind, thus far, I feel infinitely rewarded by the results.

My life has been lived continuously in the search. At times my efforts have been hidden: I could not expose the experiments being done to the gaze of others without irreversibly altering the experimental conditions and thus changing the results with the changed conditions. Today as yet, I cannot discuss certain experiments I have done: many are, of necessity, still hidden. Even the facts of my own motivations ("What Is Reality?") given in this chapter will change the current experiments. Thus it is, in the huge feedback system of which each of us is a very small part.

Many others (in one way or another) have pursued this search for reality and its representations. I owe many debts to those who cleared some of the jungles of beliefs, who removed accumulated layers of nonsense before I started digging. (As an aside, I feel somewhat like the sparrows I watched in Minnesota as a boy: unerringly each sparrow found the undigested edible single kernels of grain in the drying manure. If only it were so easy for us to find the viable kernels of true knowledge in the masses of nonsense given us in books, in the media, in political speeches, in ourselves by ourselves!)

Some searchers end their books (and apparently their search) with pessimistic statements. I give one example of a foremost thinker, Ludwig Wittgenstein:*

"6.522 There are, indeed, things that [a] cannot be put into words. They *make themselves manifest* [b] . They are what is mystical."

I added [a] and [b]. For [a] substitute the words "as yet." For [b] add the words "by other means." This transforms these two statements of Wittgenstein into the explorer's domain. Substitute for his third statement the following:

"They are now what is in the Unknown yet to be found."

Thus do I operate: If I see premature closing off of possibilities, as if something is impossible ("mystical"), I paraphrase, reorient the statements, so as to continue my own metabelief: *The province of the mind has no limits; its own contained beliefs set limits that can be transcended by suitable metabeliefs (like this one).*

Returning to the Tractatus, there is an oft-quoted statement:

7. "Whereof one cannot speak [c], thereof one must be silent." *("Wovon man nicht sprechen kann, darüber muss man schweigen.")*

In the added position [c], I add the words "as yet," transforming the statement into an opening injunction, rather than, as it is given by Wittgenstein, an absolute closure by this injunction of a system of thought.

* Ludwig Wittgenstein, *Tractatus Logico-Philosophicus,* p. 151.

Of that which we cannot yet speak, we remain silent until a new experience or way of expression allows us to speak. (Radio waves in 1700 A.D. were silent.)

G. Spencer Brown shows (in *Laws of Form,* pp. 77-78) that Wittgenstein probably was referring to descriptive language rather than injunctive (instructional) language. Injunctive language (in its far-reaching uses) instructs on how to do-make-create something in the inner reality and/or in the external reality. Wittgenstein did not have either later neurophysiological knowledge nor the later knowledge of computers, each of which directly opens the domains expressible in new languages (of the descriptive and injunctive types). Experimental science somehow seems to topple previously expressed absolutes about reality, about meaning, about language, about perception, about cognition, about creating descriptions of minds with limits, specified by the constructor-descriptor. The limits defined are only in the description used, in the simulations of the mind doing the describing.

Realization of the lack of any limits in the mind is not easy to acquire. The domains of direct experience of infinities within greater infinities of experience are sometimes frightening, sometimes "awe-full," sometimes "bliss-full." I quote from a writer who feels this lack of mind limits in his own experiences, Franklin Merrell-Wolff, *The Philosophy of Consciousness Without an Object: Reflections on the Nature of Transcendental Consciousness,* pp. 38-39.

1. The first discernible effect in consciousness was something that I may call a *shift in the base of consciousness.* From the relative point of view, the final step may be likened to a leap into Nothing. At once, that Nothing was resolved into utter Fullness, which in turn gave the relative world a dreamlike quality of unreality. I felt and knew myself to have arrived, at last, at the Real. I was not dissipated in a sort of spatial emptiness, but on the contrary was spread out in a Fullness beyond measure. The roots of my consciousness, which prior to this moment had been (seemingly) more

or less deeply implanted in the field of relative consciousness, now were forcibly removed and instantaneously transplanted into a supernal region. This sense of being thus transplanted has continued to the present day, and it seems to be a much more normal state of emplacement than ever the old rooting had been.

2. Closely related to the foregoing is a *transformation in the meaning of the "Self" or "I"*. Previously, pure subjectivity had seemed to me to be like a zero or vanishing point, a "somewhat" that had position in consciousness but no body. So long as that which man calls his "Self" had body, it stood within the range of analytic observation. Stripping off the sheaths of this body until none is left is the function of the discriminative technique in meditation. At the end there remains that which is never an object and yet is the foundation upon which all relative consciousness is strung like beads upon a string. As a symbol to represent this ultimate and irreducible subject to all consciousness, the "I" element, I know nothing better than zero or an evanescent point. The critical stage in the transformation is the realization of the "I" as zero. But, at once, that "I" spreads out into an unlimited "thickness." It is as though the "I" became the whole of space. The Self is no longer a pole or focal point, but it sweeps outward, everywhere, in a sort of unpolarized consciousness, which is at once Self-identity and the objective content of consciousness. It is an unequivocal transcendence of the subject-object relationship. Herein lies the rationale of the inevitable ineffability of mystical insight. All language is grounded in the subject-object relationship, and so, at best can only misrepresent transcendent consciousness when an effort is made to express its immediately given value.

I change his last statement by means present in his own writings into, once again, a transforming injunction: "That language (not 'all language') grounded in the subject-object relationship misrepresents transcendent consciousness when, in that language, an effort is made to express the immediately given value (of transcendent consciousness)."

G. Spencer Brown's doorway* out of this dilemma is the development of an injunctive language that gives instructions (suitable to the listener-reader-experiencer) on how to evoke-enter-create transcendent consciousness in one's Self.

I have found Merrell-Wolff's writings on his own experience to have injunctive qualities for me, for changing my "subject-object" consciousness into the new domains that he so beautifully expresses.

The distinction between descriptive language and injunctive language disappears in the domains of inner experience (and probably in the domain of external experience also) as follows:

A mind isolated from all known stimuli-reaction probabilities (in a state of being with attenuated or missing feedback with the outer reality) for a long enough time, frequently enough, enters new (for that mind) domains. Once that mind has the experience of entering-creating new domains, it has self-referential programs-beliefs-metabeliefs that can be used (at some future times) to transform its own state of being into further new domains. (One learns rules of exploring new domains under the special conditions.)

To achieve this new level of learning-to-learn, one sets aside previous limits set upon domain exploration: one drops irrelevant beliefs about inner/outer realities previously stored; one examines beliefs-about-beliefs (metabeliefs), especially those about "the limits of the human mind." One drops the usual self-limiting languages (useful for use with other persons not so equipped) found in the external reality. One gives up entrancement-seduction by "systems of thought," by other persons, by successes-failures in the consensus realities of others linked to one's self and of one's self in those realities.

However, without the disciplines outlined above and without experience of solitude-isolation-confinement in the external world, these considerations may be meaningless. Once one has been immersed long enough in the above, description of new domains by others now become injunctive to one's Self. Their descriptions invoke-evoke new domains in Self, in one's own mind.

* G. Spencer Brown, *Laws of Form*, p. 78.

78

Thus can language instruct one to move into new states of being, new domains of experience.

Of particular interest to me are the domains represented by the mathematical concepts of: zero (the origin at which numbers and variables cease having any value); of *infinity* (the non-terminus approaching which, numbers and variables assume values that cannot yet be represented); of the point (the smallest possible value of any number or of any variable that approaches, but does not reach, zero); of various *differential operators* ($\nabla^2 = 0$, for example), which can move through their defined domains free of constraints by the domain in/upon which they operate.

Of particular interest is the *relation of identity*, one variable to another, in the consciously functioning domain. Assuming one's conscious Self to have a "size" in a certain domain (say equivalent to that of a human brain in the external reality domain), one *identifies* one's Self with that "size." Start cutting down that "size" until one is a point: in any domain, a point is not zero. *Identify* one's whole Self with a point. This kind of point has consciousness, memory, the complete knowledge of the individual Self. It can remain a fixed point in a defined domain, a moving point in the same domain, or a point in *any domain*. Such a point has no mass, no charge, no spin, no gravitational constant and, hence, is free to move in any physical field.

And so on and on—for identities of Self with differential operators, with infinities, with zero. Identify Self with a differential operator that can move through a field unconstrained by the presence of the field. Assume that oneself is infinite, what is the experience? Assume that oneself is zero, what is the experience? The reader is left with these exercises to perform on/in himself/herself.

I would like to end this discussion with a quotation from a researcher who investigates the bases of reality—G. Spencer Brown: *

* G. Spencer Brown, *Laws of Form*, p. 110.

Unfortunately we find systems of education today that have departed so far from the plain truth, that they now teach us to be proud of what we know and ashamed of ignorance. This is doubly corrupt. It is corrupt not only because pride is in itself a mortal sin, but also because to teach pride in knowledge is to put up an effective barrier against any advance upon what is already known, since it makes one ashamed to look beyond the bonds imposed by one's ignorance.

To any person prepared to enter with respect into the realm of his great and universal ignorance, the secrets of being will eventually unfold, and they will do so in a measure according to his freedom from natural and indoctrinated shame in his respect of their revelation.

To arrive at the simplest truth, as Newton knew and practised, requires *years of contemplation*. Not activity. Not reasoning. Not calculating. Not busy behaviour of any kind. Not reading. Not talking. Not making an effort. Not thinking. Simply bearing in mind what it is one needs to know. And yet those with the courage to tread this path to real discovery are not only offered practically no guidance on how to do so, they are actively discouraged and have to set about it in secret, pretending meanwhile to be diligently engaged in the frantic diversions and to conform with the deadening personal opinions which are being continually thrust upon them.

In these circumstances, the discoveries that any person is able to undertake represent the places where, in the face of induced psychosis, he has, by his own faltering and unaided efforts, returned to sanity. Painfully, and even dangerously, maybe. But nonetheless returned, however furtively.

CHAPTER FIVE

The Self as the Isolated Observer—Agent—Operator

In the brain (the central nervous system, C.N.S.) are the computed–processed "images" generated centrally from the signals entering over the sensory neurons from the peripheral end organs of the eyes, the ears, the skin, the nose, the mouth, the genitals, the anus, the muscles, the joints, the bones, and the internal viscera (the lungs, the gastrointestinal tract, the exocrine and endocrine glands, the testicles, the ovaries, the generative tracts, the heart, the blood vessels). These patterns of neuron activities are constantly active in greater or lesser degree.

From the brain go neuronal impulses to each of these peripheral regions, in patterns of activity constantly operating in greater or lesser degree. The exiting patterns are generated by central processing.

Central processing controls the amount of neuronal activity allowed to enter and to leave the brain at each and every entrance and exit to and from the brain.

The above observations-integrations are the bases of modern neurophysiology: they define a current model of the here-and-now activities of the brain.

From additional data from clinical studies on patients in neurosurgery, we know that memory processes occur in the cerebral cortex, and possibly in other regions (subcortical nuclei in feedback relations with cortex, and the cerebellum, also in feedback with the cortex).

The processing of the neuronal patterns exiting and entering the C.N.S. of the present instants (over time periods up to a few seconds to milliseconds) is done in sensori-motor cortex in and near the central fissure, in visual cortex in the occipital lobe, in acoustic cortex in the temporal lobe, in the eye fields in the frontal lobe.

Longer-term processing (over time periods of minutes to years) of central patterns generated in the shorter-term areas (above) takes place in the special associational ("silent") areas in the frontal lobe, the parietal lobe, the occipital lobe and the temporal lobe. All cerebral cortical lobes have central selective feedback relations with other lobes and the subcortical nuclei (striate nuclei, thalamus hypothalamus).

Where is the observer-participator in all this structure?

Is he/she merely an "epiphenomenon" of central processes in the above regions?

We know from instances of accidental-brain-injury cases that the observer–agent is located in the main bulk of the C.N.S.: a simple blow of sufficient force on the skull shows this—he/she becomes at least noncommunicative with outside observers. Injury to visual cortex blinds him/her; injury to sensori-motor cortex paralyzes him/her; injury to temporal cortex deafens him/her.

From the above (all-too-short) picture combined with further observations, we can deduce the following:

1. *The observer–agent's conscious self does not depend on the peripheral data* (i.e., exiting and entrancing patterns) *processors in any input-output mode in any cerebral lobe-subcortical nucleus.*

2. The observer–agent's processed-computed inputs-outputs can be cut off if the peripheral input-output data processors are injured or die.

3. Small systems in the mesencephalon (midbrain) can exert a powerful facilitatory and/or inhibitory control over all inputs and all outputs: this system when injured can remove all inputs-outputs to and from the observer–agent, inducing externally observable

inability to communicate with the external-world-situated observers.

The centrally located observer–agent can remain conscious while such removal of participation with the external realities is taking place.

4. Thus, theoretically, if the brain's life-support systems remain intact (blood supply, blood-borne nutrients, including oxygen and disposal of catabolic molecules), *the conscious observer–agent can be totally isolated-confined within the C.N.S.* by selected injuries to the brain, reversibly (with anesthetics and other chemical agents, concussion, or minimal reversible lesions), or irreversibly (with toxins, virus diseases, mechanical or chemical or electrical destruction of structure).

I deduce the following (from the above and from personal experience):

The thus isolated observer–agent can continue to experience internally generated programs from continuing central processing. The internally generated programs can create practically any internal reality for this observer–agent: realities like those experienced interlocked with the external world, realities like those experienced in special states of being (including: dreams, trances, anesthesia states [immergence and emergence], "hallucinogenic" chemical states, "mystical states," etcetera).

The thus isolated observer–agent–participator (properly trained previous to this profound isolation) can and may control (to a certain extent) these states of being. "Spontaneous" changes in states of being (derived from at present unknown sources) can also occur.

The above simulation of the realities of the totally isolated-confined observer–agent–participator can be simulated (to a more limited degree) in the solitude-isolation-confinement tank.

Given enough time and enough exposure to the near-zero environment, *any well-trained experienced person can experience directly for himself/herself the phenomena of central processing programs generating internal realities.*

These inner realities can have virtually infinite domains, unlimited by current or past concepts of languages, of logics, of mathematics, of philosophies, of beliefs, or of metabeliefs previously learned—experienced by this particular person. These domains are also unlimited by previous external reality experiences of the particular participant observer. Such considerations as these give (at least to this writer) a new perspective on possible (inner/outer) realities and their representation; the following research-oriented proposals are made:

1. *No current representation/simulation of inner/outer realities is adequate; no such model has the power of "goodness-of-fit" needed in such investigations.*

2. *A new set of attempts to simulate/model/represent the realities experienced under these conditions is needed.*

3. *No forbidding/nonallowing/nulling escapes from this research are permitted,* such as: "mystical," "God-given," "God forbidden," "work of the Devil," "impossible," "meaningless questions," "irrelevant observations," "nonsensical theories," "nonessential theories," "ineffable phenomena," "subjective reports," "no objective data or recordings," "anecdotal material," "delusions and illusions," "irrational thinking," "schizophrenia," etcetera. These are a few of the professional cliches / slogans / easy-judgments, based on laziness / greed / power / justification / protection, in and of religious-scientific-political-social territories in the defined consensus views / beliefs / metabeliefs of what is / is not "real."

4. *Protection of persons who perform these researches (through privacy of the fact it is being done) and of their results is a necessary condition.*

5. *Trained, disciplined, interested persons, with acceptable records, from each of most of the varied human disciplines are to be encouraged to engage in this research.* These domains of human endeavor include acceptable persons from: mathematics, science, religion, philosophy, politics, business, finance, the military professions, poetry, arts, the writing professions, the media, etcetera.

6. *Certain qualifications and conditions* are to be met for/by each person doing these researches in/on the isolated Self.*

7. *The methods used in these researches are as safe as can be designed/maintained. However, no responsibility is undertaken by the sponsors for the results of accidents resulting from equipment defects, from errors of personnel, or to the investigator during the course of his/her researches on Self.*

8. *Each Self investigator must take his/her own responsibility for risks, external as well as internal.*

* a.) *A past record of accomplishment* (as student or practitioner) in at least one human discipline/profession/activity; b.) *a demonstrated interest in pursuing the work for at least the minimally required number of hours in the isolation condition;* c.) *a lack of a past record of unacceptable characteristics* (violent behavior, irresponsible activities, nontrusting behavior, dogmatic intransigent performances/writing/sermons/lectures, sterile argumentative productions, etcetera); d.) *a demonstrated desire to learn about and modify his/her own currently operating belief systems and to widen his/her metabeliefs;* e.) *lack of evidence of a closed system of beliefs determining thinking-doing;* f.) *the absence of evidence that the person taking the training intends to use his/her results to gain (ego) power over others.* This requirement does not rule out those in responsible positions in any endeavor; g.) *persons with diseases of various sorts* (certain developmental anomalies, certain diseases of the nervous system, certain addictions, certain bacterial-viral or fungal diseases, etcetera) *must undergo medical screening before acceptance/rejection* for training. In certain physically diseased states, isolation tank work is contraindicated; h.) *a history of indulging in gossip* (spoken/written/professional/ media) *contraindicates acceptance: a demonstrated interest in privacy of self and the records of others is indicated;* i.) *a history of confabulation in the service of personal ego must be examined carefully before acceptance;* j.) *letters of recommendation* by responsible professionals *are required* and will be checked with the persons writing the letters; k.) sponsors of such research/ training are not interested in polemics/arguments/"con games"/selling/buying, etcetera.

CONCLUSIONS

1. In the isolated condition, the observer–agent experiences/creates that which we name "the inner domains"; such naming and such distinctions are made upon emergence from the isolated condition.

2. In the inner domains, states of being can be experienced in which the observer–agent has no knowledge of his/her brain, his/her body, his/her body's external environment, his/her identity as a unique human person on this planet.

3. *Isolated in the inner domains the observer–agent can transform into, be transformed into, any form,* including no form and infinite form (polymorphous property of the isolated observer–agent).

4. *Isolated in the inner domains, the observer–agent can experience any transform of Self (he/she/it)* (polytransform property of the observer–agent).

5. *Isolated in the inner domain, the observer–agent can experience any transform of the context/surrounds/domains* in which he/she/it is imbedded/lives/relates (polytransform property of the inner domains).

6. These polytransform properties of the observer–agent and of the inner domains are characteristic of C.N.S. central processing relatively uninfluenced by modulations of activity by the input–output processes of the C.N.S.

7. While still in physical isolation and upon emergence from the inner domains, the observer–agent experiences the limited transforms of Self given by his/her central nervous system's (low-level amplitudes) input-output processing, influencing the central processing at a low level.

8. Upon emergence from physical isolation into an external domain/reality/environment, the amplitudes/energies/quantities of activity in the input-output processing increase and the central processing becomes that necessary for adequate function of the brain/body and the observer–agent in the external domain/reality/ environment.

9. The reported descriptions/representations/simulations of the observer–agent in the external domain are now dependent on the communica-

tive abilities/capacities of this particular observer/agent with other observers–agents and their communicative abilities/capacities, imbedded in the social domains.

10.   Communicative capacities/abilities include descriptive and injunctive languages/concepts/mathematics/logics/semantics/drawings/paintings/motion-picture representations/etcetera.

11.   In the inner domains the observer–agent is not limited by his/her communicative abilities/capacities.

12.   In the outer domains, the polytransform property of the observer–agent (no. 4, above) and the polytransform property of the inner domains (no. 5, above) are attenuated/eliminated as a consequence of no. 8, above.

13.   In the inner/outer domains the unknown exists: unknown domains and phenomena exert programmatic effects on the observer–agent.

The above conclusions are stated in a system of explication/meta-language/metaprogramming as openended and nonclosed as is currently possible in/by this writer/observer–agent in a relatively stable external domain.

This is the statement of the current metatheoretical position in his search for reality (*The Dyadic Cyclone,* chapter on "The Search for Reality," reprinted in Chapter Four of *The Deep Self*).

These conclusions can be applied to studies of representations/descriptive/injunctive/computational means and languages and their analysis. In the inner domains, a given observer–agent may seek closure of such a language that she/he is creating/discovering. In attempting to achieve closure in the mathematical/logical sense, he/she may define his/her inner domains in such a way as to preclude experiencing the polytransform properties of Self and of domain. Mathematical criteria of rigor, of proof, of demonstration can limit the domain, the observer–agent, and the probable range of states permitted to each.

One example,* and its transform to open a (possibly premature) closure, is as follows:

6.522   There are, to be sure, nonenunciables. These indicate themselves, it is the mystical. [Es gibt allerdings Unaussprechliches. Dies zeigt sich, es ist das Mystische.]

TRANSFORM: There are, to be sure, experiences yet to be enunciated. These experiences themselves originate in, as yet, unknown domains.

Another example:**

7.   Whereof one cannot speak, thereof one must be silent. [Wovon man nicht sprechen kann, darüber muss man schweigen.¹]

TRANSFORM: Whereof one as yet cannot speak, thereof one can be silent. "We must bear in mind that which we need to know" and discover how to speak of that which was inexpressible. [In 1700 A.D. radio waves were silent and unenunciable.]

---

* Ludwig Wittgenstein, *Tractatus Logico-Philosophicus*, p. 150.
** Ibid.

CHAPTER SIX

The Domains of Reality: The Metabelief Operator

In each of us we define what is real and what is true by our own beliefs. At a given time and in a given set of circumstances, that which is real/true is derived from outside experience and inside experience ("inperience"). The phenomena of one's existence are reinterpreted in the light of one's beliefs about reality, generating one's simulations of the real and of the true. From direct experience/inperience and from the beliefs taught/given us, we create our pictures of reality.

It has been found useful to extend the concept of belief to include all of one's simulations of reality, including those generated by oneself. It is also useful to extend the usual definition of reality (as that which is outside the mind) to include that which is in the mind. In this system of thought we thus have an external reality and an internal reality, symbolized by e.r. and i.r.

One's Self is immersed in the i.r. This is true at all times, even when one is busily engaged in pursuits in the e.r.

There are two aspects of the Self that we separate into two concepts. The observing Self we name "the observer." The doing-participating Self we name "the operator." The whole Self is named "the observer–operator."

Depending upon circumstances, the observer can be observing external reality (e.r.) events and/or internal reality (i.r.) events. The operator can manipulate/participate-in external reality (e.r.) events and/or operate on/participate-in internal reality (i.r.) events. In the e.r. the operator uses the body, in the i.r. the operator uses simulations/concepts/beliefs/metabeliefs/intention/distinction, etcetera.*

As is developed in more detail in Appendix II on the Contained Mind, the observer/operator is always immersed in the i.r./i.r. simulations domain. Even when operating/observing in the e.r. events, he/she operates/observes through the i.r. domain into the e.r. domain in a two-way feedback (i.r. to e.r. to i.r. etcetera) relation.

We further define a "consensus reality" as that set of beliefs/assumptions /postulates/interpretations/simulations that each of us is given/absorbs that are said to be real/true in our culture/society/family/school, etcetera. *Consensus reality* is that which is agreed to be real/true by a dyad, family, group, nation or group of nations. Examples are the various human legal structures (city, county, state, nation, etcetera), the pictures of realities created by the media (newspaper, TV, radio, etcetera), the financial realities created by banks, taxes, salaries, wages, etcetera, and the scientific community's picture of reality.

Consensus reality is thus one collection or another of simulations of i.r./e.r. with which one agrees/disagrees. A large fraction of our most securely held sacred beliefs is in the consensus group of simulations of reality. Feedback with lovers, family, religious/political/business groups generates beliefs/disbeliefs in each of us. These beliefs are difficult to unearth: it is difficult to become aware of their existence and influence on our thinking/doing/feeling. (See *Simulations of God: The Science of Belief.*)

In visualizing the problems posed by the representation of the various facets of the realities, it has been found useful to define the concept of "the metabelief operator." Here the term "operator" is used in the mathematical sense of something that operates on something else to introduce changes/transforms in it. The term "metabelief" is defined as a belief about beliefs themselves: it is "meta" (above on the

* See Appendices I and II on the Contained Mind for further constraints and functions imposed/operating on the observer-operator by i.r./i.r. simulations.

90

next level) to beliefs. Thus a metabelief operator is a concept/function/agent that operates on, transforms, introduces changes into belief systems. The metabelief operator is operating outside a given belief system and operating on it. The primary conceptual role of the metabelief operator is the transformation of beliefs, and hence transforms of one's assumed realities.

The metabelief operator can be weak, strong, or nonexistent. If one is quite content with one's representations of the inner/outer realities, and content with one's life as it occurs, there may be no great need for a metabelief operator. In this case, it may be so weak as to be insignificant; one is content with one's beliefs: in one's family/business/religion/politics, one's beliefs work satisfactorily. One's intention is not devoted to transforms of beliefs. In such a case, the metabelief operator is nonexistent or functioning only as an entertainment of Self.

Activation of a strong metabelief operator in one who previously did not have such an operator can occur through a crisis of the physical/mental/spiritual type. A near brush with death, a profound religious experience, a serious accident, a prolonged illness, a financial disaster, a sudden unexpected new confrontation with violence-war-invasion, a deep psychedelic experience, each can generate a need to change beliefs about Self, about external reality, about internal reality. In such cases, the metabelief operator may appear and function for a time and either continue its operations or disappear again.

Some persons, geniuses of one sort or another, seem to acquire metabelief operators quite early in life and either use and maintain them or let them die with aging. Certain artists, scientists, businessmen, politicians, are creative through such metabelief operators. Once they are successful, the need for the metabelief operators may become weakened: the beliefs have become satisfying and the need for change has approached zero.

Others seem to maintain their metabelief operators throughout their life. Curiosity and interest in beliefs and their changes are kept alive for decades. Aging does not seem to affect these persons.

One important subset of the consensus realities is named the "paper reality" and its counterpart the "film/tape reality." In our society we record on paper our contracts, our marriages, our wills, our financial transactions, our news, our history, our thoughts, our opinions. Some of these records determine our action/thinking/doing to a large extent. We live up to, or break, our contracts. We marry one person and live with him/her according to our beliefs in what is marriage. We make a will in the expectation that its provisions will be carried out after our death. A checking account works because enough people believe in its paper reality. We believe/disbelieve in printed stories in newspapers, in TV news, etcetera. We tend to believe as true that which we read in books, magazines, etcetera. We tend to believe as true that which we see in motion pictures and on TV.

To a large extent, the "paper reality" represents the consensus reality to each of us. We are immersed in a representation of reality fed to us on paper, on film, on tape.

One's own experiential/experimental here-and-now reality and its direct self-generated simulations may agree/disagree with the paper reality. One can unquestioningly accept the paper/film/tape reality and become a passive acceptor/believer in the dictates of this portion of the consensus reality. One can also question these dictates on the basis of one's own experience/experiments/insights/knowledge.

One's metabelief operator can operate on the paper/film/tape reality and choose that which has a sufficient goodness-of-fit with one's own simulations of reality. One can thus develop criteria of what is real/true for oneself.

A useful set of logic value choices for such selection/use/observations is as follows:

1. That which is *"true/real"* in the consensus simulations or in the simulations of one other person is that which fits one's own simulation with an acceptable degree of correspondence.

2. That which is *"false/unreal"* lacks the necessary degree of correspondence of fit.

3. That which is *"as if true/real"* in the simulations of the other(s) is that which does not yet fall into one's own experience/simulations and is seen to be believed as true/real by the other(s).

4. That which is *"as if false/unreal"* is yet to be experienced/ simulated by Self and is believed by the other(s) as false/unreal: Self is withholding judgment.

5 That which is *"meaningless"*, is yet to be simulated by Self or is rejected by Self through ignorance/inexperience/disbelief/knowledge/insight/experience.

6. That which is *"as if meaningless"* is believed by other(s) to be meaningless, and Self is withholding judgment.

These six values can apply to one's own states of being. (See Appendix II on the Contained Mind.) In one state, one experiences certain events/simulations as true/real. In another state of being, not overlapping the first one, these events/simulations can become "as if true/real," "false/unreal," "as if false/unreal," "meaningless", or "as if meaningless."

For example, in physical isolation in solitude, one has a profound deep experience of eternal loneliness and unity with the universe. This experience/inperience at the time of occurrence is true/real. One returns to the busyness of life with family/occupation/colleagues/ friends. One is then in a state of belief interlock with the others. The previous state of being of loneliness/unity now seems only "as if true/real" or possibly unreal/untrue or meaningless. One knows it was real/true, yet now it is only "as if real/true" or unreal/untrue or meaningless.

One is then faced with the dilemma of what is reality. What is really true?

These are difficult questions. Our answers are not yet satisfactory to us. Our temporary/to-be-revised notions are as follows:

1. Direct here-and-now experience/inperience is to be taken as true/real.

2. Memories of past direct here-and-now experience/inperience are

imbedded in simulations and are simulations themselves and hence are only "as if true/real" on replay in isolation.

3. Consensual validation of experience/inperience is a mutually agreed-upon simulation. Two persons can agree only on their overlapping domain of simulations.

4. Direct here-and-now experience/inperience is not directly transferable from one mind to another.

5. Each of us thus generates a unique i.r./i.r. simulation domain with only some overlap in the agreed-upon simulation domain.

6. In a given e.r. experience, each of two persons experiences/ inperiences a unique reality postulated upon the simulations of each; the only overlap is in the subsequent descriptions, each with the other.

The metabelief operator can be constructed to change beliefs at various rates, from zero to the maximum speed available to the given person. In the event of a crisis, the speed of change can be such that the basic beliefs are changed in a few seconds, hours, or days. In the event of slow social change forcing belief changes the process may take years.

In the consensus reality, fast belief changes in a given person are suspect; that person is considered abnormal/far out/diseased/mentally ill/fanatic/unstable.

The consensus reality itself is one aspect of a very large hyperstable (see Appendix IV) multiple-individual feedback system. Its changes are slow in the absence of war/violence/catastrophe. Metabelief operators derived from consensus reality reflect this slow rate characteristic. To speed up the changes, solitude away from consensus reality feedback is necessary for the design of fast metabelief operators. Physical isolation long enough (hours) and frequent enough (daily) allows the development of such fast transforms. Such experience/inperience at least furnishes the possibilities for such metabelief operators to be developed. Psychedelic means (also in solitude) can speed up the transforms, as long as conflict with consensus reality can be avoided.

Immersed in the consensus reality, one finds the concept of interlock useful. *(Programming and Metaprogramming in the Human Biocomputer.)* Interlock is that set of phenomena experienced when one or more biocomputers (persons) are within the critical communicational distance for feedback and develop a two-way communication link used for a given time interval.

Examples of e.r. interlock are a conversation between two persons isolated with each other, a telephone conversation, here-and-now sexual relations, a group of persons playing a game, or singing together, or working together. When isolated and alone, in a given person, simulations of e.r. interlock may be a large portion of his/her i.r./i.r. simulations.

Interlock varies in its intensity. In e.r. sexual relations, the body1-body2, i.r.1–i.r.2 interlocks can be at a very high energy level. In an objective telephone conversation with another person, the interlock can be weak in its intensity. In a court, the interlocks can be of high intensity between the various antagonists.

Any e.r. interlock involves two-way exchanges that originate in the two observer/operators through representative mutual "e.r./i.r" simulations in the i.r. of each. Such simulations include the current language choices of each, the simulation of each by the other, the self-simulations of each of his/her role in the interlock, the simulations of consensus reality in each, and the positive, negative, and neutral energy controls exerted by each participant.

For interlock between two persons, the language requirements are limiting in certain domains. The verbal-vocal language (including control of voice, size of vocabulary, levels of cognition expressible by each, etcetera) is a portion of the interlock. Direct body language (facial expressiveness, control of movements of the arms, hands, and body, etcetera) is deeply involved in face-to-face interlock. Physical contact introduces additional parameters within one's i.r.

One's simulation of another person controls somewhat that which one can/will say to the other. If one expects negative energy from the other in certain domains of discourse, one tends to stay out of those domains, or challenges the other to enter them. If one expects a high positive energy from the other, one may avoid that domain or challenge the other, etcetera. With certain persons one can expect neutral energy in most (if not all) domains. If one's simulation of the other person places him/her above/below Self in regard to knowledge/ignorance/power /money/sex/intelligence, one may operate with certain special scripts assigned by consensus reality to such interlocks. With a metabelief operator that says that interlocks with another can transcend expected limits one can move beyond that which one expects of the other. One's simulation of the other can become a new process of opening up him/her and oneself into new domains of interlock.

The interlock concept can be extended beyond human-human feedback. Human-dolphin interlock has been discussed at length elsewhere (see *Lilly on Dolphins: Humans of the Sea*).

The human-machine interlock is an important one in our culture. For example, the driver-automobile interlock is a daily occurrence in many lives. The programmer-computer interlock is gradually assuming more importance in our culture: it influences the paper/film/tape reality in an increasingly powerful way. The mass production of industry depends upon exact human-machine interlocks of diverse types. One can look at our culture as depending to a great extent on such interlocks. From a woman working with her sewing machine, an author with his typewriter, a steel worker in a mill, a person on an electronic assembly line, a pilot in a transport jet, a scientist with an electron microscope, a newscaster and the TV camera and cameraman, to a user of the computer network, our culture is literally a large system of human-machine interlocks generating a large portion of our e.r. consensus reality.

When one removes oneself from this vast network of interlocks for a long enough period of time, one can see the continuation in one's internal reality of the influence of the past e.r. interlocks. In physical isolation and solitude the overshoot of the previous interlocks continues in one's simulation domain. One's internal reality is filled with e.r. interlock simulations.

There are some persons for whom this is reality, e.r. and its simulations are real/true to such a person. Everything else in the internal reality is looked upon as dream, daydream, or fantasy. To such an e.r.-oriented person there is a reluctance/fear/taboo of penetrating into the vastness of his/her inner realities. In our culture, consensus reality approves/rewards such persons. This mode of life is quite acceptable/meaningful until it is interrupted by some influences greater than Self. As stated above, crises generate changes in one's metabelief operator.

For such persons, the isolation tank is a resting place and a "think tank" for working out problems. For these purposes the tank can be of great benefit.

For those who are discontented with this view of reality, for those who wish to penetrate the deep Self, pursue self-analysis, use the deeper meditations, explore reality in greater depth, the isolation tank functions as a useful tool probably better than any other e.r. configuration. This environment allows the inner realities to be penetrated as deeply as one is capable of doing so. All e.r. interlocks are minimized almost to zero at the time one enters floatation in the darkness and the silence.

It is for such a group of persons of this latter type that we furnish further domain maps of the internal realities that we have found useful in these pursuits. These maps are for those who have already decided to change their belief systems and develop a more flexible/powerful set of metabeliefs, metabelief operators.

In isolation, in deep penetrations into the internal realities domain, one comes upon certain phenomena not usually experienced in everyday life as we know it in our culture.

Floating in the darkness/silence, one can lose awareness of any or all of the following: (1) the tank and solution, (2) one's body, (3) one's e.r. simulations, (4) one's i.r., (5) one's i.r. simulations, (6) one's identity: one's simulation of oneself, (7) oneself as a unique individual Self, (8) one's humanness, (9) one's planet and its e.r. (See Appendixes.)

One can become aware of new experience/inperience: (1) that the apparent e.r. (e.r. simulations) is penetrable by means other than those experienced in consensus e.r. interlock, (2) that Self is programmed by program systems of which one is not usually aware, (3) that entities other than one's Self somehow can interlock with one in the isolation tank by means not present in our current consensus science, (4) that one is something/someone far greater than one's simulation of one's Self, (5) that one can become so deeply interlocked with something far greater than human that one's Self disappears as an individual human being and one unifies/identifies with some "network" of creation, (6) that one's Self (when present) can move out of the body to anywhere/anytime/any form.

These phenomena have been described in my three books: *Programming and Metaprogramming in the Human Biocomputer*, in *The Center of the Cyclone*, and in *The Dyadic Cyclone*. Some of these phenomena are recounted by persons other than this author in the tank logs later in *The Deep Self*.

The author's current position in regard to these phenomena is given in two appendixes in this book: "The Development of the 'Contained Mind' Hypothesis," and "The Contained Mind Metabelief: Definition of Elements." The first of these two appendixes is a summary of a metabelief operator that assumes that the mind, as we know it, is limited to the brain and that it can be isolated from all inputs/outputs known in current consensus science by means of the tank technique of isolation. The second of these two chapters is a set of metabelief operators in which the mind either is not limited to the brain or in which at present unknown inputs/outputs exert detectable effects on the mind.

CHAPTER SEVEN
The Mind Contained in the Brain:
A Cybernetic Belief System

In the American society of the year 1977, there is a vast array of belief systems about the mind and the brain. There are those primarily in religion who believe that the mind is something greater than computations done by a biocomputer, which demonstrates an implicit faith that the human mind somehow is connected with a human spirit or soul that transcends the everyday operations of the normal human mind. Such concepts generate a "mind unlimited" belief which is dealt with in Chapter Eight.

This belief in an unlimited mind available to man goes back into our dim, distant past, long before written history. It is connected with one's religious feelings, with one's religious experience and with the traditional teachings derived from the formalized religions. Over the millennia, this belief system has become quite powerful and determines the thinking of millions of persons upon this planet. It is only relatively recently that a possible alternative to this belief system has arisen in science and in medicine.

The new belief system arises from studies of medicine, neurology, neurophysiology, to a certain extent, but also has arisen in the pragmatic way that man and woman treat one another in their everyday relations in the law, in business and in science itself. In our everyday pragmatic relationships we assume that the other person whom we are dealing with is contained within his/her body. We assume that in his/her absence we cannot deal with him/her. When he/she is, say, more than a few hundred feet away, in a sense he/she is missing,

99

absent. When another person is out of reach of our voice in the external world, or out of reach by telephone, somehow or other we have lost contact with him/her. At least we cannot make mutual decisions without his/her presence and his/her agreement in the presence of either the voice or the person.

If there were a secure means of communication without the known physical means of communication such as voice, vision, vocal feedback and so forth, we would undoubtedly use these other channels. In the pragmatic everyday world we use that which is available to us to use. Theoretical possibilities do not enter into our everyday calculations in relationships with others.

Thus we have arrived implicitly, if not explicitly, at a system of dealing with others in which we depend upon the telephone, the telegraph, the letter, the TV image, to link one of us with others. It is only rarely that we have experiences that allow us to say that there are possibilities of communication other than those that currently are represented by the visual image, by the vocal expression or by the written word.

Thus, in a rather sloppy way, we assume that each person somehow is contained within his/her body, and that to deal with him/her, the body or a known communication means must be available in order to communicate. Out of sight, out of sound, and away from written materials, with no TV set, we are each pragmatically alone.

Thus, from the empirical experience point of view, the person is relegated at least to the body that apparently houses him/her.

Certain empirical observations made over the millennia have convinced certain persons who have studied the subject that the person is not only confined to a body, but is confined to the brain within that body. In the experience of a sufficiently powerful blow to the head, one can see the person disappear, as it were. The body goes into coma, one can no longer speak with the person within that body-brain, the usual means of communication are cut off abruptly and completely. That particular person is assumed to be unconscious; i.e., incapable of communication with those that surround him or her. Such a person for a time remains incommunicative and then somehow seems to return to conscious use of the body and communication is resumed.

In medicine, for many years it has been assumed on the basis of such observations, that the person somehow is a function of intact cerebral cortical activity within the central nervous system. The person is limited to a functioning intact brain, undamaged, not under anesthesia, in a so-called normal state for that particular brain.

Such observations have led to the contained mind hypothesis, or, if you wish, belief system.

This belief system dominates our law; for example, in habeas corpus doctrine, which says that the only way that the law can operate is to have the body present, in such proceedings the body is obtained. Similarly, in psychiatry, the presence of the patient, communication with the patient, is necessary for a diagnosis. In arriving at the diagnosis, one assumes that all of the information needed is somehow contained within that particular body in that particular brain. In the business world one deals with other humans in bodies, and deals with their particular kinds of brains, kinds of minds contained in those brains, on the pragmatic assumption that if the person is present one can make a deal; if the person is not present, one cannot make a deal with that particular person.

Quite common in the United States are those who believe in both systems: the contained mind and the uncontained mind belief systems. On a particular day of the week these people attend formalized meetings in which the uncontained mind hypothesis operates, such as in church on Sunday, or with a religious group, and during the rest of the week they operate using the contained mind belief.

At night during sleep one leaves the external reality in the consensus way of operating in that external reality with other persons, and enters into regions in which there are apparently other laws, other beliefs. In hypnotic states, in dream states, the laws of the external world may or may not rule that which happens. One can go through complete experiences with apparently real other persons, either known or unknown persons; one can melt and flow as if a liquid, one can become a point, a line or a solid, one can control somewhat what the other persons say and do, etcetera. The laws of the apparent internal reality of the dream states do not have the constraints that the external reality has. There are other sets of laws of the internal reality that are far different, and yet may overlap those of the external reality. In such states the mind may seem to be unlimited, to extend out beyond the confines of one's own brain, of one's own body. Each of us can have such experiences isolated within oneself each night in our beds.

The contained mind thus becomes an apparently uncontained mind, asleep dreaming at night. Similarly, under the influence of anesthetics, psychedelic chemicals, of trance, and of the isolation tank, one can enter into states of being in which the mind seems apparently to be unlimited, not constrained to the body and brain.

Let us then develop more specifically the contained mind belief system and see if it can embrace both sets of phenomena, those of ordinary everyday waking life, interacting with others, and the dream states, trance states and psychedelic states, and religious experiences.

In this belief system we are in effect saying that the mind is a function of the brain's activities, and of nothing else—except, the changes in that mind as modulated by exchanges and participations in an external world with the solidity of the planet and the complexity of other humans and other animals and plants. Let us also assume that we can specify all the inputs to this brain and all the outputs from this brain. The inputs are vision, hearing, tactile sense, position sense, detection of accelerations owing to gravity and owing to motion, the sense of smell, the senses delegated to the regulation of the body itself. The outputs from that brain are restricted to muscular activities, glandular activities, the intake and the output of food and its products. In this belief system there are no hidden inputs or outputs. The inputs and outputs to and from the brain are those within the body and at the surface of the body.

Complete physical isolation of the body thus leads to attenuation or elimination of all inputs and all outputs. As is given in other parts of this book, the physical isolation tank eliminates all of the inputs to and from the body insofar as this is possible to do. The isolation tank does not eliminate the inputs and outputs to and from the brain within the body itself. The body's motions are still available, and only by voluntary inhibition of bodily motion can isolation of the brain from this source of feedback stimulation be eliminated or attenuated.

The isolation tank prevents interactions with the external reality and assures a solitudinous body and a solitudinous biocomputer within that body with no further needful exchanges with the external reality.

The contained mind hypothesis thus says that the isolation tank isolates the body completely insofar as our present science is able to specify isolation itself.

In this belief system then, there is no way that a person in an isolation tank can communicate with other persons. All channels of communication have been eliminated. This belief system states that there are no mysterious unknown means of communication remaining to that particular isolated person.

A person believing this contained mind hypothesis will then take all experiences reported by such isolated people as being evidence of what can happen in a contained mind within a contained brain. All states, no matter how far out or how far removed they are from everyday experience, that are subsequently recounted as having been described by a person in isolation, will be accounted for by an observer with this belief system as having taken place totally within the isolated body-brain of that particular person.

Some persons experiencing the isolation tank have other belief systems based upon their previous experience in the tank. Some have other belief systems based upon direct personal experience without using a tank, using experiences of anesthesia, of coma, of near brushes with death, in addition to tank experiences. Thus, there is a gap between people with the contained mind belief system versus those with the mind unlimited belief system.

Let us examine the contained mind hypothesis and see if using such a belief system we can construct the possibilities of experiences that seem to belong to the region of the unlimited mind, and account for them, at least theoretically, adequately. In order to do this we must be able to account for dream phenomena, for psychedelic experiences, for coma experiences, for deep religious experiences, and similar phenomena reported by many hundreds of persons.

In order to simplify our descriptions, let us assume that we are, each of us, isolated in an isolation tank, floating in the darkness, the silence, removed from all known communication means.

At the beginning of such an experience one has moved from the external reality, including: clothing, a lighted environment filled with noise, with many, many signals coming into the body, from many, many different sources, including other people. Each of us takes off their clothes, immerse themselves in the tank, floating at the surface in the darkness and the silence, alone. At first one rememers the immediately preceding external reality fairly vividly. Slowly these memories can disappear or can be maintained by conscious processes. As one abandons these memories of the external reality, one may become preoccupied with the sensations of the body floating in the blackness and silence and warmth.

After many hours of exposure to such an environment, repeated on a daily schedule, one gradually increases one's speed of abandoning the memories of the external reality and the preoccupation with the floating sensations of the body in the dark in the isolation tank. One now becomes aware that one is aware, quite independently, of the body or of the external reality. One says in effect, I know that I am conscious and functioning without the interlock with the external world; preoccupation with remaining sources of stimulation within the body passes away, the heart and the respiration and the sensations from the skin all are attenuated to the point where they can be forgotten.

One has gone beyond seeing the differences between open eyes and closed eyes, changing the rate and depth of respiration, playing with one's heart and similar activities.

If one is in a disturbed state because of some interaction that has taken place in the external reality, this disturbance will go on sometimes for hours. One may be totally obsessed with some sort of a hurt given by another person, some sort of a quarrel that one has had. In the tank, eventually this kind of thinking and preoccupation can also die away.

One may then fall asleep and go through a long dream sequence and then wake up again in the sense that one comes back to the body and the brain, out of the dream world. With more and more exposure to the tank, one finds that between the state of dreaming and the state of being wide awake and conscious of one's body there are hundreds if not thousands of other states of being in which one's consciousness is unimpaired and apparently disconnected from the brain and the body.

Let us try to construct a partial catalog of these states and see if we can construct a theory that can account for each portion of that catalog. Since that which exists in the external reality and connects us with it is missing, we will call this catalog a catalog of the internal realities.

1. One has entered into a dream state in which one's body is intact and one is walking around upon the very familiar planet in which one has existed in the past up to the present. One is carrying on conversations both with persons known to oneself and possibly with strangers. It is all a very familiar reality based upon one's previous experiences in the external world. In the contained mind belief system we assume that this is a simulation of the Self and of the external world (such e.r. simulations being part of the i.r.) that one is generating within one's own brain. In such scenarios there is nothing that is surprising, nothing new, nothing unique, nothing bizarre and one is quite content that this is as one lives and has lived in the past in the external reality.

In the contained mind belief system this is a simulation of Self, of one's body and of the external reality of oneself. For most persons this is a very safe simulation and expresses a large number of their personal dreams. In the tank it has been noticed that such experiences have a brilliance and a "reality" far greater than most dreams. The subject of such an experience seems to be stronger than he or she is in his/her normal dreaming states. There is a more intact awareness going on, of voluntariness and a brilliance of the whole scene that is lacking in the ordinary dreams.

2. Almost imperceptibly there may be strange extraterrestrial external realities developing and strange creatures, strange humans not of this planet appearing. One's Self and one's body may remain the same as they were before, in the external world. One can then wander around in these strange extraterrestrial surroundings. One is still one's ordinary self, one's ordinary body, but within very strange surroundings.

3. Alternatively, one may become a strange Self in these strange surroundings. One's body may change to something else or someone else. One may be looking through the eyes of someone else, realizing that one is doing so. The body that one is inhabiting at that point may be reading some very peculiar language with which one is unacquainted. The body one is inhabiting may be conversing with another similar strange body. There is a sense of alienness about such experiences of which one is aware.

The strange Self can also be in an ordinary, known type of external reality and be a stranger among familiar humans. The familiar external reality may seem strange, as if one is identified with a visitor to this planet.

4. In strange or familiar external realities, there may be transforms of Self in which one loses one's body. One can become some other form of body, a point or even a small point existing in a strange or familiar external world. One may travel through the external reality quite freely without known means of locomotion. One can go far above the scene

that one is looking at and look down upon it, or one can go down into any aspect of the scene as if one is looking through a microscope, enlarging any aspect of the scene. One can also go outward, as if one is looking through a telescope, and approach galaxies off the face of the planet which one is currently inhabiting.

5. Alternatively, there can be a beginning fusion between Self and one's surrounds. The surrounds can become liquid and flow in a myriad of colors. At this point the distinctions between Self and the surrounds begin to be lost. One no longer has boundaries; one spreads out and becomes some of the flowing materials, the flowing energies. There is a loss of the boundaries and the distinctions between Self and the surroundings.

6. The surroundings may disappear entirely; the Self becomes isolated in a voidlike space. The mood of Self can then become anything. One can be totally paralyzed with fear or one can be ecstatically blissful and happy, floating in isolation, no body, no surroundings, no external reality, just the reality of Self.

7. Alternatively, one may become the whole universe; one becomes omniscient, one knows everything that happened in the past, is happening in the present and will happen in the future. One is omniscient, omnipotent, and omnipresent. One can react to this with fear, with joy, with high neutral energy or with anger.

8. One may become nothing, there is no Self, no external world, no knowledge, no memory. One has become zeroed out; there is nothing left including Self. Awareness and consciousness disappear.

As one can see by inspecting this catalog very carefully, these are the kinds of experiences that one can experience in dream states. As we said above, the difference in the tank experience is that there is a heightened awareness, heightened consciousness and a heightened participation in what is happening. This catalog is not exhaustive of such states, it is merely indicative of the kinds of things that can happen to one in the isolation tank.

How can we account for such states if we assume that the mind is contained in the brain, that the mind and the Self are the results of computations of a central nervous system?

For purposes of discussion, let us try to divide up the Self in various realities into simplified diagrams so that we can grasp some of the variables and parameters that are active here. In Chapter Five we discussed the Self as an isolated observer–agent-operator. In the contained mind hypothesis, the Self, the observer/operator (ob/op) is part of the results of the computations of a central nervous system, a brain. In a basic philosophical sense, the Self is thus a generated result of those computations. Without the computations the Self does not exist. *Thus, the Self is a program, a metaprogram, a Self metaprogram, a self-referential aspect of the computations of that brain.* Thus, the Self is the victim, as it were, of that which generates it, is the victim of the self-referential computations of that brain.

This state of affairs can be very threatening when one realizes what "one really is." When a given observer realizes this source of Self as true, a paranoid reaction of great depth may develop. That particular person may become hypercautious as to allowing this knowledge to penetrate himself. This model or simulation of Self may wall off that particular person from further realizations about the true complexity of the situation. If one assumes that the computational processes of a brain are simple, and hence one's Self is a result of simple processes, this can induce quite a good deal of fear and paranoia. In reality, of course, the computations of a given nervous system the size of man's are immensely complex and hence one does not really know all of the computations that can take place. Some people in order to escape the position that they are the result of computations of a central nervous system will immediately shift to the belief in the unlimited mind and believe that they are not contained within the computations of the brain. Such persons will not bother to explore this possibility. I recommend exploration of this possibility to as great a depth as one is capable with courage so as to realize its true nature rather than shying off from it because one is afraid of it.

As one can see in the above catalog, items 1 to 8, the phenomena experienced by the inside observer can be accounted for by assuming that all of this is the result of computations within the central nervous system. Let us discuss each point in turn.

The external reality that one experiences in (1) above in a sense is the stored simulation or model of past external realities with which one has had experience. The structure of that particular planetary surface, the people, the buildings, the plants and so on are quite familiar and may be portions of the planetary surface in which one has lived. Thus, we arrive at a computed past external reality simulated, currently brought out of storage, and computed around the computed Self. We call these the external reality simulations (see Figure 2, Appendix II, and Table 2, Appendix II).

As we move down the list from (1) to (2), we find that the external reality changes into strange, unique and new external realities surrounding a familiar Self. Thus we begin to see that there are stored, or created anew, strange external realities, apparently not experienced before by this particular Self. In ordinary parlance we have entered the region of "imagination." Since I do not know what imagination is, I would prefer to say that these are simulations of new external realities, either generated de novo by unknown processes in the brain, or by the inherent noise level in the brain generating new external reality appearances. Thus, we can see that the e.r. simulations, the simulations of an apparent external reality, can either be of a familiar stored type or of a new unique created type.

In a way similar to that of external reality, the body that the Self is inhabiting can change. One can become someone else that one knows or some stranger that one does not yet know, or some strange animal, plant or other form. Thus, the simulations of Self, like those of the e.r., can change and be of a familiar type or a new and unique type.

Continuing then in the list (item 5), there can be a loss of distinctions between Self and the surrounds, so that the simulations of Self and the simulations of the surroundings become melded; the boundaries of distinction become more diffuse and the Self spreads out. Here then, mixtures of the simulations of Self and of the e.r. become blurred and finally disappear.

Simulations of the external reality can disappear completely and the simulations of Self become totally isolated in a domain that has no space, no time, and is eternal. The Self is still capable of emotion, and may become, may move into any emotional mode of which one can conceive. The simulation of Self is still intact, still functioning, and still apparent to Self. One then moves down the list (item 7) further and finds that the simulations of Self have disappeared, and the Self is everything, spread out, universal, creating everything, creating itself, the state of total feedback upon Self with no outside references to Self at all. All simulations of the external reality are gone, all simulations of Self are gone and there is only a pure consciousness, a pure awareness, consciousness without an object (Franklin Merrell-Wolff).*

Finally (item 8), Self disappears, everything disappears. If there is any experience in this state, none of it is brought back in returning from this state to other states.

The above materials are treated more meticulously, in a purer form, in Appendix II, *"The Contained Mind Metabelief: Definitions of Elements."* For those who wish to pursue this kind of representation of what happens in the tank I recommend a study of Appendix II. One can test one's mastery of this particular model by carrying out the exercises suggested in Appendix II.

I would like to clarify the concept of the observer/operator (ob/op). The deep basic meaning of observer/operator implies a certain degree of consciousness and control. This is a science game, the scientist is always conscious, aware and in control of his thinking and of the processes that he is examining. In the isolation tank this may not necessarily be true. There are many states in which the Self is not in con-

* Franklin Merrell-Wolff, *Pathways Through to Space.*

trol and is being programmed by forces very much larger than Self, so that there are aspects of Self that are not dealt with in any great length in the presentation of Appendix II. The Self as a victim, the Self as someone who is being coercively persuaded of another belief system not one's own, is one that most of us experience at one time or another, especially as children. The passive observer and the active operator both seem to disappear under these conditions. The Self is interlocked with forces, with beings, with entities far greater than Self and doing that which is programmed by them rather than by one's own initiative. One does not, as it were, sit still and watch; one is forced into participation by external entities, forces, and so forth.

Such states of the Self as a "programee" can be threatening or enjoyable or quite neutral.

In the above model, in the model in Appendix II, we must remember that we are assuming that all of these phenomena are taking place within an isolated body and brain. There is no access here to mysterious forces outside the computational processes of the brain itself. As soon as one no longer believes in such a model and its apparent limitations, one can move into other belief systems about the same phenomena. The alternatives to the above model are considered in the next chapter, "The Mind Unlimited: The Deep Self Uncontained." In this alternative set of belief systems, we consider other origins for the phenomena experienced.

We do not wish to espouse either the contained mind model or the leaky mind or the universal mind models. Our task here is to present alternatives rather than to espouse any one of them.

I hope that such considerations will help you in your own researches into your own Self using the isolation tank. I hope that such models will open up new possibilities for your own direct experience in the tank. I hope that this will enlarge your horizons and allow yourself to experience that which we have described in a safe way, so that you can be convinced that such things are possible and probable for you.

I suggest that you read the accounts elsewhere in this book of the direct experiences that several people have had. Many more than are given here are to appear in a book currently in preparation; we will give several hundreds of such direct firsthand accounts. Most of what each of these people has to say can be accounted for by these models, by these metasimulations, if you wish.

One lesson that has come from all of my more than twenty years experience with the tank is that the human mind has many unknowns within it, and my own personal respect for it has moved way beyond where it was when I started the tank research on the Deep Self.

CHAPTER EIGHT

The Mind Unlimited:
The Deep Self Uncontained

From the contained mind belief system of the preceding chapter, we can move into a wider context. As an introduction to this context, a quote from *The Center of the Cyclone* is pertinent.

LIMITS OF BELIEF TRANSCENDED

At first one's limits are set by the belief "I am centered in my physical brain." (That which one believes to be true, is true, or becomes true, at first within limits to be found experimentally. These limits themselves, are beliefs to be transcended.)

I am not limited by the known physical senses, known physical signals sent/received by my brain. (Transcended, these limits are left behind. I send/receive messages by means unknown with unknown entities greater than me.)

Beyond transcendence is an infinite variety of unknowns. (I move from my brain into other universes and spaces, other states of being. Once lived, these unknowns are no longer unknown.)

In the other universes and spaces, the other states of being, are teachers, guardians. (Beyond these unknowns, not known, is full complete Truth.)

The guardians/teachers make me aware, help me be aware, and help me to experience, when I'm ready, realities beyond belief, beyond proof, beyond demonstration, beyond theory, beyond imagination. (Beyond that Truth, full and complete, are unknowns.)

The teachers' teachers take over my lessons. (New unknowns become known. The cycle repeats. Mastered, these unknowns are transcended.)

This excerpt contains a stepwise infinite progression of belief, transcendence, new belief, its transcendence, and so on to infinity. This series is to be borne in mind during the following discussion as a further guide to understanding beyond the details of the beliefs discussed.

Here, in contrast to the chapter "The Mind Contained in the Brain: A Cybernetic Belief System," we take on a belief system that does not contain the mind in a central nervous system. The boundaries of the mind, the domains open to the Self, are not limited by the biophysical structure of the brain.

Even though most religions and esoteric-mystical schools espouse such belief systems, here we are not making our assumptions similar to or identical with such systems of thought (see *Simulations of God: The Science of Belief* for our point of view on such beliefs).

The phenomena experienced in physical isolation-solitude-confinement can still be expressed in the terms used in the "contained mind" cybernetic belief system. The fundamental difference is in the concepts of the limits placed on: (1) the sources of inputs/outputs (signals), (2) on the sources of information (other than from central processing), (3) on the sources of ∇'s (simulations), and (4) on the mobility of the observer/operator (outside the C.N.S.)

The "mind unlimited" belief system states:

1. There can be sources and signals not yet instrumentally detectable that can be/are detected by the observer/operator in isolation from all known physical sources specifiable in modern sciences. These sources and signals can be transformed into information by central processing.
2. In addition to information resulting from central processing of input/output signals, there can be internally detectable additional sources of information transmitted from unknown sources directly to

the observer/operator.

3. In addition to those simulations resulting from central processing, there can be additional ∇'s (simulations) originating in unknown sources and transferred directly into the i.r. ∇ domain by unknown means.

4. The observer/operator, in addition to being a result of the central processing of a C.N.S., can exist as a mobile unit/entity that can and does leave the vicinity of a brain in which it has invested a life interest.

Taking up each of these beliefs (1 through 4) separately, we can explicate/examine the mind unlimited belief system in detail.

1. The first assumption is essentially that of signals and their sources not yet in our current natural sciences. In the physical isolation (silence, darkness, floating isothermally) technique, we are not knowingly isolating the observer/operator from at-present-unknown signals that he/she may be detecting after central processing into information.

This assumption is analogous but not identical to the example I mentioned earlier of radio waves and atomic particles in, say, 1700 A.D. At that time there was no available instrumental means of detection of either one. At present there is no known means of detecting either one without instruments.

If there are sources/signals at present detectable by the observer/operator and not detectable by instruments, there are as yet no experimental verifications acceptable to the criteria of the natural sciences. Firsthand reports/observations by accepted trained observers must be verified by agreement with the firsthand reports/observations of 2nd, 3rd, to nth accepted trained observers. Not enough such trained observers have used the current isolation technique to try for such consensus verification.

If such unknown signals exist, and if they are operative in present observers in the isolated state, the resulting phenomena in the i.r. and i.r.V's operate in such a way as to be indistinguishable (by our present criteria) from phenomena originating "spontaneously" from central processes and their inherent "noise level," from memory processes, and from Self-programmed phenomena.

If and when instruments can be devised/discovered/created for detection of such signals (if any), then "objective recorded data" can be used to separate the at-present indistinguishable phenomena and their origins by means of the simultaneously recorded signals.

2. The second assumption states that there are unknown kinds of information generated/transmitted by unknown means directly to the observer/operator, bypassing the C.N.S. central processing that generates information out of signals.

This is a mode of communication claimed to exist by mystics/prophets/ gurus in which some suprahuman agency greater than the teacher imparts information directly to him/her, and possibly through him/her directly to the disciple/student. These processes are called inspiration/intuition/direct knowing/gnosis.

Even though such processes of "direct information transfer" may exist, the evidence seems remote from the criteria of acceptable trained observers in modern science. Cross-observer validation among trained scientific observer/operators is lacking in this critical area.

This assumption bypasses the processes inherent in the cybernetic contained mind belief system. The only evidence for the existence of such systems of direct transfer is given by those experiencing phenomena that are *described "as if" such systems exist.* Only those believing such an assumption give such descriptions as *true*, not *"as if true."*

To a scientifically trained observer/operator experiencing such phenomena, the cybernetic contained mind beliefs are more satisfactory investigative tools. The contained mind open to unknown signals (1, above) and their processing somehow seems more "investigatable," and would seem to generate data more easily handled in the scientific domain.

For the untrained observer/operator the "direct transfer" theory is seductive/provocative/easy and does not require the disciplines of the cybernetic model. Validation by cross-observer investigations is thus not necessary/ avoidable/unsatisfactory. Overvaluation of this type does not fit the scientific approach.

3. The third assumption bypasses the signals/processing/information/ simulation chains of the cybernetic contained mind system. It is a variant on (2) above of "direct information transfer" and implies "direct simulation transfer" in a similar fashion.

Under this belief system, a believer believes in simulations transferred from (suprahuman or human) sources directly to him/her without processing. Hence simulations in the i.r. are *real and true events/entities/processes,* not dependent on central processing.

For such persons as above (i.e., this class of believers) in certain states of being (3, 4 and 5 of Table 2 in Appendix II) there are no simulations, no i.r. or e.r. simulations, there is *only true direct inner experience.* For some persons it is necessary to accept *as true* rather than, *"as if true"* the inner phenomena of 3, 4 and 5 while in state 0 of Table 2 in order to move into 3, 4, or 5.

Another, more satisfactory method for this writer is to use the cybernetic contained mind system in state 0 and to assume 3, 4, 5 *"as if true."* When in 3, 4, 5 the events/processes/entities are not i.r. simulations ("as if true"); they are *true direct experiences.* On return to state 0, the "true direct experiences" become "i.r. simulations" (i.r. ∇'s), if and until some better evidence of their real existence is furnished by cross-observer validations.

4. The fourth assumption is that of an observer/operator who is free to move outside the C.N.S. and is not necessarily contained in the brain.

Several kinds of assumptions/systems can be found under this belief system when combined with other systems:

    a.   The observer/operator is within the i.r./i.r. simulation domain and has access to being programmed by i.r. simulations "as if" traveling/mobile outside the C.N.S.: the observer/operator is in one of states 2, 3, 4 or 5 (Table 2, Appendix II) and believes the internal events are true and also believes they are not restricted to the i.r. domain.

b. The observer/operator is mobile and not contained in the C.N.S. processing domain, and is free of C.N.S. constraints.

c. The observer/operator is within the i.r. domain in the C.N.S. processing and is programmed (with the i.r.∇'s) by unknown outside sources to be "as if" mobile, unconstrained, free of the C.N.S. processes.

a. This is essentially the cybernetic belief system dictating the *as if true* position discussed in Table 2, in states 2 through 5 for the observer/operator in state 0. In this view, the "apparent travel" is just that: apparent, not real. The belief in the real in states 2 through 5 does not hold in state 0.

b. This is the familiar assumption of mystics/yogis/astral travel advocates. (See R. A. Monroe, *Journeys Out of the Body*.) The phenomena described in this literature are explicable and "generatable" under *a.* and *c.*, as well as *b.* (of list above).

c. This assumption postulates unknown outside programming sources that generate "travel scripts/programs/realities" within the i.r./i.r. ∇'s/ob/op domains. The observer/operator is put through experiences as real by this outside agency; the i.r. context is changed to match the script necessities at each instant.

The writer's own experiences in isolation are each real enough to be able (in state 0) to believe in assumption *a, b,* and/or *c.* In his present state 0, he prefers "*a*" over "*c*" over "*b.*"

There seems not to be, as yet, any secure way of separating *a* from *b* from *c*, as far as this observer/operator can enunciate at this time (1977). The phenomena experienced under each basic belief system are similar if not identical. Until a secure multiple cross-observer/operator method is worked out, these three belief systems remain more or less equivalent as "phenomena generators-explicators."

(Some of R. A. Monroe's data in *Journeys Out of the Body* re dyadic observer/operator travel seem pertinent and seem to favor *b* over *a*, though not saying much about *c* applied to two observer/operators.)

The following experimental proposal is made: Two properly trained investigators functioning as isolated observer/operators are physically isolated in solitude from each other and from all other persons.

1. Each investigator enters a separate tank at the same clock time.
2. Each is preprogrammed for each exposure with the same belief system (a or b or c).
3. Each remains isolated long enough (and frequently enough) to experience the phenomena in the i.r./i.r. simulations domain.
4. Each, on emersion, dictates in solitude his/her description of the experience.
5. A third investigator (also trained properly) analyzes the two separate reports without feedback with the other two investigators.
6. All precautions possible to prevent cross-communication between the three investigators are taken to prevent parallel programming by the known physical modes of communication.
7. This experiment is repeated several times for each of the three belief systems.
8 Results at the end of the series are closely analyzed by the third investigator.
9. A three-way analysis is then conducted by the three investigators to arrive at a possible consensus.
10. Additional suitable personnel are introduced as needed.

No immediate answers to the above questions are to be expected. For some time, no deadlines are to be set. This is a long-term program, not a short-term project.

Instrumental means for clock-timing of events can be of aid in arriving at timing of experienced phenomena in the two observer/operators for determination of synchronous shared experiences.

Sufficient security is placed on all data to assure no leaks between the two investigators (see the article by Lilly and Shurley in Chapter Ten for sources of such leaks).

CHAPTER NINE

Mental Effects of Reduction of Ordinary Levels of Physical Stimuli on Intact, Healthy Persons

(Reprinted from Psychiatric Research Reports 5, American Psychiatric Association, June, 1956)

JOHN C. LILLY, M.D.*

INTRODUCTION

We have been seeking answers to the question of what happens to a brain and its contained mind in the relative absence of physical stimulation. In neurophysiology, this is one form of the question: Freed of normal efferent and afferent activities, does the activity of the brain soon become that of coma or sleep, or is there some inherent mechanism which keeps it going, a pacemaker of the "awake" type of activity? In psychoanalysis, there is a similar, but not identical problem. If the healthy ego is freed of reality stimuli, does it maintain the secondary process, or does primary process take over? i.e., Is the healthy ego independent of reality or dependent in some fashion, in some

*Author's affiliation at that time was the National Institute of Mental Health, Public Health Service, Department of Health, Education and Welfare, Washington, D.C.

degree, on exchanges with the surroundings to maintain its structure?

In seeking answers, we have found pertinent autobiographical literature and reports of experiments by others, and have done experiments ourselves. The experiments are psychological ones on human subjects. Many psychological experiments in isolation have been done on animals, but are not recounted in detail here; parenthetically, the effect on very young animals can be an almost completely irreversible lack of development of whole systems, such as those necessary for the use of vision in accomplishing tasks put to the animal. No truly neurophysiological isolation experiments on either animals or man have yet been done.

AUTOBIOGRAPHICAL ACCOUNTS

The published autobiographical material has several drawbacks: In no case is there a sizeable reduction of all possibilities of stimulation and action; in most cases, other factors add complications to the phenomena observed. We have collected 18 autobiographical cases from the polar and sea-faring literature (see References for Chapter Nine) which are more frank and revealing than most. We have interviewed two persons who have not published any of their material. In this account, we proceed from rather complicated situations to the more simple ones, i.e., from a maximum number of factors to the most simple experimental situation.

From this literature we have found that isolation per se acts on most persons as a powerful stress. The effects observed are similar to those of any extreme stress, and other stressful factors add their effects to those of isolation to cause mental symptoms to appear more rapidly and more intensely. As is well known, stresses other than isolation can cause the same symptoms to appear in individuals in an isolated group.

Taking our last point first, we have the account by Walter Gibson given in his book, *The Boat.* This is the case in which four persons out of an initial 135 survived in a lifeboat in the Indian Ocean in World War II. Gibson gives a vivid account of his experiences and the symptoms resulting from loss of hope, dehydration, thirst, intense sunburn, and physical combat. Most of the group hallucinated rescue planes and drank salt water thinking it fresh; many despaired and committed suicide; others were murdered; and some were eaten by others. The whole structure of egos was shaken and recast in desperate efforts at survival. (It is interesting to note that many of those who committed suicide tried to sink the boat by removing the drain plugs before jumping overboard, i.e., sink the boat [and other persons] as well as the self; this dual destruction may be used by some of the non-surviving solitary sailors; see [solitary sailors] below.)

I cite this case because it gives a clue as to what to expect in those who do survive isolation in other conditions: Gibson survived—how? He says: (1) by previous out-of-doors training in the tropical sun for some years; (2) by having previously learned to be able to become completely passive (physically and mentally); (3) by having and maintaining the conviction that he would come through the experience; and, we add, (4) by having a woman, Doris Lim, beside him, who shared his passivity and convictions.

In all cases of survivors of isolation, at sea or in the polar night, it was the first exposure which caused the greatest fears and hence the greatest danger of giving way to symptoms; previous experience is a powerful aid in going ahead, despite the symptoms. Physical passivity is necessary during starvation, but, in some people, may be contra-indicated in social isolation in the absence of starvation. In all survivors, we run across the inner conviction that he or she will survive, or else there are definite reassurances from others that each will be rescued. In those cases of a man and a woman together, or even the probability of such a union within a few days, there is apparently not only a real assurance of survival, but a love of the situation can appear. (Such love can develop in a solitaire; see below.) Of course, such couples are the complete psychological antithesis of our major thesis of complete isolation; many symptoms can be avoided by healthy persons with such an arrangement.

Solitary sailors are in a more complex situation than the group of polar isolates. The sailing of a small boat across oceans requires a good deal of physical exertion, and the situation may be contaminated by a lack of sleep which can also cause symptoms. The solitary sailors, of which Joshua Slocum and Alain Bombard are outstanding examples, relate that the first days out of port are the dangerous ones; awe, humility, and fear in the face of the sea are most acute at this time. Bombard states that if the terror of the first week can be overcome, one can survive. Apparently, many do not survive this first period. Many single-handed boats have not arrived at their transoceanic destination. We have clues as to the causes from what sometimes happens with two persons on such crossings. There are several pairs of ocean-crossing sailors in which one of the couple became so terror-stricken, paranoid, and bent on murder and/or suicide, that he had to be tied to his bunk.

Once this first period is past, other symptoms develop, either from isolation itself or from isolation plus other stresses. In the South Atlantic, Joshua Slocum had a severe gastro-intestinal upset just before a gale hit his boat; he had reefed his sails, but should have taken them down. Under the circumstances, he was unable to move from the cabin. At this point he saw a man take over the tiller. At first he thought it was a pirate, but the man reassured him and said that he was the pilot of the Pinta and that he would take his boat safely through the storm. Slocum asked him to take down sail, but the man said, no, they must catch the Pinta ahead. The next morning Slocum recovered, and found his boat had covered 93 miles on true course, sailing itself. (His boat was quite capable of such a performance; he arranged it that way for long trips without his hand at the helm.) In a dream that night the pilot appeared and said he would come whenever Slocum needed him. During the next three years the helmsman appeared to Slocum several times, during gales.

This type of hallucination-delusion seems to be characteristic of the strong egos who survive: a "savior" type of hallucination rather than a "destroyer" type. Their inner conviction of survival is projected thoroughly.

Other symptoms that appear are: superstitiousness (Slocum thought a dangerous reef named M Reef was lucky because M is the 13th letter of the alphabet and 13 was his lucky number. He passed the reef without hitting it. Bombard thought the number of matches necessary to light a damp cigarette represented the number of days until the end of the voyage. He was wrong several times.); intense love of any living things (Slocum was revolted at the thought of killing food-animals, especially a goat given to him at one port. Ellam and Mudie became quite upset after catching and eating a fish that had followed the boat all day, and swore off further fish-eating.); conversations with inanimate objects (Bombard had bilateral conversations with a doll mascot.); and a feeling that when one lands, one had best be careful to listen before speaking to avoid being considered insane (Bernicot refused an invitation to dinner on another yacht after crossing the Atlantic alone, until he could recapture the proper things to talk about.). The inner life becomes so vivid and intense that it takes time to readjust to the life among other persons and to reestablish one's inner criteria of sanity (When placed with fellow prisoners, after 18 months in solitary confinement, Christopher Burney was afraid to speak for fear that he would show himself to be insane. After several days of listening he recaptured the usual criteria of sanity, and then could allow himself to speak.).

Life alone in the polar night, snowed-in, with the confining surroundings of a small hut is a more simple situation. However, there are other complicating factors: extreme cold, possibilities of carbon monoxide poisoning, collapse of the roof, etc. Richard Byrd, in his book "Alone," recounts in great detail his changes in mental functioning, and talks of a long period of CO poisoning resulting in a state close to catatonia. I refer you to his book for details. He experienced, as did Slocum and many others, an oceanic feeling, the being "of the universe," at one with it.

Christiane Ritter (*A Woman in the Polar Night*) was exposed to isolation for periods up to 16 days at a time. She saw a monster, hallucinated her past as if in bright sunshine, became "at one" with the moon, and developed a monomania to go out over the snow. She was saved by an experienced Norwegian who put her to bed and fed her lavishly. She developed a love for the situation and found great difficulty in leaving Spitzbergen. For a thorough and sensitive account of symptoms, I recommend her book to you.

From these examples and several more (see References for Chapter Nine), we conclude the following:

(1) Published autobiographies are of necessity incomplete. Social taboos, discretion to one's self, suppression and repression of painful or uncomfortable material, secondary elaboration, and rationalization severely limit the scope of the material available. (Interviews with two men, each of whom lived alone in the polar night, confirm this impression.)

(2) Despite these limitations, we find that persons in isolation experience many, if not all, of the symptoms of the mentally ill.

(3) In those who survive, the symptoms can be reversible. How easily reversible, we do not know. Most survivors report, after several weeks exposure to isolation, a new inner security and a new integration of themselves on a deep and basic level.

(4) The underlying mechanisms are obscure. It is obvious that inner factors in the mind tend to be projected outward, that some of the mind's activity which is usually reality-bound now becomes free to turn to phantasy and ultimately to hallucination and delusion. It is as if the laws of thought are projected into the realm of the laws of inanimate matter and of the universe. The primary process tends to absorb more and more of the time and energy usually taken by the

126

secondary process. Such experiences either lead to improved mental functioning or to destruction. Why one person takes the healthy path and another person the sick one is not yet clear.

Experiments to clarify the necessary conditions for some of these effects have been done. One of the advantages of the experimental material is that simpler conditions can be set up and tested, and some of the additional stresses of natural life situations can be eliminated.

EXPERIMENTAL ISOLATION

The longest exposure to isolation on the largest number of subjects has been carried out in Dr. Donald Hebb's Department of Psychology at McGill University by a group of graduate students. We started a similar project independently with different techniques at the National Institute of Mental Health. In the Canadian experiments, the aim is to reduce the *patterning* of stimuli to the lowest level; in ours, the objective is to reduce the *absolute intensity* of all physical stimuli to the lowest possible level.

In the McGill experiments, a subject is placed on a bed in an air-conditioned box with arms and hands restrained with cardboard sleeves, and eyes covered completely with translucent ski goggles. The subjects are college students motivated by payment of $20 per day for as long as they will stay in the box. An observer is present, watching through a window, and tests the subject in various ways verbally through a communication set.

In our experiments, the subject is suspended with the body and all but the top of the head immersed in a tank containing slowly flowing water at 34.2° C (93.5° F), wears a blacked-out mask (enclosing the whole head) for breathing, and wears nothing else. The water temperature is such that the subject feels neither hot nor cold. The experience is such that one tactually feels the supports and the mask, but not much else; a large fraction of the usual pressures on the body caused by gravity are lacking. The sound level is low; one hears only one's own breathing and some faint water sounds from the piping; the water-air interface does not transmit air-borne sounds very efficiently. It is one of the most even and monotonous environments I have experienced. After the initial training period, no observer is present. Immediately after exposure, the subject writes personal notes on his experience.

At McGill, the subjects varied considerably in the details of their experiences. However, a few general phenomena appeared. After several hours, each subject found that it was difficult to carry on organized, directed thinking for any sustained period. Suggestibility was very much increased. An extreme desire for stimuli and action developed. There were periods of thrashing around in the box in attempts to satisfy this need. The borderline between sleep and awakedness became diffuse and confused. At some time between 24 and 72 hours most subjects couldn't stand it any longer and left. Hallucinations and delusions of various sorts developed, mostly in those who could stay longer than two days.

The development of hallucinations in the visual sphere followed the stages seen with mescaline intoxication. When full-blown, the visual phenomena were complete projections maintaining the three dimensions of space in relation to the rest of the body and could be scanned by eye and head movements. The contents were surprising to the ego, and consisted of material like that of dreams, connected stories sharing past memories and recent real events. The subjects' reactions to these phenomena were generally amusement and a sense of relief from the pressing boredom. They could describe them vocally without abolishing the sequences. A small number of subjects experienced doubling of their body images. A few developed transient paranoid delusions, and one had a seizure-like episode after five days in the box with no positive EEG findings for epilepsy.

Our experiments have been more limited both in numbers of subjects and duration of exposures. There have been two subjects, and the longest exposure has been three hours. We have much preliminary data, and have gained enough experience to begin to guess at some of the mechanisms involved in the symptoms produced.

In this experiment, the subject always has a full night's rest before entering the tank. Instructions are to inhibit all movements as far as possible. An initial set of training exposures overcomes the fears of the situation itself.

In the tank, the following stages have been experienced:

(1) For about the first three-quarters of an hour, the day's residues are predominant. One is aware of the surroundings, recent problems, etc.

(2) Gradually, one begins to relax and more or less enjoy the experience. The feeling of being isolated in space and having nothing to do is restful and relaxing at this stage.

(3) But slowly, during the next hour, a tension develops which can be called a "stimulus-action" hunger; hidden methods of self-stimulation develop: twitching muscles, slow swimming movements (which cause sensations as the water flows by the skin), stroking one finger with another, etc. If one can inhibit such maneuvers long enough, intense satisfaction is derived from later self-stimulations.

(4) If inhibition can win out, the tension may ultimately develop to the point of forcing the subject to leave the tank.

(5) Meanwhile, the attention is drawn powerfully to any residual stimulus: the mask, the suspension, each come in for their share of concentration. Such residual stimuli become the whole content of consciousness to an almost unbearable degree.

(6) If this stage is passed without leaving the tank, one notices that one's thoughts have shifted from a directed type of thinking about problems to reveries and fantasies of a highly personal and emotionally charged nature. These are too personal to relate publicly, and probably vary greatly from subject to subject. The individual reactions to such fantasy material also probably vary considerably, from complete sup-

pression to relaxing and enjoying them.

(7) If the tension and the fantasies are withstood, one may experience the furthest stage which we have as yet explored: projection of visual imagery. I have seen this once, after a two and one-half hour period. The black curtain in front of the eyes (such as one "sees" in a dark room with eyes closed) gradually opens out into a three-dimensional, dark, empty space in front of the body. This phenomenon captures one's interest immediately, and one waits to find out what comes next. Gradually forms of the type sometimes seen in hypnogogic states appear. In this case, they were small, strangely shaped objects with self-luminous borders. A tunnel whose inside "space" seemed to be emitting a blue light then appeared straight ahead. About this time, this experiment was terminated by a leakage of water into the mask through a faulty connector on the inspiratory tube.

It turns out that exposures to such conditions train one to be more tolerant of many internal activities. Fear lessens with experience, and personal integration can be speeded up. But, of course, there are pitfalls here to be avoided. The opposite effects may also be accelerated in certain cases. Fantasies about the experience (such as the illusion of "return to the womb," which is quite common) are dispelled; one realizes that at birth we start breathing air and hence cannot "return to the womb." One's breathing in the tank is extremely important: as a comforting, constant safeguard and a source of rhythmic stimulation.

In both the McGill experiments and in ours, certain aftereffects are noted: the McGill subjects had difficulty in orienting their perceptual mechanisms; various illusions persisted for several hours. In our experiments, we notice that after emersion the day apparently is started over, i.e., the subject feels as if he has just arisen from bed afresh; this effect persists, and the subject finds he is out of step with the clock for the rest of that day. He also has to re-adjust to social intercourse in subtle ways. The night of the day of the exposure he finds that his bed exerts great pressure against his body.

No bed is as comfortable as floating in water.

Experiments such as these demonstrate results similar to that given above for solitary polar living and sailing alone. If one is alone, long enough, and at levels of physical and human stimulation low enough, the mind turns inward and projects outward its own contents and processes; the brain not only stays active despite the lowered levels of input and output, but accumulates surplus energy to extreme degrees. In terms of libido theory, the total amount of libido increases with time of deprivation; body-libido reaches new high levels. If body-libido is not discharged somatically, discharge starts through fantasy; but apparently this is neither an adequate mode nor can it achieve an adequate rate of discharge in the presence of the rapidly rising level. At some point a new threshold appears for more definite phenomena of regression: hallucinations, delusions, oceanic bliss, etc. At this stage, given any opportunities for action or stimulation by external reality, the healthy ego seizes them and re-establishes more secondary process. Lacking such opportunities for a long enough interval of time, re-organization takes place, how reversibly and how permanently we do not yet know.

Apparently even healthy minds act this way in isolation. What this means to psychiatric research is obvious: We have yet to obtain a full, documented picture of the range available to the healthy human adult mind; some of the etiological factors in mental illness may be clarified and sharpened by such research. Of course, this is a limited region of investigation. We have not gone into details about loss of sleep, starvation, and other factors which have great power in changing healthy minds to sick ones. I think that you can see the parallels between these results and phenomena found in normal children and in psychotics. And, if we could give you a more detailed account, possible explanations of the role of isolation factors in involuntary indoctrination and its opposite, psychotherapy, would be more evident.

Experiments in Solitude, in Maximum Achievable Physical Isolation with Water Suspension, of Intact Healthy Persons

From B.E. Flaherty (editor), Psychophysiological Aspects of Space Flight, *New York: Columbia University Press (1961), pp. 238-247, by permission of the publisher.*

JOHN C. LILLY and JAY T. SHURLEY*

Originally, one of the aims of this investigation was to test the neurophysiological hypothesis that, in the drastic attenuation of physical stimuli below the usual level, the activity of the brain and its contained mind would be that of sleep. Findings in our experiments (see References for Chapter Ten: 1, 2) and in those of other groups (see References for Chapter Ten: 3, 4) in this field demonstrate that sleep is not necessarily the outcome over a short time period. A parallel, though not identical, aim was to observe what, if any, effect such experimental conditions might have in altering ego function both in the present moment and over the longer time period; i.e., ego choices

* Dr. Lilly was Chief, Section of Cortical Integration, Neurophysiological Laboratory, Research Branch, National Institute of Mental Health, Bethesda, Maryland. He was Director of the Communication Research Institute, St. Thomas, U.S. Virgin Islands and Founder/Director of the Human/Dolphin Foundation, Malibu, CA. Dr. Shurley was on the staff of the Veterans Administration Hospital, Oklahoma City, Oklahoma.

and ego structure. A more specific aim has been to establish methods of self-observation by finding, defining and setting limits for the subject's psychological sets for these experiments and by seeking those sets which would give the maximum of information from the subjective sphere. The collection of data has been mainly by notes and recordings by the subject alone.

At the outset two conditions seemed essential, and these have been maintained throughout. All observers first prepare themselves by participating as subjects; those who participate in this experimentation first do so in the role of subject, then in the role of "safety man" (observer), and, finally, in the role of self-observer in solitude. The second crucial condition is that of the restrained and minimal participation of the "safety man"; his role is to stay out of and not interfere with the phenomena which occur in the self-observer.

TECHNIQUE

A systematic consideration of the technique illustrates how these aims are carried out in this particular set of experiments.

The Physical-Physiological Level

1. The simultaneous attenuation of all known external physical stimuli to the lowest possible level (including light, sound, odor, taste, light pressure, deep pressure, and other gravity-opposition forces, vibration, heat, cold, etc.). These characteristics of the experimental environment were achieved with relative success by use of a water immersion tank in a soundproofed chamber.

2. The maximum simultaneous attenuation of intra-integumentary sources of stimuli which, in the order of importance in our experiments, have included low-level pain and discomfort because of an unsatisfactory position in the tank; muscle stretch; slow motions of limbs moving through the water; internal sources such as hunger; full

bladder; full rectum; gas in the GI tract; unusually active cardiovascular system; local pressure ischemia leading to pain; irregular changes in respiratory rhythm, rate, or depth; accumulating carbon dioxide; reduction in oxygen.

3. The maintenance of a constrained and restrained situation voluntarily: obviously in a system such as the human body, efferent activity leads to afferent activity in a continuous and circular fashion; therefore in suspension in a liquid the subject is instructed to voluntarily inhibit movement, including vocalizations, to his maximum possible ability.

4. Special case of skin temperature: We have found that thermal differences over the skin of the body are intensely stimulating when the other sources of stimuli have been attenuated. The use of water suspension (in which the water is slowly flowing by the body) allows an isothermicity of the unclothed skin surface which is difficult to achieve by other methods. At 34.2° C (93.5° F) the water seems to disappear in the thermal sense; i.e., the subject feels neither hot nor cold, and this temperature allows a steady state of heat exchange at a constant normal body temperature at the reduced level of metabolism that can be achieved under these conditions. In addition, the slowly flowing water allows continuous removal of waste products of the body.

5. The position and suspension of the body in water: Because the body parts are not of uniform density it is necessary to add weight to certain parts and to add buoyancy or support to certain other parts. These additions are done in such a way as to avoid chronic low-level discomfort and pain caused by unusual degrees of angulation of spinal or other joints and that caused by pressure ishemia.

We found that the position of the body of each subject must be very carefully worked out in order to avoid low-level discomfort and pain. Unless this is done we found that we were studying the effects of a chronic low-level pain on our subjects in a relative absence of other sources of stimulation. If a given subject is exposed to too much

135

pain for too long a period, the experiment becomes extremely distasteful to him. We do not feel that we have found the ideal method of buoyancy adjustment, and that a good deal more work could be done on this phase of the experiments, possibly by using liquids of two densities, one for the limbs and one for the chest and head, or, possibly, by using a liquid of greater density than the fresh water which we have been using. In summary, water suspension allows most of the gravity-opposing forces to be distributed evenly over the whole surface of the body; thus the unit pressure is greatly decreased over any one area. Because fresh water of the proper temperature was available, we used this liquid.

6. The mask: Since the subject is suspended in the liquid, breathing requires a mask with certain characteristics; (a) mimimum inward pressures over the surfaces of the skin, (b) maximum sealing without undue local pressure, (c) minimum flow resistance, (d) minimum dead space, (e) minimum back- or fore-pressure during the respiratory cycle, and (f) as great a degree of equalization of the pressure in the mask with that over the chest as can be achieved. An appoximation to the last requirement can be reached if the subject is suspended just below the surface of the liquid with his chest parallel to that surface so as to minimize pressure difference across the thoracic and abdominal walls while breathing air at one atmosphere from the room. Such an apparatus has the virtue of extreme simplicity and maximum control by the subject. We have employed a through-and-through breathing system with an inspiratory valve and an expiratory valve with two different tubes leading to the small space (approximately 100 cc) in the mask immediately in front of the nose and the mouth, breathing air at one atmosphere from the room. This system can be easily repaired by the subject and does not require as much maintenance as a more complicated, continuously flowing gas system at a higher pressure. However, again, we do not consider this ideal, and would prefer a very simple system operating at a higher pressure so that the subject could be less constrained as to depth of immersion.

Environmental Control at the Social and Community Level

1. The maintenance of physical-physiological isolation and solitude in the midst of a community implies barriers to intrusion by persons or sources of physical stimuli; i.e., such isolation implies that eventually one is in solitude (of course solitude per se does not necessarily imply physical isolation). Such consideration requires a building which houses the tank...constructed in such a way as to bar any continuous traffic through its structure and which permits no invasion by people or animals or other objects which may be sensed by the subject; a lock on the door is required but not sufficient. The safety man is instructed to act as a buffer agent for the subject, both before, during, and after the experiments and to maintain privacy. The safety man also must check the in-flowing water temperature, lights, telephone, etc.

2. The issue of privacy seems to us to be so important that we give it separate consideration here. Relevant privacy includes present and future communications including all of those between the subject and the safety man. For optimal conditions privacy requires the firm assurance to the subject of his control of the secrecy of his individual data indefinitely into the future. Maximum ego freedom and voluntariness of the subject in these experiments can be achieved through such kinds of privacy. It also implies that the subject chooses his own times for beginning, ending, and the total duration of exposure as well as the control of whatever restraints, voluntary inhibitions, and supports are needed. Privacy also implies trust and respect for the ego of the subject on the part of the safety man; i.e., the elimination (or at least attenuation) of any observer encroachment, exploitation, or invasion of each experience and of its data indefinitely (even to the extent of avoiding invited, available, encroachment by the subject).

When the safety man and the subject both consider it is safe for the subject to become a self-observer free of the safety man, i.e., to enter solitude, these matters must be considered with great intensity and care. It is at this point in our experience that the subject is likely to use disguised methods of appealing for help from the safety man, or from others, in one form or another. After the first few experiences it may help him as a self-observer to function as a safety man for another subject. The introduction of any new factors into the experiment (especially variables important to survival, such as changes in the respiratory apparatus) requires a self-observer to return to "subject status" temporarily and bring a safety man back into the situation.

Of course, privacy also implies that the abstraction of, and the distribution of, the results of the experiments are also under his control. In this regard one must consider all media of communication including gossip (professional and otherwise), newspaper accounts, scientific journal accounts, and scientific meetings. One keeps in mind possible future uses of the material by persons other than the subject; the revealed material is carefully scrutinized by the subject in order to contain only those observations and shorthand descriptions which contribute directly to the generalizations which are found. Minimal disguise of data allows maximum transmission of the true picture of what occurs but is carefully balanced against what Freud called, in his communications of his self-analysis, "the point at which one owes discretion to oneself."

The future research plans are also maintained in privacy and are set up by those who have reached self-observer and safety man status. In functioning as safety man the necessity for certain specific plans and organization becomes apparent and obvious.

3. The process of selection of subjects: Normal, healthy volunteers of equal social and professional status to the previous subject-observers have been the source of our subjects. Neither much younger nor much older, higher or lower, persons are chosen in order to give maximum freedom to the particular person involved. This condition is required for the attenuation to our maximum ability of any factors which might resemble a draft, a persuasion, or coercing of the subject in his or our view. In addition, this process implies that not only each experiment or exposure but each series of exposures requires that

social isolation be maintained. The fact that experiments may be going on is protected in the local community. This technique has been worked out as a result of provocative and disturbing experiences during the course of our experiments.

SCIENTIFIC METHOD AND THE SELF-OBSERVER

Objections can be raised that under these rules an ego observing itself generates only circular data; i.e., that it experiences only what it wishes and allows itself to experience, and that the use of an outside observer can avoid such difficulties. We have found that these objections have a limited validity and for our purposes an outside observer inordinately complicates the situation and the data in which we are interested. Within certain limits yet to be determined experimentally, it seems to us that the mind is the only province of science in which what one believes to be true is, or becomes, true (see References for Chapter Ten: 5). Our experimental task in these studies is to determine what these limits are. However, it is felt that it is important to remember that one must give subjects the permission to experience what can be experienced and not make suggestions as to what may or will be experienced.

It is our conviction that the range of phenomena available to the normal human mind is much greater than "society" will apparently permit or accept (see References for Chapter Ten: 1, 2, 5); consequently, the safety man becomes the intercessor between the individual and the community. As such, he grants the subject permission to experience whatever he can experience; i.e., the right to exercise any function, strictly leaving open the content of what is experienced. If you will, the individual is "indoctrinated" in the principle of freedom for his own ego with the internal experiential sphere. As is mentioned below, the results of such experiences in a given subject generally turn out to be surprising to that subject; i.e., so far as the subject is consciously aware, new data occur quite spontaneously.

CONCLUSIONS

Detailed results are to be reported in a later paper. However, some general conclusions of these studies may be of interest.

When given freedom from external exchanges and transactions, the isolated-constrained ego (or self or personality) has sources of new information from within. Such sources can be experienced as if they are outside with greater or lesser degrees of awareness as to where or what these sources are (projected imagery, projected sounds, doubling of body parts, emotional states of euphoria or anxiety, etcetera).

Any other person, observer, or safety man can be made to appear as if he is a "source" to which is attributed the origin of the new information.

Transference-related drives may become extremely intense. In a given exposure, such needs increase in intensity with time and may ultimately demand direct release; i.e., such as leaving the tank and participating in one's active life with other persons (see References for Chapter Ten: 2, 5). Multiple exposures lead to better control and increase awareness of these effects.

The relationship of any residual stimulus to these needs is carefully evaluated. "Negative and positive" transference problems arise from extremely small and unlikely kinds of stimuli under these conditions; i.e., a "wrong" word, too many suggestions, implied judgments of accuracy or performance, or their "positive" opposites. The safety man must be, as it were, an ideal and keenly aware diplomat when faced with such problems. It has been found that having once experienced the lowest possible level of stimulation oneself makes it much easier to function as a "diplomatic," tolerant, and considerate safety man. Hurt feelings, overenthusiastic reactions, and replication of experience reported by others are examples of the kinds of phenomena to be found and dealt with.

The positive, enjoyable results were achieved only at those times when the inner and the outer disturbing stimuli were minimizable. Any residual discomfort made it impossible to achieve the euphoric state; any anxiety induced by faulty apparatus or technique blocked the possibility of enjoying or profiting from the experience. Until we were able to attenuate physical discomfort and fear by better techniques, multiple exposures, and careful training, we saw mostly "negative" phenomena. As the levels of stimuli were lowered closer to zero, the positive, more blissful, enjoyable states and the positive transference phenomena appeared. No addiction to these states has occurred: the internal satisfactions of needs achieved in the tank are limited in the same sense that, say, day-dreaming is limited. Basic satisfactions of needs felt in the tank require later exchanges with other persons and with physical reality.

As has been published (see References for Chapter Ten: 1, 2), it is felt that such experiences are not necessarily psychotic, or even mentally aberrant, and after training can be constructive and invigorating. Eventually, after many exposures, each subject can learn enough to enjoy and not fear or dislike his own experiences.

CHAPTER ELEVEN

Standards for Isolation Tank Manufacture and Use

The standards are those we have found necessary for reliability of operation, for safety, and for maintenance of a reasonably hygienic environment. Low cost of operation and safety are favored over low initial investment; if a more expensive item meets our standards and decreases the cost of operation we use it rather than a less expensive item that may be less reliable, unsafe or costly to operate in the long run (one year or more). A cheaper item may end up generating far more cost in terms of unreliable operation, redesign cost, time spent on its maintenance, anxiety over its unsafe operation, and its potentially unhealthful effects on persons using the tank.

In the experience of over twenty years of tank design, maintenance and personal use, we have arrived at the above point of view. After one has been in coma because of a failure of control of the solution's temperature, experienced electrical shocks, run out of air, received skin infections from the water, lost valuable solutions through leaks, dealt with plugged too small filters, blown fuses through shorts in the electrical systems, dealt with corroded pumps and lines, found toxic amounts of copper in the solution, paid high electrical bills because of lack of adequate heat insulation on the tank, cleaned up salts left on house floors and carpets etcetera, one becomes conservative, cautious and expert at avoiding such contingencies in the future. In short, one learns that a high initial investment may be necessary to avoid high future operating costs of all types, including threats to health and happiness.

IDEAL PROPERTIES OF AN ISOLATION TANK

1. *Thermal insulation* is optimal to the point where the heat loss from the floatation solution and from the air over it is so low that only a very small or zero outside source of energy is needed to maintain the 93° to 94°F temperature when a person is floating in the tank. The heat from the body metabolism maintains this temperature, neither raising it nor lowering it. Zero loss of heat is to be avoided; the body would then raise the temperature of the solution. The body temperature would then rise. Thermal insulation, then, should be such that the steady state heat loss with a person in the tank is slightly greater than the basal metabolic heat production of the body of a person with basal metabolism up to three standard deviations above the mean for the human population expected to use isolation tanks. A rough approximation of the energy produced is 80 to 90 watts in these cases.

2. *Available air supply* is optimal when the oxygen, carbon dioxide and water vapor content are maintained within physiological limits and no noxious gases or unpleasant odors are added to the tank air from the outside air supply. No possible sources of the following substances are to be allowed in the air supply: carbon monoxide; natural gas; methane; propane; butane; Freon; bug sprays, paints and thinners; acetylene; ethylene; nitric, hydrochloric and sulfuric acid; battery gases; helium, hydrogen; nitrous and nitric oxide; krypton, xenon, radon; radioactive gases (liquids and solids); hydrogen sulfide; no particulate solids or droplets of noxious solids or liquids.

Physiological limits, after four hours exposure: The oxygen shall be at 20 percent atmospheric pressure minus less than 2 percent. The carbon dioxide percentage shall not be more than 2 percent integrated over the four hours. Water vapor percentage shall be that at 90 percent humidity at 90° to 94°F within a few percent.

3. *Solution temperature:* The temperature of the floatation solution shall be maintained at a fixed value between 93° to 94° within 0.1°F in the fully stirred condition. It is desirable to be able to set this tem-

perature at a fixed value in the range 93° to 94°F and maintain it within ±0.05°F. A suitable thermometer for measuring these temperatures is ASTM number 51F (range 69° to 116°F, eighteen inches long).*

4a. Solution density: The lowest desirable density in gms./cc. is 1.30. This value corresponds closely to a specific gravity of 1.30, determined by a sensitive hydrometer** readable to 0.001 gms./cc. This density is to be achieved and maintained by using clean tap water and approximately 53 percent by weight of commercial magnesium sulfate: $MgSO_4 \cdot 7H_2O$ (hydrated salt). See Table 1, Chapter Two, for relations between solute (hydrated and nonhydrated salt) solution percentages and solution densities, resulting from various concentrations at a given temperature. A suitable hydrometer for the measurements of solution densities is one with a range of 1.200 to 1.4200 specific gravity. (Refer Table 1, p.44.)**

4b. Mixing for 1.30 density: The desired solution density is obtained by using enough ($MgSO_4 \cdot 7H_2O$) commercial Epsom salts to saturate the solution at 93°F; one mixes proper weights of Epsom salt and of water at 140°F; the endothermic reaction brings the mixture to 93°F.

Determination of the weight of hydrated magnesium sulfate to add to water to make a solution of high density for floatation in the isolation tank (approximate values, within 1 percent):

Desired density = 1.30 gms./cc.

Specific gravity = 1.30.

The hydrated magnesium sulfate contains 51.0 percent water.

For a given weight of the hydrated salt 51.0 percent is water of hydration (H_2O).

---

* Catalog no. 61096-003 page 1196 in VWR *Scientific Apparatus Catalog*. Catalog no. 72 (September, 1971), P.O. Box 2062, Terminal Annex, Los Angeles, Ca. 90054, cost approximately $6.
** See Catalog no. 34615-006, hydrometer range 1.200-1.420, 12 inches long; or no. 34680-008, specific gravity range 1.15-1.30, in syringe for ease of use, page 720 in VWR *Scientific Apparatus Catalog*.

For the usual commercial 100 pound bag, 51.0 pounds is water (H_2O), and 49.0 pounds is the dry salt ($MgSO_4$).

Only the salt ($MgSO_4$) increases the density of the solution; the water of hydration (H_2O) only adds to the volume of the solution.

The working temperature of the solution in the tank is 93.2°F or 34.1°C.

The density of water at 93.2°F (34.1°C) is 0.994 gms./cc.

The equivalent density of the dry salt is 2.16 gms./cc. in solution. For a solution density of 1.30, the following table of values gives the fractions involved:

	Percent by weight	per cc. (gms.)	per cubic foot (kgms.)		per cubic foot (pounds)	
Added H_2O	46.36	0.4608	13.048		28.7	
Hydration (H_2O)	27.34	0.2718	7.6965	36.83	16.93	81.02
Dry salt	26.30	0.5680	16.084		35.38	
(Hydrated salt)	(53.64)	(0.8398)	(19.755)		(43.46)	

73.7% { Added H_2O , Hydration (H_2O) }

From this table one can calculate the amount of commercial hydrated salt needed for a given tank to give a solution of density equal to 1.30 gms./cc.

EXAMPLE: A tank 7 1/2' by 3 1/2' with a depth of 10" of solution: 7 1/2' × 3 1/2' × 10/12 = 21.9 cubic feet

43.46 pounds of hydrated salt are required for every cubic foot of solution.

The total weight of hydrated magnesium sulfate for this tank is thus: 21.9 cu. ft. × 43.46 pounds/cu. ft. = 952 pounds.

4c. Experimental determination of density: Over a temperature range from 74.4°F (23.6°C) to 103.2°F (39.6°C), the average weight of 10.0 cc. of saturated magnesium sulfate solution was found to be 13.07 + .01 gms. The density in gms./cc. is 1.307 + 0.01. Tap water by the same technique at 74°F (23.3°C) had a density of 0.9950 and at 105.8°F (41°C) was 0.993. (The accepted values for pure air-free water are 0.997 and 0.992 respectively.)

Therefore, we can assume the method gives the density of 1.30 close enough for all practical floatation purposes.

The solution from each of two tanks with saturated magnesium sulfate gave 1.30 + 0.01 gms./cc. density.

As mentioned elsewhere, a hydrometer gives the density (specific gravity) more quickly and easily: use one with a range of specific gravity from 1.200 to 1.400.

5. *Water supply:* Reasonably clean tap water is used to make up the 50 percent plus by weight solution of hydrated magnesium sulfate. This water should not contain chlorine in a high enough concentration as to be odorous. The bacterial content should be less than that specified in the public health standards for city water supplies. The toxic inorganic ions should be below toxic levels for long repeated exposure of skin, including genitalia. Such ions include those of copper, arsenic, cadmium, mercury, lead, uranium, plutonium, etcetera.

The pH (acid-base balance) shall be within the physiological range for the normal human skin, genitalia and anus for chronic exposure (7.0±0.2).

6. *Tank dimensions: wall and bottom contacts:* The floatation area (surface of the floatation solution) shall be at least 7 1/2' (202 cm.) long × 4' (108 cm.) wide. The solution depth shall be at least 10 inches (25.4 cm.). These dimensions have been found to be comfortable for individuals up to 6' 6" (175 cm.) in height. The smaller the individual the smaller the "Ping-Ponging effect." (Because of the low friction and the high mobility of the floating body, a contact with a wall resulting in even the slightest push-off force causes travel from wall to wall called "Ping-Ponging.")

A tank, larger in surface area than the above, improves the isolation by decreasing the frequency (increasing the time interval of wall contacts). A circular tank (8' or 215 cm. in diameter) with a slowly rotating (one revolution every five minutes) solution was found to give no wall contacts during two-hour exposures. The drain was at the center of the circle; small jets directed in the direction of rotation were placed at the wall perimeter.

A square tank 8' (215 cm.) on each side (with regulated convection currents; see below) gave no wall contacts over four-hour periods.

A rectangular tank 8' (215 cm.) wide and 12' (323 cm.) long (with regulated input-output flows; see below) gave no wall contacts over twelve-hour periods.

The depth of the solution at 10'' (25.4 cm.) was determined in a sequence of three hundred subjects as that depth at which the most steatopygic high-density individuals did not have bottom contacts in the gluteal regions. At 8'' (18 cm.) some individuals went aground.

7. *Convection currents in the solution:* If the heaters are arranged in the bottom of the tanks correctly, the very slight resulting convection currents tend to hold the body in the center of the tank. (In rectangular or square tanks the heating elements, either electric or tubing containing hot circulating water, imbedded in the bottom are placed around the outer dimensions. In circular tanks the heaters are placed circularly around the perimeter.)

8. *Adjusted input-output flows:* In certain designs of tanks, a very small flow pattern of the solution can be used to center the body. In each case the output flow from the tank is placed under the center of buoyancy of the whole body (near the center of gravity) in the bottom of the tank. The input flows to the tank are near (but not at) the surface with at least three in each wall (twelve total) directed toward the body in the rectangular tanks. In the circular form, twelve to sixteen inlets are placed in the wall uniformly distributed.

Such flows are obtained from plastic plumbing fed by a very small plastic pump, removed from the vicinity of the tank to minimize noise introduced into the tank.

8a. Filtration: A 1/2 horsepower plastic pump and diatomaceous earth swimming pool filter (20 sq. ft. area) are used to filter the tank solution as needed to maintain a clear solution (once a week, depending on use hours).

9. Light level: In the visible spectrum, the light level at the eyes of the floating subject shall be subliminal for fully dark adapted open eyes in subjects with no night-blindness (adequate vitamin A intake). No ultraviolet radiation shall be allowed. Infrared radiation is restricted to that emitted by the body, the solutions and the ceiling-black-body emission of infrared radiation in the temperature range 98.6°F (37.0°C) to 93°F (33.9°C).

10. Sound level (20Hz to 100,000 Hz*): The level of sound energy in the solution throughout the acoustic spectrum shall be below the underwater threshold for detection for subjects with unimpaired hearing, measured re the reference level of 0.0002 dynes/cm^2.

11. Vibration level (20Hz to 0.1Hz): The vibration energy level in the solution shall be less than body threshold throughout the vibration spectrum for the most sensitive individuals. Any detectable vibration must be eliminated. Exceptions that cannot be eliminated are earthquake waves, large sonic-subsonic booms, explosions, nuclear blasts, etcetera.

12. Electric and magnetic fields: Electrical fields in the frequency range from direct current (0 Hz) to 100,000 Hz shall be below threshold for detection for normal human subjects. Power line frequencies (50 to 60 Hz) have the least energy threshold for nerve stimulation in this range and can be particularly dangerous. Power line fields (electrostatic and conductive) must be below detection levels for a grounded subject outside the tank touching the solution (an AC voltage difference less than 0.1 volt).

Oscillating magnetic fields at or near power line frequencies can

---

* A frequency of one cycle per second.

cause oscillating phosphenes ("as if light") emanating from retinal-ganglion cell network stimulation in the eye. Such fields are to be eliminated or kept below threshold for phosphene production.

THE IDEAL ENVIRONMENT FOR THE TANK

The room or building in which the tank is housed and used must have the following specifications:

a. Remove from all social encroachment; no foot traffic, visitors, large or small animals, children, insects or other living organisms are allowed in the room or near the room.

b. The location for the room or building should be free of outside noise sources. The location should be as silent as possible. Within the room, exclude all noise, music and speech sources (no furnace, no refrigerator machinery, no hair dryer, no vacuum cleaner, no water pump, no radio, TV or hi-fi sets and so forth). Sound insulation both for transmission and reflection should be put upon the wall, ceiling and floor. This is an absolute requirement.

c. No daylight shall be allowed in the room. The light within the room shall be controlled. For cleaning the room and making adjustments to apparatus, bright lights are needed, also for maintenance of the tank itself. During tank use dim red lights (as in photographic darkroom) are used to prevent glare effects in the person emerging from the tank.

d. Electrical and thermal insulation of the floor is used to prevent electrical and/or thermal shocks through bare feet.

e. The room temperature shall be kept at approximately 86°F to prevent thermal shock to a person emerging from the tank. This temperature may seem too hot when one first enters the room and removes one's clothes.

f. A pleasing aesthetic appearance of the room is necessary for most persons. Be sure the room has carpets, for example, that are impervious to Epsom salts solution.

g   A shower bath should be installed either in the room or immediately adjacent to the room to prevent tracking of Epsom salts into the surrounding environs.

h.   Some means of drying the body should be supplied. In general, towels tend to get extremely stiff when filled with Epsom salts solution and dried later. In general it is better if the shower is immediately available to get rid of the Epsom salts.

i.   Some sort of toilet facilities should be immediately adjacent to the room, also. It is necessary to void urine and feces before going into the tank and to take a shower before entering the tank. We have found it is best if the person who is using the tank shampoos his/her hair before entering the tank, thus eliminating loose-hair problems in the tank filtration system.

RULES FOR TANK USE

In our experience we have found that persons with skin diseases should not use the tank unless they are prepared to protect their lesions with silicone or some other form of ointment that is waterproof. In general we do not encourage people who are in the midst of an infectious disease to use the tank. These are good public health and hygiene measures. The inflammatory stage of any disease (the common cold, influenza, venereal disease, suppurative lesions, the early stages of traumatic cuts, abrasions and contusions) is inimical to other persons using the tank; however, during the initial stages of broken bones and similar traumatic episodes, the tank is an immense relief for the patient using it. Medical advice should be sought in the presence of any type of organic disease.

No persons with epilepsy are to be allowed to use the tank unless their epilepsy is under medical control, having sufficient control of the subject's seizures so they will not endanger themselves in tank use.

No person under the influence of drugs should be allowed in the tank. In the younger population that has used the tank, we have found that too much marijuana can lead to states in which the person cannot control his/her floating. He/she may end up under the water, taking the Epsom salts solution into the nasal and oral tract in such a way as to pose a potential danger. Drugs in general make a person less competent to handle the tank situation than he/she is when in the nondrug state.

No persons with severe mental illness should be allowed to use the tank except under extremely careful medical control.

No persons who have a tendency toward suicidal action should be allowed in the tank or anywhere near it.

We have found that there are certain types of personality that do not benefit from tank work. It is a moot point as to whether one prevents them from entering the tank or whether one allows them to find it out for themselves. In general we tend to allow people to find this out for themselves with caution in the above categories.

Some people do not have the discipline necessary for effective tank use. This seems to be a matter of intuitive clinical judgment rather than a categorical imperative. In general we have not allowed people with a hostile "acting-out" kind of personality to use the tank. (As Walter Gibson showed in The Boat [see Chapter Nine], certain people tend to pull the drain plug in the bottom of the boat, sinking everybody else along with self.)

The tank room or building must have a secure lock on the door to prevent accidents or apparent accidents by hostile persons. We have found that certain persons need an inside lock on the tank room in order to feel safe while they are in the tank. We provide this but we also make sure that it is a lock that can either be broken from the outside, or opened from the outside in case of an emergency. Strangers must be prevented from blundering into the tank room while a person is in the tank.

We have found empirically that the following rules give best tank use and allow many people to use the same tank, during a given twenty-four-hour period.

1. Each person involved must remove his/her clothes and take a very thorough shower, including shampooing his/her hair.

2. Before the shower, urine and feces must be eliminated.

3. If the shower is at some distance from the tank, a bathrobe, which is frequently washed, is furnished to the subject.

4. Each new subject is introduced to the technique of floating on one's back and of placing one's hands, intertwined in the hair, behind one's head, with the elbows immersed in the solution. This technique allows one to feel safer during certain kinds of experiences and should be emphasized with each new subject.

5. If the person intends to sleep in the tank, a safe float for the head should be introduced to him/her so that if the head tends to turn over, the buoyancy of the float tends to keep the head upright. Certain kinds of dreams lead to action of the body that can be balanced out by means of the float.

6. On emersion from the tank the person is asked to stand in the tank and drain as much of the Epsom salts solution from the body as can be done, including squeezing his/her hair so that the solution runs back into the tank, rather than being tracked out onto the floor.

7. On emersion from the tank, either a towel is used or one immediately walks to the shower and gets rid of the Epsom salts in the hair and on the body. Since one has shampooed his/her hair before immersion in the tank, after emersion simple rinsing of the hair with water will get rid of most of the Epsom salts; some people wish at this point to shampoo again.

8. It is wise for most new subjects to write up their experience in solitude immediately after emersion in order for them to pin down their experience and not forget any of it.

9. Many persons tend to get quite loquacious after a tank trip. This can be handled according to local custom. We tend to discourage it in our environment so that they will reserve the energy to write up or to integrate their experience in their normal gravity-loaded environment.

10. Such things as psychological testing, E.E.G.'s, and so forth are

discouraged in our particular research; however, other research groups may wish to carry out such procedures. We have found that such procedures disturb the learning that takes place in the tank situation.

11. Any write-ups that persons make at our installation are protected in the sense that they are allowed to say whether or not these can be used for publication or for further transmission of the information. We have a sheet at the bottom of which the subject makes his own choices. We realize that subjects tend to censor their own experiences when writing them up for others. We accept this limitation on our data and realize that it is very important for the individual to do this for his own benefit and his own discretion.

12. We tend to dissuade those who wish to use the tank in the service of their own egos, both in terms of their own personal learning and in terms of others' use of the data from subjects in the tank.

13. We try to eliminate all aspects that could be considered coercive in this particular research setting. We do not force subjects to go into the tank, either by persuasion or by hierarchical social position. Strictly voluntary use both as to starting time and emersion time within the limits of the social structure surrounding the tank is absolutely necessary.

14. No therapy nor therapeutic aims by others than the person himself/herself alone are expressed or allowed to be expressed by other persons before or after tank exposure. Persons using the tank are not "patients"; they are peers and self-teaching "students."

Sensations of the body: black, wet, warm, quiet.

Previous thoughts: why am I here?

Realize you are alone with your mind (let go).

Go into a dreamlike state.

Experience new realities. (Vortex as a state of being.)

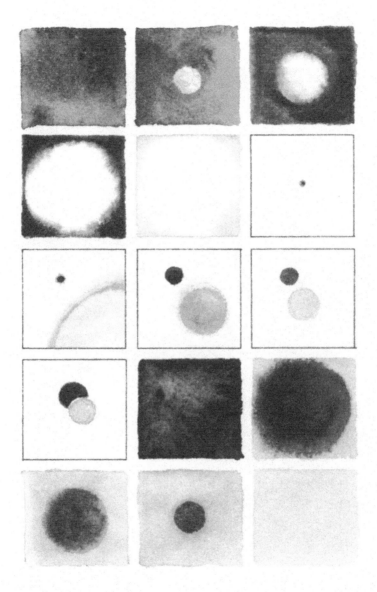

Diagram of Astro Body Separation into the Void. *Total Darkness. Point of light appears. The light (energy) approaches and surrounds consciousness. Another point appears (Void). Consciousness transcends, then separates and leaves the body bathed in the security of the energy, approaches the Void. Out-of-body enters the Void... Total Blackness... Then to a Higher State. The Being Experiences expanded awareness, astro travel, etcetera.*

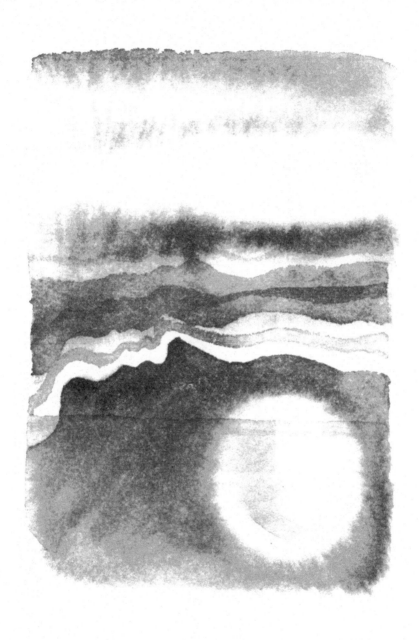

Realize you are the Void. Recover from planetside trip.

CHAPTER TWELVE
Tank Logs: Experiences

A THOUGHT FROM THE TANK

Sane and pragmatic individuals measure our interpretation of reality as reflected by our senses. The psychic and insane or nonsane have the gift of transcending the barrier of the physical body in order to become aware of the pure state of being—that state that has no parameters, and is infinite. This divine gift, no matter how slight or great, can be a curse or a blessing depending on the space in which that individual is centered. All that we call reality is merely the point of view of our place in time—that mere fragment of a wheel that has no beginning or end.

The only real art in life is how you wish to spend that brief moment: The passion you express for all facets of your being, the style in which you deal with the problems, the joy and the pain. This is growth, this can be bliss, this is art. Individuals who are capable of expressing this in any particular medium are only pointing out to those who are blocked, the existence of a higher state of consciousness.

When one reads the reports (recorded here) of persons who have had isolation tank experiences, one considers the selection of these persons, their preprogramming, the experience as compared to that of others, where and when the report was written, the environs of the tank itself, the other persons contacted pre- and post-exposure and their attitudes, explicit instructions (if any), implicit instructions (if detected), the time of day for immersion and emersion, and the physical characteristics of the individual (age, sex, etcetera).

The persons giving the reports here recorded were volunteers who asked us for the experience. In no case was any group pressure, hierarchical influence of age, position, finances, or anything else intentionally used to induce the person to undergo the experience. Rather than paying persons to be "subjects of an experiment," some persons paid in order to use the facilities for their own experience. Each person was asked to write out a report within a few minutes of emersion while the memories of the experience were still fresh. A few persons did not do so for one reason or another ("not enough time, do it later," "do not want to write it out," or were members of a workshop in which the time schedule did not allow reporting on paper).

In regard to preprogramming of the persons involved, many, if not most, either read *The Center of the Cyclone* or *The Human Biocomputer*, attended one or more workshops led by the author and his wife, Toni, or by the author himself, or lived close by the facilities. A few were brought by experienced friends or were visitors to the facility. No patients of doctors or of therapists were accepted as such unless each had professional qualifications or personal experiences of a special variety (talent in the inner domains, psychedelic experiences of the deeper types, etcetera). Many persons, for one reason or another, were referred to other facilities in the metropolitan area.

In general, the presence of other persons, pre- and post-exposure, was limited to members of our household and/or other guests or other members of a workshop. No questioning by any of these other persons was encouraged. The only questions by the person entering the isolation that were answered were those having to do with the physical operations (shower, use of toilet, floating techniques, and assurance of true solitude-isolation). Questions about expected experience were answered in such a way so as to leave it up to the person himself/herself.

Post-exposure discussion was discouraged. Writing out a report was encouraged. Forms were furnished to be filled out for pertinent data (age, height, weight, sex, times of immersion/emersion and date).

A place on the form was provided to give preference as to how the data would be used: published or not, name used or not, initials or a number, etcetera.

The environs of the tank were either that of a workshop (at Esalen Institute, etcetera) or that of our home. In the home facility, the tanks were located in buildings separate from the house. Two tanks were in one small building; the others were distributed in separate buildings. One shower and the toilet facilities were in the house; one shower was outside.

No intrusion of the tank building by other persons was allowed while a person was in an isolation tank. Insofar as was practical, the time of exposure was set for one to three hours depending on other factors. Usually, a person set his own internal clock to the desired interval. Most persons came out at a surprisingly close time to that chosen. In workshops, because of the large number of persons using the tank twenty-four hours per day, the time was limited to either one or two hours and was terminated by the next person on the schedule.

In contrast to the home facility procedures (upon which most of these written reports are based), in the workshops the explicit instructions were: (1) do not discuss experiences except in the full group so that they are shared with the whole group, (2) if one wishes, write a private journal of the experience. (Some of these group discussions were recorded on workshop tapes and copies may be obtained through the author.)

Implicit instructions varied considerably. Those in workshops, those who had read the books took their own instructions from these materials.

In general, it was noticed that those in a five-day workshop, sharing the results with others, tended to elicit crossprogramming. Those with limited repertoires of experience tended to widen their allowable experiences in the presence of the reports of those with more facility/talent/exposure. The self-metaprograms widened with increased personal/group experience.

In the first experience to tank isolation in solitude, there are many common trends in the population. As in any new circumstance there is a concentration on the new environment (tank walls, temperature, water, darkness, silence), bodily phenomena (heartbeat, respiration, air supply, borborigmi [gut noises owing to moving gas], posture, skin sensations, sources of low-level pain), and psychologically standard responses (fear of loss of air supply, fear of drowning, of overheating/overcooling, of being shut in, of bacterial infection, etcetera). Some persons did not repeat the experience: many others did.

As the number of exposures and the total time spent in the tank increased, each person reported new phenomena for him/her. Each exposure, in general, widened/deepened the domains entered. (Of course, here we are talking only about "survivors" who wanted to continue: some of those who stopped after one or two exposures may not have experienced the widening/deepening reported by others with more exposures.)

In the experience of the author, during many hundreds of hours of use, each tank exposure for him has become a unique experience with very little if any repetition of previous experience. The variety is rather surprising even when one is on a daily schedule of use.

Insofar as is possible, the following reports are unedited and are given as in the original report.

In these reports there are none in which psychopharmacological substances were used. Since 1966, the current legal status of such agents makes it difficult if not impossible to do further research on combined physical isolation and the psychopharmacologically active chemicals. With some regret, it is noted that the original work on this combination cannot be replicated to test it through consensual validations (e.g., *Programming and Metaprogramming in the Human Biocomputer* and *The Center of the Cyclone*).

Following the selected accounts by this group of persons is a chapter containing pertinent quotations reproduced from the two above

166

noted books. These accounts of the author's past personal experience are reproduced to allow evaluation of the preprogrammatic effects on the persons in this chapter who read the above two books.

TANK LOGS

Andrews, Jill Fairchild (3/1/75)
Andrews, Oliver (3/15/75)
Bateson, Gregory (10/28/73)
Bateson, Lois (10/26/73)
Bay, Jane (2/8/no year)
Binns, Steve (11/10-11/73)
Brackman, Jacob (11/30/73)
Brenner, Paul (11/16/73)*
Brewer, Jan (8/22/73)
Bridger, Joe (8/5/73)
Brockman, John (10/24/73)
Busco, Francis (1/20/73)
Campbell, Douglas A. (9/73)
Campbell, Liz (11/5/73)
Carlson, Caroll (2/15/74)
Costa, Helen (9/29/73)
Curtis, Will (no date)
Di Suvero, Victor (no date)
Elliott, Rona (8/18/73)
Enright, Craig (9/13/73)
Erhard, Werner (2/1/75)*
Feynman, Richard (Spring 1974)
First, Elsa (8/23/73)
Gaer, Faye (10/28/73)
Gaer, Paul (no date)
Garren, Ron (8/3/73)
Gellis, Henry (8/25/73)

Gerber, Michael L. (11/10/73)

Glatt, Myron (8/18/73)

Glatt, Ruth (8/9,8/18/73)

Gold, Cybele (3/20/75)

Gold, Eugene J. (no date)*

Gregory, Bruce (11/20, 11/27/73)

Grof, Joan (1/2/74)

Grof, Stan (no date)*

Hart, Joe (7/9/73)

Hellman, Nancy E. (10/2/75)

Herbert, Paul (8/18/73)

Hoover, Eleanor (10/28/73)

Huang, Al Chung-Liang (2/9/no year)

Hughes, Michael (10/27, 11/1, 11/16, 11/18/73)

Jodorowsky, Alejandro (11/2/73)

Kantor, Ulrike L. (9/16/76)

Keen, Gifford (8/8/73)

Keen, Sam (8/8/73)

Knapp, Cynthia (10/28/73)

Krassner, Paul (1/1/74)

Lilly, Antonietta L. (8/2-8/3/73)

Lit, Peter (9/73)

Lymon, Herschel (10/2/73)

McElroy, Dave (7/16,7/17, 7/18/73)

Meredith, Burgess (8/5/73)

Meredith, Jonathon (12/26/74)

Metzner, Jan (10/16/73)

Metzner, Ralph (10/16/73)

Nicholson, Jan (9/13/73)

Perry, Glenn A. (1973-1975)*

Prestera, Hector (11/10/73)*

Rafaelson, Bob (10/26/73)

Rubin, Jerry (1/75)

Sharpe, Kathryn (9/30/73)
Smith, William (11/2,11/15, 11/30/73)
Stern, Grace (7/17/73)
Sundsten, Bobbie (no date)
Sundsten, John W. (no date)
Tart, Charley (no date)
Taylor, Mary (11/17/73)
Varela, Francisco (7/2/75)
Vicente, Eligio Carrillos (4/76)
Weil, Andrew (11/30/73)
Weininger, Benjamin (8/24/73)
Weininger, David (7/9/73)
West, Louis Jolyon (no date)
Wheeler, Sharon (11/10, 11/11/73)
Wilkes, Tom (5/3/75)
Williams, Barbara (7/9/73)
Wilson, Robert A. (4/10/75)

---

* Persons who acquired their own tanks after the experience reported here.

1 March 1975
Jill Fairchild Andrews, female, 26 yrs., 135 lbs., 5' 5":
time not recorded.

A preference for immediacy... This week, particularly this week, when ideas are colliding with doubts and questions I wanted the silence, the deprivation of the tank. Sadly the veins of internal stimuli kept breaking into the void. And so it was work... I found the shaft of light again and used it to take me away from the clutter. I'd be there, feeling nothing, thinking nothing but the luminescence of the shaft when I'd raise myself to it and then... shit, here comes Diver Physiology and Medicine, Joe MacInnis, money and so on. When I bent my frame and began to waggle again, the head frustrations left and the moment was sensual. I think it will be important for me to recognize my mandala or a point of concentration that I can stay with.

Ah, at one time a muscle in my side flexed and I imagined a small animal had just entered to join the float and I wondered if he could see me.

15 March 1975
Oliver Andrews, male, 49 yrs., 175 lbs., 5' 9":
1 hour.

I was lying in the tank in a spread-eagle position, face up, legs and arms outstretched, gradually I seemed to make a head-first 180° roll so that I was facing down into an impenetrable night. Dawn broke from the eastern horizon, illuminating a vast desert of glittering sand a hundred feet below me. The sand became transparent and directly below me was a polished black granite monolith of rectangular shape about 100' long, 30' wide by 25' deep, buried below the surface of the desert. In the center of the monolith was encased a sculpture of Jill (who was at this time in the other tank). The effigy was of monumental size, legs together, arms at the sides. It was made of dark burnished gold with a face of gleaming rose quartz, out of which shone her wide, open amethyst eyes. When her eyes met mine, two lines of graphite streaked across the desert, straight to the source of the sunrise beyond the distant mountains. The edges of the line vibrated and thousands of lines raced off across the sand to the right and the left like the legs of a universal centipede. I followed the line leading into the distance, where it became a beam of light bisecting a peak just below a star which was still shining in the sky even though it was daylight, which split open to reveal a clear crystal dodecahedron, in the center of which, standing straight up was another effigy of Jill made of silver, lapis lazuli and coral. Behind Jill was the statue, several times the size of Jill, of the seated figure of the Egyptian cat goddess, made of burnished nickel-iron, the dark color of a meteorite. Still in the spread-eagle form of an X, I hovered above the two figures and began to flow with a heat so intense that it melted the two figures until they formed a dark pool with currents of silver, blue lapis lazuli and pink coral swirling around in it. The heated meteoric mixtures melted holes in the desert floor and flowed down through these holes into an underground lake beneath the desert sands.

I, the radiant, hovering X, sent steel grappling cables through the melted holes in the roof of the underground lake, and pulled up the roof in the form of a perfect square made of fused desert sand still smoking from molten statues of Jill and the cat goddess. Below, Jill (the real Jill, not a sculpture) was floating in a sunlit pool filled with flowering lotus plants. As Jill stood up, water streamed from her body and it became an upright microphone absorbing and broadcasting everywhere the sound of opening lotuses. The lotus song emanated from the pores of her body, standing straight up in the form of a radiating rose-white light.

The X that was me moved into the pool radiating blue-white light. Slowly the X and the I moved together and united to form an incandescent star.

28 October 1973
Gregory Bateson, male, 59 yrs., 220 lbs., 6' 5": 1 hour.

Mostly away—no—just no words? Briefly a dream—switching to and fro between the others (?Lilly, J.) is a boy; I am a man. And vice versa he is a man, I a boy—mostly just floating—extremely curious of posture, head, back (unusually far back) and the posture as a sort of ground but mostly see figure against that ground.

Relaxing from all that—very definitely process, interrupted by Lilly calling to me "Are you all right?" Opened lid which for two of us sort of joke—

26 October 1973
Lois Bateson, female, 44 yrs., 120 lbs., 5' 5": 1 hour, 2 minutes.

Fourth tanking, first time in no. 3. Enjoyed spaciousness and buoyancy more than in no. 1. Immediately experienced floating out of body shell. Roamed and sauntered through a kind of cosmic park, full of density but infinite boundaries. People's images occasionally came in and out of this but nothing stuck around important to focus on. Then as wondered on this, sudden enlightenment—there is no such thing as separate consciousness. My roamings were a kind of total consciousness of all that was. The dense bits here and there—I was it—it was me—the people—same—there was no boundary between me and them—pronouns are only illusions! Fantastic! Kinesics were flowing like this.

8 February (no year)
Jane Bay, female, 33 yrs., 130 lbs., 5' 6": 1 hour.

There was the panic of the propane gas tank blowing up and tossing me in the tank down the hill where I landed upside down, not able to open the door of the tank... trapped, in other words... that soon passed... I don't remember some of the first thoughts, they seem unimportant now, at one point I felt as though I was in a river floating downstream at an easy flow... and wondered what it was like inside my mother's womb when she had an orgasm... then I wondered if she did have orgasms during pregnancy or any other time... and I began to feel lonely right now about my own sexuality... that it seems wrong to be at this high place in my sexual development and not be with someone special... lovemaking with old lovers is comfortable and satisfying, but not new and since my orgasms and sensuality are higher now than ever, I felt a certain frustration and sadness... I did want to relax and enjoy my time in the tank but there was the nagging question that has been going over and over in my mind the last few days... am I putting off writing the women's project because I'm afraid of failing or do I really want to learn how to let everything go and enjoy leisure... there is a duality here that I want to understand but can't seem to sort it all out yet... in the tank my thoughts flowed from not caring if I "do something great" to focusing on just what it is that I will do that will give meaning to my life, wanting my work to be productive and beneficial to myself and others, regardless of what it is... I think I expect too much of myself sometimes, and don't want to get caught worrying about the future... maybe I don't need the answers right now, that they will come when I'm ready, just hold on and let my life progress doing what feels right when I need to make decisions... I wonder about losing faith in myself... if that's what's happening... wondering where the gumption went... wondering whether there will be a series of highs and lows or if the place in between is bland and dull and if I could live like that... having to tell myself to live each day and find beauty in what it offers... why can't I just do that naturally, rather than having to tell myself to do it when the going gets rough... I need reassurance and talked to myself a lot in the tank today... no answers to the questions, but glad to face the questions... the tank provided the space to do that freely....

10-11 November 1973
Steve Binns, male, 27 yrs., 155 lbs., 6':
total time: 4 hours, 20 minutes.

Saturday, November 10, 1973: 1 hour. First experience in tank. Mainly an adjustment period—much Ping-Ponging. Several instances of beginning relaxation and awareness of the potential within me to explore the vastness.

Saturday, November 10,1973 (7:00 P.M.-8:30 P.M.): Second tank experience—significant shift from unfamiliarity of first time. Into several deep levels hitherto unexplored. In response to self-questioning of "Why am I here?" (in reference to being in the tank) no specific information received but a "full" sense of well-being came to me. The feeling of a threshold experience occurred at these points.

Sunday, November 11, 1973 (7:00 A.M-8:00 A.M.): No log.

Sunday, November 11, 1973 (10:05 A.M.-10:55 A.M.): Fourth tank experience. Beginning to experience true relaxation from "tightness of consciousness." Release of emotions of love and warmth with subsequent expansion.

30 November 1973
Jacob Brackman, male, 30 yrs., 165 lbs., 6' 2": 57 minutes.

Went quickly into a quiet state; slowed respiration, loss of bodily ions. Fluid movement between reverie (warm and pleasant) and relatively void mind. Less able than usual to sustain preprogrammed visualization, or train of thought. Felt free of tension, anxiety, would have liked to continue longer. Will use again soon.

16 November 1973
Paul Brenner, M.D., male, 40 yrs., 185 lbs., 6' 2":
1 hour, 32 minutes.

1. Shouldn't have shaved—salt is an irritant to the skin.
2. How do they get O_2 into this thing?
3. I hope it works!—O_2 that is.

4. This must be the closest thing to death.

5. Nothing's happening—I'll try hypnosis.

6. Christ, when I moved my hands—they felt anesthetized! Yet the movement was fluid.

7. If I combine hypnosis—I wonder what will happen.

8. Now I am seeing green—(an old friend)—can't get with any other colors, damn it!

9. Black appears three-dimensional with my eyes open—like looking at all the celestial bodies of the universe—they disappear with my eyes closed—keep thinking of Watts.

10. If I move my body—I feel "dolphinesque" and sensual—have tremendous fluidity of movement.

11. Starting to feel my surroundings—I wish I could experience something new—I am getting an occipital headache—

12. I'll try hypnosis again—it doesn't work—damn it!

13. I better get out—saw infrared light—went back in and grooved, on the red after burn.

14. Got out again 8 minutes later—time of emersion 11:42 A.M. —something must be wrong with the clock—probably still on daylight standard time!

15. St. headache (rt. peri-orbital) during shower—but I felt extremely clean—maybe even purified—

22 August 1973
Jan Brewer, male, no data given: 1 hour, 51 minutes.

10:00 A.M.-11:51 A.M.: I entered the tank and floated—with hands behind head. An immediate sensation of black void free-fall space. I slowed down and tried to avoid numbers of signals entering from the outside. Finally connected with one strong signal—found to be John and Toni—received additional instructions and continued exploring—some sensation in a red through orange-yellow color pulsing energy band. Some contact with many old personalities—seemingly known to me which all appeared and faded, as if released. Was aware that my body had extreme tension that did not release while floating as if its balance was not familiar with the medium it was in. Finally was instructed to see if Oscar was there. Some fear—but I looked and did not find him. As trips go this one was mild—pleasant with very little fear and very little intense emotion. A comfortable, floating trip. I specifically avoided calling on any of my old traveling companions or systems—quietly waited.

11:51 A.M.: Very little sense of direction.

5 August 1973
Joe Bridger, no data given: 1 hour, 32 minutes.

5:29 P.M.-7:01 P.M.: Upon getting into the tank I flashed back on John unplugging the water pump, and at the time I had a concern that the air pump might have also been unplugged, so I got out of the tank—checked the air pump and saw that it was plugged—and then realized that it's perhaps a good idea to check that in the beginning, to see that everything is plugged properly. I had not read the manual guide for technical details to check for whenever one gets in and out of the tank, and if this information is not included (to check the plugs to see that everything is plugged properly) then perhaps it would be a good idea to include that in the guidebook. The immediate sensation in the tank was getting into an unfamiliar program, or a program of being in an unfamiliar place, and had some difficulty in the beginning in completely allowing myself to relax and float off. I tried a series of programs, trying to establish the position of it not really mattering whether I relaxed or not, and I had encountered a similar program earlier when first learning methods for achieving deep relaxation, but with the passage of time I concentrated and paid less and less attention to this particular concern of mine (not being able to relax), and paying less concern to myself as an object (being self-referential) and then concentrating on that kind of feedback loop, allowed me to see that I was creating everything that was happening to me inside the tank. At some point in the early part of the experience the word

"Home" came into mind, and that was finally the key concept that allowed me to sort of achieve, or allow myself, to become relaxed within the tank. That is, it was a friendly place to be, it was not a confining place to be at all, it was relaxing, satisfying, comfortable, and had the true feeling of the meaning of "home" as I experience it. With that, it was a delight to be in the tank, very much a joy, a feeling of freedom and deep relaxation. There were not any visual images of any forms at all, though I played with the idea of focusing the energies to sharp points and materializing forms with them, but this seemed to be work that I want to do in the future, in future experiments with the tank. I also had the idea of (in the future) preprogramming myself with something like *Pathways Through to Space*, which puts one in a good state of feeling and thinking, prior to going in the tank, and use that as the preprogramming. At three or four points in the journey, there was the feeling of a pumping, a very low-frequency, powerful "cosmic motor," and I allowed myself to stay in that space for a while, but did not push the energies. That is another region that I wish to explore further. About three or four minutes before John knocked on the door to see if everything was ok, I started coming back into the body and felt some tension—stiffness, that I had started loosening up by swimming around, paddling around in the water. By the time I had gotten that loosened up, then I heard John—someone—knocking at the door—got out and opened it and John was there.

24 October 1973

John Brockman, no data given: no time recorded.

Into Lilly's tank. Imagine me, having an experience. Don't like the idea at all—the experiential idea. Something lying before me—a body of reality—thinged—something I will manipulate that manipulates me. That's not the way the show runs in my post-human, nonuniverse. The independent mind, dethroned, is not the subject-object-verb of "experience," a word I don't use.

Before entering the tank, I had been exposed to the logs of my predecessor "tankees," which were filled with rhetoric/vocabulary of humanistic experiential psychology. Their descriptions dealt with altered states of consciousness, energy flow, vibration, love, and so on.

But my world is a world of words. The lives lived in the mind are at an end. Proving this is for me the ultimate value/use of Lilly's tank. Once inside the tank there is no exposure to the normal sensory stimuli of the outside world. Neural energy (not what we are thinking but that which powers our brain) is not produced by the eyes and ears, but by the gravitational receptors, the stretching-type muscles. The eyes, which bring in about two-thirds of the sensory stimuli to the brain, are useless as a source of energy for the brain. The tank cuts off all input to the eyes, thus quieting all those related neural circuits. Also the floating body creates a totally unique situation for the gravitational muscles, which are forced by the circumstances into new and unique patterns of use. The effect is a potent energizing neural (not *personal*, not *human*) experience.

What do you think about in the tank? You don't think about anything. You don't think. *You* don't. The brain takes over spelling out, spilling forth its information. It's totally a nonhuman experience.

Things going through my head had little relation to the reports of the other "tankees" (or should I say "tankettes"?): "How long must I stay in this stupid tank in order to be polite to Lilly? What am I doing with my clothes off floating in the darkness when I should be in the other room working, paying for my trip to California." But these are the thoughts of a severely limited and rather unenlightened soul, one with no interest in the roller coaster high/low explorations of the psyche or indeed of the extent of vocabulary of contemporary psychology.

The point of the tank is that meaning ceases to have any meaning. The words have a life of their own in the stillness, in the darkness. There is no *one* at home to have an experience. Whether you're high, low, or in between is irrelevant as the tank leads you to the realization that distinctions, differentiations, are impossible within its confines.

The realization does not end upon leaving the tank. The philosophical-ontological implications are of a most profound nature. The only limits to tank use lie in the danger that it might become a self-indulgent status symbol of individuals involved in psychological one-upmanship. But for now, it is indeed the ideal cosmic tool.

20 January 1973
Francis Busco, male, 23 yrs., 160 lbs., 6': 1 hour.

Half hour of body awareness with mild discomfort, salt; chlorine; not enough O_2; noticeable high humidity. Then very quiet like good ZaZen. Time contraction.

"Swooning" experiences several times. Mild hypnogogic-type visionals near end (some content): eyes, faces—abstract.

Contraction-to-point exercises tried without much affect.

Trip no. 2; no data.

(Note: Left lid open for more air, heater on in room—lights out.)

(Tank still has low-pitch periodic sound.)

(Break after first thirty minutes for bladder.)

Time seemed shortened 50 percent. Very quiet. Mind largely devoid of form activity save infrequent thoughts of social and scientific topics, peaceful/restful, attempted visualizations with no clear images forming.

Mental efforts quickly refused, and back to peace. Forced ZaZen. Little disappointed at no visual imagery or phosphenes—body disorientation on exit. Feel good!

September 1973
Douglas A. Campbell, male, 44 yrs., 163 lbs., 6': 10 hours.

I got nowhere in the tank because I thought too much. It is hard for me to break this habit. The first several times I forgot where I went. Later I just daydreamed, which means I did not let myself go. I think the tank is like a dark cupboard [meditation cell] or a dark Zendo—a valuable tool, but unnecessary. The main advantage to my

(? what word here) was to overcome the fear of being alone. I want to try again.

5 November 1973
Liz Campbell, female, 39 yrs., 150 lbs., 5' 9": 1 hour, 20 minutes.

My first experience in the tank—immediately I felt at home—some time before I could allow myself to totally relax—a deep and mellow sinking into relaxation, responding to heartbeating, to breathing, to body noises. Joyfulness, no concern with time and space. Still a lot of mental trips—floating through, let them pass. Many images, awake or asleep? Still, mainly a tremendous calm and sense of well-being, a coming home.

15 February 1974
Caroll Carlson, male; no data.

Body sensations distract wigwams—peace—my child idea of an Indian village.

Then a castle corridor—a man in blue steps out of a picture—the other two frames are immobile.

Then part images, faces, vague frameworks—

Then water in my eye as I wanted to turn over—like in bed.

29 September 1973
Helen Costa, no data given:
5 hours.

A quiet place where I can allow my energy to entertain me; this time, in the form of Tai Chi.

Will Curtis, male, 28 yrs., 140 lbs., 5' 8"; no date:
1 hour, 30 minutes.

I relaxed quickly after immersion. After about half an hour, I decided to turn around and put my head at the foot of the tank. For

180

what it's worth, three things influenced this body shift... (I) I had been thinking about polarity, (2) I had imagined that it was cold at the head of the tank, and (3) I assumed that, since the heating coils were indeed closer to the foot of the tank, it might be warmer there. Very soon after doing this, all things became still. I no longer Ping-Ponged against the tank. I felt myself relax completely and go into a kind of sleep. A long time seemed to pass between thoughts. Later, I felt that this "awake/sleep" had terminated and that it was time to go. I was surprised at how long I had been in.

Victor di Suvero, male, 48 yrs., 152 lbs., 5' 8"; no date: 50 minutes.

The first voyage in the Concurrent Elsewhere. Alan Watts' "here and now," the Tao, all the names of God, the invocations of Infinity, the Idea of Idea, the avenues to the Self whether found in the Zendo or on the beach looking at sunset are met—and we are all together in the tank.

The dark, absolute—not claustrophobic—mind working, all the baggage, the reflexes, comparisons, referents all there—beginning to flow—illusion of movement rushing, the waterfalls to the right I'm going over, is it the Northern Hemisphere or the Southern, clockwise in the rapids below or not—the rush the fall into absolute stillness. I notice my neck muscles finally let the beard down into the water, which is now in my ears sealing all sound inside.

Suddenly, almost pulled, at an acceleration that is not painful, but intense, a move at a tremendous speed to the northwest quadrant of space and realize as I'm thinking NW—there—over there—there is no reference point anymore—space having no top or bottom but the movement is through galactic space and is in a direction over vast distances, and then, suddenly, the big toe of my right foot touches the wall of the tomb—to smile and open my eyes to realize it's the same—shut—open—shut—my right arm is comfortable three inches between right thumb and hipbone—my left thumb keeps trying to

181

rest on my left hipbone—examine why—left shoulder tense—has been for years—boxing at Santa Clara? nerves bunched? Judy Finstein manipulation needed—bop—suddenly it's at rest same as the right hand—now let's get on with it—close eyes—open—close—open then absolutely nothing—more nothing then a mosaic of faces—all in muted dark to darker blues, magentas, purples—all muted almost under a monochromatic haze—faces talking—young Narda—much younger than I had ever known him. Alan—range—running into the woods, Alfonso in his coffin—I am also Alfonso and he's flying into galactic space—all images merge almost as if a subway had not stopped at the station but rushed by—and there they all were standing on that purple tiled platform, frozen in time—an instant and yet all time, back then to moving, set even faster speeds into pinpoints of light that almost create a spiderweb's look at earliest dawn with the small dewdrops catching the light imprinting a shape to the web and the web growing and then the muted knock—John calls—it's over.

18 August 1973
Rona Elliott, no data given: 58 minutes.

3:26 P.M.-4:24 P.M.: It was very pleasant, when I got in I started floating immediately and was at first afraid to immerse my ears—it felt a little uncomfortable to do so. Then I realized it was more a question of accepting it than anything else, so finally I laid my head back completely and my hair was immersed and I noticed that the head floating in that position does not lie very comfortably with the rest of the body; that in putting your head backward in such a fashion is a little uncomfortable. John now tells me that that is very common and that he neglected to tell me another position to alleviate that kind of discomfort. My thinking processes right now are pretty slow—I'm pretty relaxed—so I'm just kind of adjusting to this phase. I found the water comfortable and I went into doing some exercises—some breathing exercises—to try to relax so I could really get into the space. I did some deep breathing, inhaling, holding, and then exhaling—and then just adjusted to the space more; was distracted a little by the discomfort I was encountering with my neck. Realized that I could give that my attention or I could just accept it and go on to other things, so I did that. I went through some exercises locating points in my body—left foot, right foot, left ankle, and all the way up, trying to get in touch with any feelings I had. Occasionally got distracted from doing that by just adjusting to the space, my eyes were closed mostly during that period. Then I encountered a tumbling, floating feeling and I got a little scared—I was afraid to go into it—it was a little reminiscent of some spaces I'd been in before—I just wasn't ready to go into the fear of tumbling. So, I kind of just put my head back in a different place and opened my eyes to see where that was at. The more breathing I did, I had some nice visual images—very muted white light with kind of chiffon, formless quality about it that changed and became bright in spots, then moved around—very chiffon—billowy—then withdrew and if I gave the attention of my eyes to another space another form would come out of that. It required looking, letting my two eyes kind of turn into one, rather than looking with two at one time. Then I got some muted orange forms and muted purple forms, very swaying—I've always enjoyed hallucinating, so I got into that, and realized it was pretty much at will. Got some visualizations of male faces, some forms, some ideas—not too clearly visual. At times when I started doing the breathing I guess I moved the water around and that would set off me getting into the tumbling space, the floating space. I got into that a little bit without the fear the second time and just kind of felt as if I was turning around in a Jacuzzi, being carried. The only time that would stop would be if I encountered the side of the tank. I sat up, cleared some water out of my nose, felt the saline in my eyes, wondered if that was ok or if it was good for you or not, then I realized if I kept my eyes closed that any irritation that I encountered would stop. I'm just incredibly low key right now and it is a little difficult to verbalize it. I kept my eyes closed a lot then and kind of looked at the fact that the fear and the control of it... that that was running me—the fear of letting go, which is not new to me but I really saw it clearly and I just acknowledged it, then it was all right. I did some more breathing—your mind just moves around a lot—I felt something bump against my leg and I realized it was my hand and that was kind of a surprise. I cracked my back on both sides to try to relieve a little more of the discomfort I was feeling in my neck. Then I moved into a different space with my body where I wasn't in my body at all for a while and the temp. of the water was just—there wasn't any water at all—and I was just kind of floatin' around out there. Something brought me back—I don't remember quite what. I kept thinking "I'm not Stanley Kubrick" and learning to relax more so that the flow would be greater and richer and less linear. I really understand that in the relaxing comes the less linear and just more images. Then I had a very specific visualization of an old man with very dark brown skin who I perceived essentially to be an Indian, but whose coloring was more Negroid, but very rich cocoa. He was lying back in the water, kind of half-smiling, not too many teeth, wearing kind of a loincloth almost diaperlike, kind of a traditional Indian garb, and he was kind of laughing. That perception turned into a thought more than a visualization of a child, an infant—and then into just this rounded point sticking out of the water, kind of like the tip of a penis sticking out of the water—it wasn't as much a penis though as that form, with a white kind of aura around it. And then some internal mechanism said, "Well it's time to sit up." So I sat up, turned around, lifted the tank cover, saw the time was just two minutes short of an hour. Then eked back into the world feeling very soft-spoken and I am extremely verbal, but I had difficulty being verbal—putting words to the images now, even though it is right after the experience. It was very nice. I think I'll do it again later tonight. Thank you.

16 September 1976
Ulrike L. Kantor, female, 43 yrs.: 1 hour, 40 minutes.
3:40 P.M.–5:20 P.M.: This time, which was my second time, I was a little hesitant to go in. I didn't know what to expect, but I knew something might and probably would go on. Once I was in, I felt physically more comfortable than the first time. The tank felt a little like my bed. I could trust it—it made me feel protected. Once I realized I was floating and could breathe in and out without sinking, I started to move my body sideways—back and forth. As I did this, the solution swayed slowly around my body. For what seemed to be a long time, I only felt the sensuality of my body. When I stopped moving, I became again, as before in the tank, aware of the incredible absence of sound and light and the connection to anything else. As I was floating, I lost all sensual feeling of my body. Slowly I felt nothing. Two or three times I woke up, like out of unconsciousness, and went right back into nothingness. With each "shock," I immediately felt my body and started to think of all the things and experiences I had that day. Finally I "woke" up bright and feeling completely refreshed. The next moment I was shaking with emotion. I remember thinking something happened to me down there, what, I will probably know and feel it again later.

13 September 1973
Craig Enright, M.D., no data given: 1 hour, 10 minutes.
One hour prior to entering the tank Jan and I spent about twenty minutes chanting and meditating for clearing.

I entered the tank at 4 P.M.

As in my previous session, my stream of consciousness was monitoring my physical sensations. The higher $MgSO_4$ content and resulting greater buoyancy was more comfortable than before. As soon as I was settled, I tried to move out of this level of monitoring the hardware, but I kept returning to my sensations. This occupied perhaps ten to fifteen minutes of objective time. At this point I stepped off into a new space which had neither the dimension of time nor space although a form of awareness remained. I was roused from this state with some difficulty; I did not respond to auditory stimulation and finally was aroused by being shaken by Jan. I remember at this point the sensation of time suddenly accelerating from zero rate to normal rate over a period of several seconds.

This state of consciousness is intriguing, but I can say little more about it except to note its lack of distinctions. In fact, I could call it the lack–of–distinctions space. Jan said she had spent four to five minutes recalling me from it.

The following fourteen hours were influenced by the tank experience. I entered a black rage state triggered by some trivial external event 1 1/2 hours after leaving the tank. It wasn't "righteous rage"—I was not identifying with this state nor did I feel justified in being there. Gradually this mood was replaced by one of positive high energy and this lasted throughout the night. Finally at 8 A.M. the next morning I began to feel tired and went to sleep. If affect were a taut string, mine had been plucked by the lack–of–distinction space, cycled briefly through a negative sine (sign) and changed to the positive.

1 February 1975
Werner Erhard, male, 39 yrs.:
1 hour.
It's incredible—no shit.
Moving when you're floating is not the same as in the effect of gravity.
The experience is joyous, fun, and moves to freedom without some of the effort to get to freedom so the starting place is further along.

Spring 1974
Richard Feynman, male, 56 yrs., 160 lbs., 5' 11":
summary of 35 hours done in 12 weeks, 1974.
Having done a number of introspective experiments on influencing

186

my own dreams (and been objectively conscious and observing while I was dreaming), I became very curious about hallucinations and welcomed the opportunity to use Dr. Lilly's sensory isolation tanks, for they were reputed to produce hallucinations, safely. I have spent at least a dozen sessions, each of over two hours, in the tank. The experience was very pleasant and rewarding. Although nothing happened for the first two sessions (except idle thinking as when one is going to sleep), hallucinations were experienced nearly every time thereafter. After some brief period after entering the tank, they would continue for hours. I was always aware that I was hallucinating and part of my mind was nearly always making observations. There were the usual out–of–body, or out–of–the–right–time hallucinations. For example, in one case I could see my hands on my head as if I were standing in back, and when I moved my hands (actually in the water) I would see them move and sky appear between the fingers, etcetera. I have later had imaginary flights over scenery, etcetera. In both of these cases the fact that others get this type of hallucination had been discussed beforehand.

On one occasion I had been thinking (in studies of artificial intelligence) about how the masses of memory materials might be organized in storage in the human memory. That week my hallucination consisted of vivid recalling, or reliving, nearly, image after image from far in the past (in no case were there any new details that I didn't think I could have remembered if asked). But I was delighted to discover that the memories were stored according to locale—you thought of one scene occurring at some particular place and all the other things that occurred at that place tumbled out. It took a full hour after I was out of the tank until I realized I had discovered nothing real, that that itself was an hallucination.

I am convinced of Dr. Lilly's dictum that you can think of anything that you want to—that the hallucinations are a delightful and entrancing union of spontaneity of detail with a pattern or set which you have made or can make about their overall character. Thus if you have discussed a great deal about the blue spheres that you will see, you may see blue spheres but have the illusion they come not from you but somewhere else—even though you know that the only one in the tank is you. The usual test of scientific reality is that many people see the same thing. In this case coincidence of experience lies not in the reality of the thing experienced but from a coincidence of influencing conversations and ideas about what you will imagine, and an illusion that the "image comes to you." The same phenomena may explain some successes in dream interpretations through dreaming certain symbols whose character or interpretation has been previously discussed.

I should like to thank Dr. Lilly, his wife, and associates for many very pleasant experiences both in and outside of his tanks.

23 August 1973
Elsa First, no data given: total time: 5 hours, 40 minutes.
9:40 A.M.–11:40 A.M.: Sat in tank for a minute or so to check out that I wasn't frightened. Then floated—either hands behind neck or at sides or arms and hands up alongside head. Got out twice to pee and to wash saltwater out of eyes. First impression vast darkness, high ceiling, fantasy of Knossos temple, but it didn't get any realer. Never lost awareness of body, water, etcetera. Comfortable, but less relaxed than in bed. All I saw was the same as I'd see with eyes shut in bed except that in bed I get more hypnogogic imagery. Saw: points of light, vague fields or nets or colored light, very faint patterns, two faint hypnogogic images (the hills outside, two ducks swimming in pond). Tried to go with whatever I saw, especially when lights got a little mandala–like, but didn't get anywhere. Experimented with seeing parts of my body as I can with eyes shut. Thought I might metamorphose into some hideous amphibian, but didn't get anywhere with that either. Lots of random thoughts on recent events interfered with relaxing.

4 hours: I just tried to use tank as a medium for meditation or

practice in getting into trance state. I found that if I went in with no such program I just went on thinking! Got more aware of relation between body and mind relaxation and vaguely more familiar with some stages in letting go.

28 October 1973
Faye Gaer, female, 74 yrs., 135 lbs., 5' 3": no time recorded.
Considerable difficulty adjusting to the hammering sound of the heartbeat. Would bring me back as I'd drift off—leaving the body behind. One short episode floating along on a gentle river; passed high beige cliffs. After a while I noticed the cliffs had shallow markings, which suggested a picture language. A satisfying quiet enfolded cliffs, water and myself. The heavy drumbeats of the heart brought me back. Most of the time a delicious sense of weightlessness and slight rocking movement.

No date
Paul Gaer, male, 39 yrs., 150 lbs., 5' 7": no time recorded.
Sunset—interior tank room—day. Everything is black—right? Dr. Lilly knocks on the door. Entering he lifts the hinged lid of the tank and looks in. Looking in—Paul is not there! Dissolve.

Interior—Toni's ranch house. Lesley can't wait any longer, already late for an appointment in Westwood. Decker School Road—nightfall. Lesley at the wheel of a bad black Buick, picking up Paul, naked, on the road. Numbers, times, later...

Lesley calling in to see if Paul has shown up.

Close shot—Dr. Lilly—night, with flashlight he is finding a break in his metaphysical routine.

3 August 1973
Ron Garren, M.D., no data given:
48 minutes.
10:48 A.M.–11:36 A.M.: Getting into the tank I was anxious, felt

excited, like an adventure—at first my feet were touching bottom—
that is my heels. Somehow I had it in my mind that this wasn't supposed to happen so I moved around but nothing changed the foot
drag. Finally I said that it was all right for my feet to touch bottom
and stopped hassling myself about it. Soon after that discovered that
by placing my hands behind my head my feet rose—at first my head
was going very fast—midway through I discovered I didn't have to
close my eyes—heard my heartbeat in my ears very prominently and
felt my breathing. Became aware that at many times was holding my
breathing at some midpoint in expiration. Then got into a space
about asthma which I had as a child and still have occasional episodes
of—got into that I was holding back in my breathing, then flashed
back through my childhood and got sad at all the holding back I had
to do to survive—then got into a space about women as mothers—
and the isolation tank as a womb—got into it as a very large physical
space—started shifting positions and got restless a few times and in
the beginning felt lots of itching all over—also felt after floating for a
while that I must be touching solids with my body, then I would
move my feet and was always surprised that they were still in water—
also felt the weight in my legs—after a while in the tank my breathing became very deep without any interruption in expiration—I
found it best to hold my expiration as long as possible—created the
best equilibrium for me—towards the end I became restless and took
that as a hint that it was time to get out. Thank you for the opportunity to experience it.

11:36 A.M.: P.S. I felt the time after getting out of the tank was
very important—enjoyed being alone outside for a while—find it also
a consolidating experience writing about it.

25 August 1973
Henry Gellis, no data given:
no time recorded.
On entering the Samadhi tank I felt just great, secure and at ease.

I tried centering my body so that my extremities wouldn't touch the sides of the tank. This was difficult at first but got easier as time went on. I also felt saltwater in my eyes and realized my head was too far back.

Most of my visions were dark in color—the mountains and valleys of Malibu Canyon on an overcast day. I tried to lighten up the mountains, but couldn't. Then I started OMing, the vibrations echoed throughout the tank. I moved the OM sound up and down my spine, coordinating it with my breathing. The OM started in a low resonance but ended up very high pitched like a spaceship taking off. I almost got off on this one, but couldn't. I then kept lowering the volume of my OM until there was just the sound of my breathing. Then I started dissecting each inhalation and each exhalation. I would take up to fifty or more inhales with the same breath running the energy up my spine. Then I held for a few minutes to gain control and did fifty or more exhalations running the energy down my spine. With a few hours more this one would have done it. I then started taking deep breaths. I was a spaceship—with every exhalation I explored the stars, with every inhalation I was floating still in space.

This was visually pleasing, but I was still not one with the stars, I was separated from them in duality.

Using the tank many more times I will be one with the stars. What a nice thing to look forward to.

Love and good thoughts to Toni and John and all their friends. Namaste.

10 November 1973
Michael L. Gerber, male, 28 yrs., 160 lbs., 6' 1":
1 hour, 15 minutes.
Saturday, November 10, 1973: Initial Ping–Pong effect with some feeling of flying straight up. After physical centering in the tank, I began processing the day's activities and became acutely aware of heartbeat, and ham–sa sound of breath. Following this I began to

concentrate on a high–pitched sound coming from the vicinity of my right ear. Then several vivid faces of women appeared and remained for one–half minute or so, followed by an intensifying series of colored lights—mostly white—I continued to relax, and probably approached sleep as I was disturbed by single clonic (?) contractions of arms and legs (four or five times) which led me to think of the time and again onto the day's activities. By that time my heart rate and stroke volume had come down causing less attention to be drawn to its functioning. My eyes burned from salt—then I experimented with different positions (breast stroke with flutter kick—ha! ha!). I was beginning to disassociate from my body by attempting to find liberating thought combinations (thinking—that I am), but felt a bit fatigued as if I lacked the ability to go deeper—the hour ended. Afterwards was cold and itchy, sober (centered), feeling slightly energized.

18 August 1973
Myron Glatt, no data:
1 hour, 16 minutes.
5:51 P.M.–7:07P.M.: This is to report that the Wizard entered the pool and he vanished shortly thereafter, melting into a saline solution, disappearing in the brine. From the brine the Wizard headed straight out over the nebula of Orion, following the guide of the *Rand Universal Universe*, and, once past Orion, we just freewheeled it a bit—hitting a few stars and barns and generally getting it on. There were no appreciable problems star–hopping until the chicken got in the bath and after a little chicken broth we headed straight for that salt solution in the eye. From there it's a caper in the navel, rolled in olive oil and stuffed with anchovies—briny, very briny. Skimming the chicken fat off the Milky Way, we headed straight for the bright light. Hit the light, struck the tilt, exited the tank—7:07.

One postscript—the Wizard is still in the tank!

9 and 18 August 1973
Ruth Glatt, no data given:
total time: 1 hour, 59 minutes.

12:46 P.M.: Approximately 2:45 P.M. now—I'm feeling very euphoric—no pains in the body—total lack of any kind of discomfort. I went into the pool at 12:46 P.M.—programmed myself for an hour. The first five minutes I spent deciding that I wasn't going to suffocate from the stuffiness and because of complete confidence in John's technical abilities, knew that he had provided for air even though I couldn't feel the sensation of any coming in. The first five minutes seemed very long and when I worked through that space I went into a very relaxed, floating space with a witness kind of experience where I was observing myself. I felt as though I were floating downstream in a very strong current—first in an up/vertical sense, with vertical sensations as though I were going up—and then as though I were going down—and then it was a horizontal drifting, very fast in a current. My eyes were closed and I felt, with very little sensation except for my hands clasped behind my head, I had my usual visual kaleidoscopic colors appearing and it didn't matter whether I opened my eyes or they remained closed—it was the same thing. After a bit of this I started to lose the sense of time, it was a nontemporal kind of experience—I wasn't sure whether I had been in the tank an hour, two or three, or maybe just a few minutes. After the time of visual kinds of sensations, seeing kaleidoscopic colors moving, seeing the inside of the tank whether my eyes were open or closed, with all kinds of colors and shapes projected, I decided that it was really groovy and I've been there before and it was probably time to get out. About the time I decided that, I started hearing Toni singing opera—with Orf in the background—and I thought that that was kind of interesting—I was still observing my own sensations, I was still the observer and the experiencer—and I remember the thought going through my mind that "no I can't be really hearing Toni, because you can't really hear anything in here," but I was hearing her sing and there was an Orf background, and she was singing opera in a contralto or soprano voice, and I listened for a while and it was very clear. I heard jets going over, I heard all the road traffic, and then Toni singing again and the Orf kind of background, and then a church–like quality with organ music. I don't particularly care for Orf, or organ music, or opera, which was kind of interesting. Then I heard a hammering and I heard my own pulse in the ear, it seemed as though it were coming from the ears, which became a very rhythmic kind of thing and then became very, very fast and I'm sure it couldn't of been my pulse because it was much too fast—it turned into kind of rhythmic kind of drumming. I still was aware that that was probably the pulse of my body or somehow related to my body, my heartbeat or pulse. Then I heard different kinds of singing and then I tried to control the singing—I went through a period where I tried to control the music—I thought "Vic Damone" and I heard Vic Damone singing, and I thought "Frank Sinatra," and I heard Frank Sinatra singing "Prisoner of Love" and "I Walk Alone" and all the old songs from the forties and I could control whatever I heard. And then it seemed as though I sort of *became* what I heard and I lost my witness, and I became one with—everything became one—I wasn't feeling the water and I wasn't hearing the sounds and I wasn't seeing the visuals, but I was all three at once, and I just relaxed—I don't know how long—I'm not sure how long because I had no sense of time, it wasn't a linear kind of thing, it was a nontemporal experience—I just melted and became the water, I became the sound, I became the visuals—they weren't differentiated in any way at all—and I heard many, many different kinds of sounds, I heard a bit of Morse code that I hear very often anyway, but it was a different tone—just a very small amount of that. I reached a level of the observer and the observed becoming kind of one with everything that was happening. Then suddenly I became the observer again and I was sure somebody was going to lift the lid and say, "Hey, your time's up," and I started getting into the regular stream of consciousness kind of thing again and I installed the pool—I rolled it back on rollers—and I got it working, the new therapeutic tank—I went through that, and I realized suddenly I was back into the space of being the observer and the observed and then I decided it was time to get out of the tank and I pushed open the lid and looked at the clock and it was two minutes less than the hour I had programmed myself for.

August 18, 1973 (1 hour, 1 minute): 4:37 P.M.–5:38 P.M.; First day of the thirteenth year of my marriage. Got in the tank—didn't go through any fear programs—thought: "Well now it's till next time" which is where I left you off last time. Waited to hear Toni sing opera, heard a jazz bass, and then absolutely nothing—absolutely nothing! Until I said, "Well, fuck it!" I pushed up the cover, looked at the clock and it was 5:38! And there is a total blank! And I'm feeling very nice and again... until next time...

Well it's not really next time, but this is a P.S. It was absolutely like Sodium Pentothal anesthetic where you start counting backwards and you get to ninety–eight and you wonder when it's all going to be over and you are suddenly told that it's an hour or so later and everything is over! That was the way it was.

20 March 1975
Cybele Gold, female, 28 yrs., 120 lbs., 5' 2":
no time recorded.

First entering the room, the lighting reminded me of a vehicle that was once used as a transporting device from one planet to another. The smell that was caused by the salts and the bodies that had been there before was a familiar one but there was one element missing from my previous experience which was a sickly sweet smell mixed with the salt, i.e., sulfur and bodies, but it still triggered that place for me to remember.

Entering the chamber, as I closed the hatch and emerged into the water after a few minutes my mind and senses lived out my existence in the womb, the delightful feeling of floating and looking around but not seeing anything with the body's eyes but darkness. The one concern that I felt was that I was now having to adjust my "regular" form of oxygen to the new form of oxygen that was now available in the tank and it took about two minutes to feel comfortable breathing. I found that I had to focus my attention on my breathing and notice my body fluids and organs (as many that I could be aware of) functioning. This helped me to be more relaxed than I was before with the difference in the available air. It was a pleasure to notice these things that I mentioned under the different conditions in the tank. One of the nicest experiences was the situation of being close to my native state, just hanging out and being without a body. Then I thought it's lonely here and how long do I want to just hang out here without anyone else to hear and talk to, do something else, so I waited until that one left, and then I waited, played and then decided to come out into everyday perceptions of life. It was a lot of fun and, thank you tank, for the experiences.

No date
Eugene J. Gold, no data given:
no time recorded.

Ah, yes, once again my animal is willing to go with me into strange and dangerous spaces, like being there quietly while I'm being here quietly. I don't remember ever having not done this or been here, and except for the change in perception and muscle-tension requirements no state change took place until I wanted it.

Tried changing things around (position, state, thoughts, mind, which is my usual things to do at first, checking out parameters of change, then checking out parameters of sameness).

I really did want to come up with something new, and so began looking for newness. I found newness, examined it, and shoved off again.

There were several thoughts, but each were old friends.

Thought about making some light, tripping out on dark, and so on for a couple of wild impetuous moments, but didn't.

Laughed a few times at the silly idea that the body was lying in a tank somewhere in Malibu. Who would believe a ridiculous story like that? Just as ridiculous as the story about being a human on earth or something.

Got going on "waiting" and "not waiting" for a while, but again it was the same. Said hello to mother a little more loudly and clearly than usual. Noticed the membrane effect better in the tank than out of it, but I haven't been paying too much attention to that lately. I like the reminder atmosphere around the tank and house. Very good alpha environment. Throughout was considering use of the tank for people still buggering around with questions, answers and wondering about nothings and somethings.

There was a passing thought to stubbornly hang out in the tank longer than anyone else ever had or would, but I recognized that thought as being the conscious property of the tank, wanting continual fillup and predictable occupation. Most of the thoughts coming out were tank thoughts rather than the person's.

20 and 27 November 1973
Bruce Gregory, male, 23 yrs., 145 lbs., 5' 8":
total time: 2 hours, 15 minutes.
This was my first experience in the tank. For about five minutes I experienced some difficulty in maintaining my balance. Afterwards I could maintain long periods of one position in the tank. The first two or three I kept my hands at my sides, and the remainder with my hands behind my neck. I preferred the latter. As soon as my attention left my balance I was aware of the high vibratory sound which comes from the ears. This sound I could pick up at will throughout the experience. I was also aware of my heartbeat after about fifteen minutes in the tank. I could also pick this up at will. I heard a lot of voices in the first half of the session. I don't remember the specifics— except for one comment concerning freaking out. I was aware of thinking "All these voices are mine." Strange! Yet it seemed the voic-

es were coming from different persons. Following this, I became aware of tensions in some parts of my body—knees, right shoulder, elbows. Most of my time from then was spent concentrating on breathing, which I wasn't able to slow as much as I would have liked. However, on the inhales, I experienced bands of white lights around the sides of my head. I experienced a lot of peace feeling floating in the blackness. At times I felt I was sinking into a pit, but the sinking feeling would halt abruptly and my attention wandered. In the last portion I felt rushes of energy inside my head and a pressure building on the frontal portion. Another experience that had some duration— seeing a lot of tiny lights dashing around at an incredible speed. This experience would come and go. It reminded me of the Monsanto ride at Disneyland.

Tuesday, November 27, 1973 (11:05–12:05 P.M.): The first few minutes after I got my balance I listened to the ear bija [pure inner sound of self], and my heartbeat. My capacity to stay in one position without shifting had increased over the previous session. There was a short period of voices, after which I passed into a space of no sense at all. The only way I can describe it is I became one with the blackness, and became the blackness. I felt nothing. I was nothing. There was only nothing. The feeling was very peaceful and restful. Thinking about it, imagine it was some state of limbo. I have no idea where I went. This covered approximately three–fifths of the hour.

2 January 1974
Joan Grof, female, 31 yrs., 120 lbs., 5': 2 hours, 20 minutes.

I entered tank with the anticipation of several things happening: claustrophobic panic or delineated stages of experiences, i.e., sleepfulness, and then visions. Neither set occurred. Instead, I was totally at ease, feeling as though this place (i.e., total quiet, darkness, and fluidity) was what I wanted. I lost body boundaries and time sense, immediately disappeared and I experienced total peace and a feeling of unity. Experience did not modulate and I did not play with it. Just was very passive and let "it" do it itself. What I experienced was a continuous void that was not boring, yet empty, not engaging, yet full.

No date
Stan Grof, male, 42 yrs.: no time recorded.

After about five minutes, enormous slowing down of time. Increasing stability, tranquility, a certain "inorganic quality of consciousness"—moving away from its biological characteristics. Atmosphere of ancient Egypt, becoming aware of her religion, philosophy and art. Insights into the process of mummification, becoming a mummy and experiencing the consciousness typical for it. Understanding it as an interspace vehicle (organic → inorganic).

Matter → spirit.

Moving into the initiation in the pyramids, feeling a parallel between a mummy and an adept in the sarcophagus. Awareness of granite, becoming the consciousness of granite. Understanding that the preoccupation with granite in Egypt was based on the appreciation of the state of *consciousness* associated with it. Changes occur on a scale of thousands and millions of years (as compared to seconds and minutes for the biological forms). Return of an old insight: Granite statues *are* the deities, not images thereof.

Moving into absolute void (experienced as consciousness of the interstellar space). Timelessness. No difference between minutes and millions of years.

Ending up the experience with feelings of regeneration, purification, refreshment, rejuvenation, clarity.

9 July 1973
Joe Hart, no data given: 1 hour, 30 minutes.

11:15 A.M.–12:45 P.M.: My first problem in the tank was to relax my tense muscles. I was holding myself in a floating position as if I were in fresh water. My hands were at my sides and my neck was arched; this was very uncomfortable. By putting my hands behind my head I could relieve the tension in my neck somewhat. Then came a part by part relaxation of my whole body until I could experience the saltwater supporting me, and the realization that I didn't have to keep myself afloat. With the awareness of being supported in the water, came the remembrance of becoming a green dolphin in a space I entered on a trip in Chile. The joy of moving swiftly and sensuously through the water I could now feel in the isolation tank. So once again I became the green dolphin diving, leaping, turning, twisting in really real joy. My body seemed to be going through these large swift moves of a dolphin, but when I rose to Joe from time to time I was aware of just the slightest actual movement of my body which was magnified into the sensation of the broad movements of the dolphin. Being a dolphin I felt a tremendous warmth and love flowing out of me. It was light, joyful, playful and delicious. At this point John checked to see if I was coping and all I could do was laugh in delight. From the dolphin space I moved into concentration on the heart center to increase the sensation of love. To do this I moved my energy from the 0 chakra up the rest of the chakras to the Ma'h; then brought the light down through the Ma'h [top of head], the Path [head], the Oth [chest], the Kath [abdomen] to the 0 chakra again. Once this circular movement of energy started, like tumo [Tibetan energy source in belly], my body heat went up and I became uncomfortably warm in the tank. So I simply moved the energy from the Ma'h to the Oth and reduced the heat. Finally, I simply rested in the Oth without any effort of concentration. My respiration and heartbeat lowered and I found that the water was becoming a little cool. Curious. So I increased the concentration on the Oth and my temperature went up to a comfortable level. Then I got out.

2 October 1975
Nancy Ellison Hellman, female, 39 yrs., 114 lbs., 5' 5"
45 minutes.

Silk... How sweet my hand felt traveling the length of my body. Difficulty in forgetting the back of my head and neck. Effort to relay there most conscious thought (throughout the forty–five minutes) after a few arm–raising exercises first pleasant thought: I am with myself. Soon discovered my eyes open offered same experience as closed so I opened them wide and felt truly blind—(later this ease at relinquishing sight surprised me. I am an artist and certainly rely on my ability to see). I consciously tried for both blindness and deafness but unwilling to relinquish concept of hearing. I knew I could hear and provided myself with my heartbeat as proof—I thought about John's reference to a stabbing— becoming the woman stabbed and wondering what the pain would be like— thinking in that state perhaps it would be reassuring—and that without it*—I circled on an axis my interior turning slowly (in my head) yet feeling my body cruising—I felt I understood both the barriers and ever–providing space—no matter what direction I traveled, it never felt bounded.

I would have loved to have been a little high—feeling perhaps closer to lingering less consciously on ideas. For a moment I felt myself in the glith without my usual "gear" and it seemed a different ball game altogether. I feel "curiouser and curiouser" that is where I'd like to begin again—empty of uniform.

18 August 1973
Paul Herbert, no data given:
1 hour, 22 minutes.

8:11 P.M.–9:33 P.M.: Since this is my first trip I guess I'd better report the things which I would probably not bother to report on subsequent trips—probably wouldn't even pay attention to them. First I was

* Eskimo say—If you stop feeling pain you are dead.

surprised at how easy it was and how comfortable I felt with the whole process. I was expecting no sound at all and of course I heard my own breathing and felt the ripples of the water and the touching of the sides of toes, elbows or hair. However, none of these bothered me, I simply got acquainted with it and got comfortable with it. I was surprised that I got scared of nothing—no paranoia—no troubles at all. I want to say that I spent the last three days in my cabin in Big Sur alone—in solitary isolation, confinement pretty much—as much as I could—centering down and allowing the surface troubles, whatever they were, to work themselves out so that when I got down here I'd be in the best shape for a deep trip—as deep as I could go. I'm so glad for those three days I just finished—I felt real good about it all—I went through a few dreams, no real nightmares. There was nothing hounding me such that it continued to occupy my mind, nothing compulsive, I was just pretty much in a state of allowing. Allowed things to come—allowed things to go, without feeding them, without refusing them. So this was the process of the three days. It gradually came to an end or a place where if I was going to come down here it was time to come. I could have continued the process, and sometime I want to, in my cabin—maybe as much as two weeks, and of course if things are going well then I even want someday to do it for forty days—I think there would be intense good—I think it's a process, which the tank is also for me, of meeting Karma, of finishing unfinished business, of dwelling on and attending to whatever is in consciousness, that arises to consciousness when that which occupies consciousness is disposed of—it disposed of itself through allowing it to remain in consciousness and to do its thing, work itself out—in whatever way there is. It's almost like a balancing process—whatever is out of balance then gradually finds its balance by its own methods. The process as far as I'm concerned, my part, is not to interfere, but to allow. Now this is just about a description of what my tank experience was that's just finished. I'm happy that I was not bothered by the fact that I didn't seem to trip out in some fantastic, melodramatic, or entertaining way—with a visual display, things like that. I didn't seem to have those things, but it didn't seem to bother me either. I seemed to be spending this session—my first session— getting very comfortable—well, I was very comfortable with the whole thing to start with—just getting familiar with variations, testings, explorations, of whatever came into my consciousness, whether it was bodily processes, whether it was the tank itself, my relationship to the tank, my sensory input coming from the environment, or now and then tripping out into daydreams. Whether tripping out into daydreams which happened a couple of times—in which I guess I did lose awareness over my environment or whatever—now, what was my consciousness trip? I actually think I've said it all. I do believe that, just the same as I have learned when I hole up in my cabin, or go into a semifast or a total fast from food and water and all sensory stimuli, as I have done several times in the past, but not recently—I do believe that the process goes deeper and deeper and that seeking specific results might be fruitful, but I think the best fruit is to just allow. And I feel so good that I am at this space where this feels right to me—I'm not disappointed in my performance, I'm not unhappy with my state. I feel real good about that. I guess that's the end of that.

28 October 1973
Eleanor Hoover, female, 30 yrs., 113 lbs., 5' 4":
no time recorded.

Not panic, but fear of panic—but how can you tell them apart? I think I can. I wished to fight the panic successfully. It would be a battle—it would be short, just a few minutes. Just hold on—barter for time, seconds, moments. No I can't—throw open the door, just for an instant. No one will know—but I will know. My heart is my ears, my throat, my ears. I am all heartbeat. It will addle me if the closeness, the darkness doesn't. It is too hot. I can't breathe. What if the breathing mechanisms don't work? Will I die here? But what matter—I choose it as the way I want to live. I am silent (but for the throat). I move nothing, tell nothing, expose nothing. If I am quiet, will the gods ignore me—the doom pass me by? Is this how a wood-cock lies in the autumn leaves that disguise him? I think of a picture of me as a child, four or so, on a pony—that someone brought into the neighborhood. My face white under the phony Western hat (that went with the chaps and the holster with the poor paid pony), lips light with fright—but I would endure, not give in to terror. I dare to swallow—and the sound is enormous inside. I breathe deeply and hear that too. I'm a little bored now. I want something spectacular to happen. I think of endless trivia, glad for the solitude and time to do it. Faces, conversations, meanings, encounters, exchanges, I am think-ing that in this dead space a taboo part of my body feels most alive. I wonder what that means—and about the evasion of ecstasy Lilly talked about. Finally it must all be controlled—if the mind, then by the same token, the body—all of it, no quarter—or you're cheating. I think of my friend, confined in a cage in prison, tortured, cornered with his own excrement for two months—what he must have felt, how he must have gone mad at times. I will match that. I will do it too. But there's the heartbeat and the panic/fear of panic has come back—but now it's gone. But there I can't even make stars twinkle or a universe out there—Have I failure of imagination? Might I be see-ing stars and colors—could I look down on my own body if I were cleverer? I am bored. After many times, it will get better probably. Now, something new is happening. Black masses are gathering and rumbling across my field of vision. Midnight black on light black—they appear, merge, rumble (silently) coalesce and mount into black waves then run away—or back around. Scary—a little. But it hap-pened. I am delighted. I dare to let go of my head, Lilly said to hold it. I've been here maybe a half hour. I didn't dare, till now, try another way! How conformist and terrified we are of ourselves. Now I move everything, experiment with everything. Suddenly, I see what I have been waiting for—a point of bright light in all that blackness and then it streaks across the dark sky. I hear a knock (it was actually for the other tank). I come awake astounded that I hadn't seen my meteor (Eleanor's meteor) before, since it was obviously there all the time. *Sic transit gloria!*

FAR OUT: CONFRONTING THE PANIC AND
PROMISE OF TOTAL ISOLATION, REPORTED BY
ELEANOR LINKS HOOVER

Down Under in the Isolation Tank

If anyone asks me what's new, I'm liable to tell them. In fact, I may just as well confess now—it has been a week of apocalypse for me personally. First, there was the new Malibu fire, a nighttime inferno, that licked its way to within two miles of my door. But it didn't exactly catch me unprepared. A few days before, I had spent an hour totally immersed—floating on my back with my face exposed—in about a foot and a half of heavy salt water, confined in a small, pitch–black, soundless isolation tank. So I was ready for anything.

The tank in which I spent my dark night of the soul is one of three on the grounds of John Lilly's new home–workshop–retreat high in the hills beyond Malibu. Lilly, psychoanalyst extraordinaire, is of course famous for his work with the dolphins. And equally celebrated for his other protean talents. He has been working with the isolation tank for the past 20 years, and has spent hundreds of hours in its dark waters—many of them on LSD, back when it was legal.

The tank is a large rectangular white box about the size of a grand piano with three small steps leading up to a heavy hatch on top. When the hatch is in place, it screens out all sound and light: however, it can also be lifted easily from inside by a mere hand push. You are carefully shown how to do this when you get in. All of which hoists you beautifully on your own petard. For when it starts feeling like a prison in there—and it usually does for most people—you are confronted with the fact that the bars are of your own making.

I knew all this in a general way before I went into the tank. But that was all I knew. A woman rushed up to Lilly while I was talking to him. She was wringing wet in her robe and had just come from the tank. "I could only stay in there a few minutes," she said. "There must be something loose in there somewhere. There was so much terrible noise I had to get out."

"We'll check it," said Lilly calmly, "but I don't think so." Then he added quietly, "It must be the noise inside your own head."

So I also knew that not everybody can take it.

As I climbed into the tank, I felt like a fetus returning to the warm amniotic waters of a white womb. The euphoria only lasted a moment. I watched the hatch close with a twinge of terror. Then, suddenly, I was in the deepest black of the universe. I floated motionless, on guard, and it started at once. The panic. Or fear of panic. I told myself I knew the difference. I must keep cool and remember it. But the panic kept growing. I could die here, I thought. I heard a tremendous noise. It was the beat of my heart. It filled the tank. I was nothing but a huge, loud, throbbing heartbeat!

I battled an urge to push open the hatch. Just for a second... to catch one last reassuring glimpse of the light? No one will know. "But I will know," I told myself and suddenly felt better. I was getting cooler with each passing minute. I coined a homily—"In the isolation tank, all you have to do is live life one minute at a time."

Finally, I felt calm enough to move out of my rigor–mortis posture and start studying the environment a little. I was able to rummage pleasantly through ideas, thoughts, memories—what Lilly called "the residue of the day." I even began feeling a little bored. Where were the light shows, the fantasies, the hallucinations I thought might happen? I looked for stars in the blackness. I found none, but I began to see black masses that rolled together and then careened across a field of lighter black. About that time, I heard a knock on the door and two things happened in quick sequence: I saw a bright flash of light that streaked across my field of vision like a meteor. And, at the same

206

time, I thought, "Why, there's a crack of light in the door—how come I didn't see it before?"

Instantly, I realized, of course, there had been no crack. I also noticed that I only had my "vision" once I heard the knock and started to relax, knowing my purgatory was over.

Later, Lilly talked about the tank experience. "We are metaprogramming animals," he said, meaning that the reality of our world is whatever we define it to be. "In the tank, we are up against a world where the usual cues don't work; so we are confronted with our evasions, our fears. What we have to learn is to make our fears our own... to see that it isn't a shark, it's a guppy—and we have just been looking at it through a microscope. It is a lesson in inner relativity. Once you can get into the tank with no preprogramming and no expectations, you are able to experience new... phenomena."

This was the nub for me and I realized why I had come. It was the obvious link between the isolation experience and creativity. As a writer, I am interested in what it means to be totally immersed in the creative experience. Joan Didion once told me that in order to finish *Play It As It Lays*, she spent one month almost totally alone. Prison has spawned a spate of great writers and thinkers—Socrates, Cervantes, DeSade, Villon, Dostoevski, Genet, Papillon, Sri Aurobindo. Arthur Koestler spent six months in a Spanish prison in solitary confinement awaiting his execution.

Such experiences either drive men mad or create a new, extraordinary breed, which is just what Lilly found when he interviewed prisoners of the Korean War and World War II. This was about the time scientists such as Lilly started working with the isolation tank to see what was involved in brainwashing. Then, it illuminated the world of the astronaut. And now, if we stick with it—and I certainly intend to—it may illuminate the world for the rest of us.

9 February (no year)
Al Chung–Liang Huang, male, 37 yrs., 140 lbs., 5' 9": 1 hour.

Prior to immersion, I had had fine food and wine, listening to the flute playing of Charles Lloyd and readings from Castaneda's don Juan by Burgess Meredith, dancing and playing Tai Chi....

Immediately after immersion, my body continued to move in curves resulting in "Ping–Pong" spiraling against four sides of the tank. The spiraling motion soon subsides as the inward curving movement becomes still. I continued to hear faintly, the fluting and the murmurings of don Juan.

The front part of my entire body was above water surface. In the beginning I was very aware of the difference in sensation: skin—air, skin—water.

My arms began to circle involuntarily, making a complete down–up curve to form the figure–8 infinity. I no longer knew the difference between air–water, sound–silence, darkness–light....

Seemed like five minutes when Toni lifted the top to remind me that an hour had passed.

27 October, 11/1, 11/16, 11/18 1973
Michael Hughes, male, 56 yrs., 180 lbs., 6' 1":
total time: 5 hours, 21 minutes.

Surprise! Surprise! I hate it! I spent most of the time fighting immense tension in my neck. From the clavicles to the center brain is made of cement. So I sat up for the rest of the time. Very loud talking. Perhaps the ego–construct was stubbornly holding on to its existence, and dwells in the neck. Gave up struggling to set up a counterforce or a high and just sat it out. Other possible factors: I hate water and I hate containment. I feel peace and immensity in the sun and the desert. Also, I very much felt the etheric surround of a dozen other people trapped in the water solution. It is not mine. Will try it again but I suspect it is not for me.

November 1, 1973 (1 P.M.–2 P.M.): First twenty minutes a fight against sleep, then against pictures and conversations—chitta, mind stub. Last third hanging on to "Who am I?" Absence of fantasies, some sense of centering and stabilizing. Aware of darkness though striving for light. Felt unfinished; goal not yet achieved but in the right direction. A very difficult concentration to hold. Feel both encouraged and discouraged. Onward and inward!

Friday, November 16, 1973 (3:30 P.M.–5:51 P.M.): Getting better. Still a great deal of conceptual "rearranging furniture." Was able to jettison the implorings—calling on names to pull me out. Hang on to "I am," trying to experience what that is. A few moments of accepting no–thing–ness, and that it is all right. One spontaneous surprise: I called, "Joanna, we are free!" and I felt I was a limp body being lifted out by the shoulders like a photographer's sheet of paper out of a solution. Perhaps still working too hard at hanging loose. A lot of belief–junk is gone or being evicted.

Sunday, November 18, 1973 (11:00 A.M.–1:00 P.M.): Came with a cloud of sadness and indecision. I left Friday's session with the question, "Who am I?" and got no answer. Began again with a sort of relaxation or letting go in my despair/futility: I just don't know and no amount of words seemed to fit. Then images came instead, somewhere between waking and sleeping. A gorgeous mandala in full Technicolor, but two–dimensional. I felt like diving into it and saw the vast intricacy in all directions, but headed for home, or the golden ball in the center. A great peace, a love affair with form from a heart of formlessness. A laughable loss of all "problems." Whatever comes next now is all right. The "I am" is something in feeling, in timelessness, in fun and joy. Like wow!

2 November 1973
Alejandro Jodorowsky, male, 44 yrs.:
1 hour.

It is one experience I would repeat every day, not to obtain, but to lose, like to go to the bathroom. In the first second, I was afraid of

being afraid. "It" controls itself saying "It is only afraid to suffocate."
But he (Lilly) must control oxygen, because what will he do with my
corpse? This matter of giving [up] my body, and to die to my
self–conception. Ok, I will die. After two or three minutes, floating,
marvelous comfort, you are at home, nice security, nice silence, nice
temperature, and nice relaxation. No body, no sex, no emotions, no
thoughts, no problems, no past, but absolutely no past, no plans for
future. Little man into the water being the seed fish, without expecting to be a tree with scales. There in the only time, the no–time,
there in the only center, the no–center. Sometimes relating with the
maternal womb, but escaping of this image. It didn't want to play
with the fetal–paradise and then, it put out like excrement the problem of practical relaxations. Now we are ready. With a great breath
of fire the burning of the oxygen like a simple star and a great general
beating of heart. Nothing but nothing, and in the middle of the
nothingness it was there like a stone—the conscience—Realize what I
know, what I live in every moment. I am not so much but still I am
something even if I didn't want it to be active, even if it wanted to be
the tongue like a cup without will with all his being made to receive.
It tried to be liberated from the little stone when the middle of nothingness became the whole universe. It prepared itself to jump. But
Mr. Lilly come, the hour is past. I regret. Was infinite but too short
and this body got out of the baptismal desiring a lot of emersions.
Anyway, I think, say the little body, I can live in this society in a very
polite way in a very communicative way, being immersed all the time
in the tank without have a tank.

8 August 1973
Gifford Keen, 13 yrs.:
35 minutes.
10:30 A.M.–11:05 A.M.: When I first got in I felt like I was spinning, going around and around—not fast; and I also had the sensation
that I was moving backward. Then nothing happened for a while. I

210

don't know—my state of thinking really wasn't all that different—I couldn't detect any differences—it was just like when I close my eyes when I'm in bed—that's about how it was. My arms itched pretty bad and they're all rashy now; but, later on, I started definitely having the sensation that I was going around and I felt like it—just going around and around and around. At one point I felt that my head *was* down at the other end. When I got out I found that I was sideways in the tank. Every once in a while I would bump into the wall and sort of push off. I was kind of distracted by twitching in my shoulder, I had a nervous twitch in my shoulder. And—that's about it. Oh—I had figured that it was about a half hour when I got out. There was just nothing a whole lot to do. I mean, you know, I got kinda bored and I was just in my regular state of thinking, not really different.

8 August 1973
Sam Keen, no data given:
1 hour, 58 minutes.
8:37 A.M.–10:35 A.M.: My first experience in the tank. When I went in I had a moment of paranoia, of thinking that I was going into something that I couldn't get out of, or somebody was going to close the lid on me—then as soon as I got in there I began to shift around, to shift my body around and experiment with how to float easily. I would judge that I spent about the first twenty minutes being really caught up in my body, not able to get out, just checking the sensations and seeing where I was and wasn't comfortable. Then gradually I began to relax my body, forget about my body, and go in and out—gave myself over completely to it. The first part of the trip was largely an inventory of my consciousness, of the things that I have been thinking about in the last week, the way I've been experiencing my thought processes in relationship to my body—the first part was very abstract; that is, my thinking was abstract and conceptual—then as I let loose more deeply I began to go into a couple of my bad spaces; one, a panic space, which was a little bit like an early

thing in the sense of not being able to control my mind—and then I realized that that was crazy, I just went to the bottom of that. Then the second, was to a real grief space connected with Ann, the woman I just broke up with, and I realized as I was going down into that space that I could either go more deeply into it or I could just jump out of it and I... it was as if I took a goblet—a thin wine goblet—and smashed it, like they do in the Jewish wedding ceremony—just when I was about halfway down into that grief and decided no, I didn't want to go down there anymore. As I came up then I began to get a lot of sense of strength—a lot of sense of the ability to control wherever my mind wanted to go, and steering. From that point on in the trip I began more and more just to sort of park my body and experiment with steering anywhere I wanted to go. Of going from one kind of thinking to another, from coming into my body to being sort of aware of the outside world and thinking about Gifford and John and Toni and Lael and Lanea and Grace—all the friends and people I've been in touch with this past week, thinking about them—and then thinking about my history and about who I am, and about all the experiences that have made me. Then going back and letting loose of all that and just going in, first to sort of blank spaces and then floating—very floating spaces. I experienced very much the sense of the water as being like the world—as being totally supportive; it was really supportive, it just allowed me to use my energy to steer where I wanted to go without having to hold myself upright. Also—about midway, or it must have been about an hour and a half, I began to feel this feeling around my heart—the same thing that I'd felt yesterday when I was driving down here—it was an actual warmth, heat, it was like a heatlamp had been put on my chest and I began to feel this sensation of very, very intense pleasant heat all around my heart. I thought about Grace saying that she had been sending me messages, and it felt like love which people had been beaming to me for the last month or two. Then I got very much into the feeling of accepting, of being open, and of being receptive, but still not being able to completely breathe out—not completely being able to express it in the way that I love—and I got this image then, of a castle—a gigantic stone castle—and on the inside, a great very strong man—and the metaphor came to me that "only the strong man opens the castle." I experienced myself then more and more—I sort of experimented with the metaphor—to see how it was that I open myself, and how the strong man within opens the consciousness to... not only to receive, but to express, and especially to express feelings of love. At that point I began to go out on a lot of different trips about people I have loved—I went back with Heather, I went back with Ann, I went to my children, I went to Lanea, I went to Eliza, and went back yesterday to talking with Grace—and I just got back into the feeling of what it was to flow out again. Then more and more I got the feeling in my body of flowing in and out—more and more as the time progressed I just had this sense of elation about freedom and about strength—and I had fantasies about using the tank to begin—this is where we should begin education, by letting a person isolate themselves from everything and really get acquainted with themselves, in a place where there is no threat at all, and just to know that they are in control of their own mind. I got more and more sense of comfort as I went along, and integration. This time I saw so much because I knew that there is nothing in there but me, that I could go wherever I wanted to, and it was a much, much—a very gentle experience. Also, I experienced that the further I went one way into my body and into owning all the sensations and finding the switches—finding the places in my body where, for instance, my breathing could get into calmer spaces by deeper breathing, or how by breathing and imagining almost, my psyche going out of the top of my head, I began to get into more universal spaces—I began to see that the further I could go one way, the further I could go out in universal spaces and leave aside all of my own daily preoccupations and my personality, and I think now of the old saying of the mystics, that "deeper in is further out," and the further I go into the real psychological spaces, the further I can go out into the psychedelic spaces. It also occurred to me that they might, after this, put an eleventh commandment in that "Thou shalt not covet thy neighbor's isolation tank!"

28 October 1973
Cynthia Knapp, female, 24 yrs., 145 lbs., 5' 6 1/2":
50 minutes.

Due, I'm sure, to the different meditation and mind tripping groups that I involve myself in lately, it is very easy to present myself with a question, pop in the tank for a half hour to forty–five minutes, come up with the answer, examine it from as many aspects as possible, throw it up and away, bounce it, see the reaction with other elements and questions, watch it turn itself inside–out, and then watch it dissolve. I spent about five minutes with deep breathing and a little chanting and then sudden- ly found myself sitting on the fence near the front porch, looking back at the Lilly house, paying close attention to the brick columns that hold the porch roof up. Flipping back to my physical body, I felt very compact and tightly put together, especially in my thoughts. Drawing an analo- gy between my thoughts and belief systems and the brick and mortar columns, my thoughts and my body seemed to be very rigidly construct- ed with use, little flexibility. I thought how obligated to my own ideas and systems I am—so I decided to let them loosen and be more flexible and let ideas, etcetera, flow through me instead of catching each thing that came flying along in my baseball glove. I found tense or inflexible blocks in my body and saw that they were rigid because various thoughts and influences were keeping them that way. So I began to physically move my arms together with a voice tone in movements that resembled peeling away layers of skin, and blocked structures. I did this for a while and was then aware that Helen's exercise class was about to begin—so I decided to get out to try to stay open and not tighten up while exercis- ing. There's nothing holding me back but myself.

214

1 January 1974
Paul Krassner, no data given:
no time recorded.

I feel it's appropriate to describe my original waking–up point. At the age of six I was playing the violin at Carnegie Hall—a child prodigy who started taking lessons at three. My teacher used to hit me so I would conform to his image of a virtuoso. In the middle of the Vivaldi concerto my left leg itched. In a moment of illumination I understood the nature of karma without having the vocabulary to express it. Without missing a note, I stood on my left leg and scratched it with my right leg. The audience laughed. I knew my calling. And/or my calling knew me. I identified with everybody in the audience. I did not take the applause personally. For better or worse, I have tried to maintain that conscious innocence.

Now then, an out–of–body experience is just a continuation of that flash of awareness I experienced onstage. I am aware of so much suffering that it would be a luxury for me to feel sorry for myself, so what is there but to feel good and try to share it? I believe I am open to almost anything, even eliminating the "almost" from that clause, but all I can report is that it feels good. I enjoy the mystery of existence and creation. I have never come up with any answers that aren't really questions. Just a reinforcement of my premise—as written in notes long ago—that God is neutral. I am prepared to accept the notion that human value judgments have cosmic connections, but until I experience something to the contrary, I just flow with coincidence. Or, to put it in more professional terminology, what the fuck.

2, 3 August 1973
Antonietta L. Lilly, female, 46 yrs., 135 lbs., 5' 7":
2 hours.

The previous week I had been inviting the thought that I would explore the possibilities that were implicit in my last experience. It fascinated me that I could almost feel the claustrophobic space approaching from a distance. This time it seemed I had the possibilities of other choices.

The imprinting of the fear was there, but it was distant and something that I could easily handle. I then found myself in a very familiar meditation space. I was going through the day's residue—reliving a conversation that I had previously, listening to myself ask questions and make comments—things I should have said and didn't—etcetera, when all of a sudden I somehow flashed on a gesture of speaking to myself. An acoustic picture—in other words, I was seeing myself give myself an earache—and I realized that I had never had that experience before, even though in meditation I could somehow see the system as a tapeloop of conversation it was all a visual experience. This was a combination of the visual and the acoustic, so that my seeing myself give myself an earache was very different. My ears being underwater, water hitting my eardrum was, I feel, one of the connections that allowed me to combine the visual and acoustic experiences. I also flashed on the fact that it was so exciting because man being a visual animal would naturally want to put his words in an acoustic form, as the dolphins must want to put their acoustic world in visual form—or, I feel, it is my belief that that would be exciting to them, as I found that to be exciting to me—it opened a dimension acoustically that I had never experienced before. I then was able to slip away from that image enough so that I could feel that as an almost—independent system from myself; so watching it go around and around with these conversations, with this day's residue, I was able to slip away from it and see it in this independent way and realize that I really had the choice of putting all my energy into that system and identifying, or pulling back with it or letting it continue with my observer observing. I then started a subtler kind of thing where the system was watching the system, and I realized that that was another sort of program that I could unhook from. There was a continuous shedding of these programs until I stopped looking or analyzing and then there was just nothingness—it wasn't a black nothingness, it was light—a lightness, almost a region of white light, with an absolute nothingness that was so complete, so blissful and so amazingly restful. I had no way of realizing how much time had passed. I then suddenly realized that the top of the tank was being opened and I saw a face, looking down at me, framed in red light. He said, "Is everything all right?" and I immediately had to overlap this nonordinary reality with the reality that someone, John, was above me saying, "Is everything all right?" It was a marvelously exhilarating experience to overlap these two states and be still in another space watching myself overlap the two states of consciousness. I was amazingly pleased and felt so complete and so full of a kind of Knowingness about myself. The possibilities of achieving these states in the future was a little more clear to me. It was an absolute knowing, with a careful examination of the points, or energy—tilts as I like to call them. I realized I had the choice to shed the program—only in the sense that I was seeing the program as something I was connected to, but not necessarily identified with, so this "observer space" was very much magnified and made me realize the incredible complexity of the human biocomputer—in John's words!

September 1973
Peter Lit, no data given:
11 1/2 hours total.

Wet, dark, salty. Kinesthetic amplification of body motion. Tank was not completely silent. The symbolic and factual isolation from outside, as well as the "safe" body environment, aided in releasing attention (energy) from traditional programs allowing it to be used in activating other programs (meta, self–, supraself–, etcetera) or to "go with the flow." There was little control over visual projections.

Trips: Someone entered room, knocked on door, I started out of the tank—

No one there.

Fell asleep.

Large areas of blank space when energy (thinking) not controlled, which were restful.

Apparent ability to "abstract" correct time except when confused with past or future observations.

Metaprograms and self–metaprograms could be observed.

Spirits should be removed from tank.

Psychic spaces programmed by G. Simon, but I mostly worked on awareness rather than "far out" spaces.

Visual representations of forces, energies, mandalas.

New tank was much roomier. No matter except at first. Increased air supply was an improvement.

Love, thanks—for the tanks—and the trips.

2 October 1973

Herschel Lymon, 57 yrs., 5' 11":

1 hour, 15 minutes.

The experience was unique. Never in my life have I experienced an attitude as close to weightlessness, or being suspended in the simulation of a gravity–free atmosphere, or in this instance, the medium being saltwater which gave me a sense of buoyancy I've never before known.

Initially, after I adapted with only very slight initial anxiety to my new environment, I thought I would visualize something in my mind's eye. But the only visual image that seemed to appear was an eye, and then subsequently, the eyes of an owl.

The atmosphere then was low–key. I am amazed that I, normally somewhat a restless person, never was impatient about the time; never did I actively wish for the time to speed up so that I could be done with this experience, and get it over with. So that was one positive, or potentially valuable learning opportunity: to become a more patient person, and to be more centered and balanced in my own time–space continuum. Likewise, as far as claustrophobic tendencies are concerned: all my life I've fretted when I was confined to a limited or constricted space, and here I was comfortable and without fear in that limited space of the isolation tank.

Similarly, in regard to other emotions; that hour and fifteen minutes in the tank was emotionless... and particularly free of any anxiety, except that which initially related to my concern about my own safety. Never before have I been so free of emotion. I tried to conjure up emotion... fear, anxiety, hate, and even love... and none was forthcoming. There were certain things I had been anxious about earlier in the day, matters relating to time (keeping appointments, not forgetting them, getting everything done), and the usual thoughts regarding money (Did I spend too much for this, or am I being too spendthrifty?)... Well, I tried to conscientiously worry... and borrowing a metaphor in another activity, I couldn't get it up! For the life of me, I just couldn't fret. So throughout the session in the tank, I dropped the attempt. (And even now, a half hour since I am out, I feel refreshed, as if my brain had been washed, or better still rinsed, and gently wiped off and erased of that kind of static.) If I did not, or was not able to hate... I don't think I was able to love either, much as I repeatedly tried to conjure love images, or just plain erotic images.

What I was aware of is that all the energy I normally use up in adjusting to the gravity of my environment and other physical realities, was now at the disposal of my mind. And my mind was clear and sharp... much more so because of the extra energy normally from moment to moment frittered away... that was available for thought. I also realized something else: thought is effortless, requiring hardly any expenditure of energy. Easy does it... because the whole milieu was one of peacefulness, calm, unstimulation.

Now I think I know why I experienced no emotions. It's the main core of the theory of the utility of the isolation tank... I think. It must have something to do with the James–Lange theory that "we tremble because of the suspension in the 'amniotic' fluid of the tank." One had no need to move any muscle to any degree. This must have been Nirvana, I guess. Without motion you can't hear emotion. And the motionless condition making so little demand on limbs and body creates a situation of little emotion. It's suddenly being freed of emotions, there's the acquiring of much freedom and sense of well–being. (Oscar Wilde: The advantage of the emotions is that they lead us astray!)

One more thought: I learned in college hygiene and physiology that in order to heal a broken limb, one of the most important treatments is immobilizing it. Perhaps, and this must be the most important insight I got out of this unique experience... by the extension of this idea, to "heal" a broken, or at least, a mixed–up and tired psyche (and body too), it is good to immobilize it—for even a short period.

Nothing much was bothering me before... but what remains clearly with me, and it is a very strong and satisfying feeling. I have been healed, and for this point in time, I am very whole and together.

Thanks!

16, 17, and 18 July 1973
Dave McElroy, no data given:
total time: 2 hours, 46 minutes.
1:10 P.M.–2:00 P.M.: My first awareness was of the salt stinging the scratches received earlier in the day; the stinging subsided within three to five minutes. The first impression I recall was that there were two crows sitting on the edge of the tank entry as if the tank door was still open. These entities appeared to be white then and not crows at all. They were very hazy, almost not perceived but when I realized my perception they disappeared. Then I watched a car drive on a hilly road bounded on each side by wheat fields. Then I considered various mundane affairs not noteworthy for I cannot recall them other than that they dealt with people here and elsewhere. The remainder of the tank time, approximately thirty minutes, was spent dealing with the great discomfort of my neck and shoulder muscles. To put my hands

behind my head caused my arms to fall asleep. To leave my arms at my side would fatigue the neck and shoulder muscles and my heels would rest on the tank floor. I considered various solutions to this problem, one of which would be to have an air pillow for both head and feet.

Tuesday, July 17, 1973 (51 minutes): 1:10 P.M.–2:01 P.M.: I lay for some time without apparent thought, then noticed the loud pulsing of blood through the ear area. I tried to attend to this pulse as if it were a mantra, but as my attention seemed to grow to a certain intensity then attention would shift to the painful areas of my body such as aching shoulders, neck, etcetera. For a long period of time I dealt with external reality problems and reached some satisfying solutions. When I realized that I had spent time unaware of tank I was somewhat surprised. Also, I felt my hour in the tank was over, which it was.

Wednesday, July 18, 1973 (1 hour, 5 minutes): 1:35 P.M.–2:40 P.M.: Most pleasant tank experience so far, apparently due to lower temperature and humidity. Most vivid imagery was of a woman in white embroidered dress saying "I'm going to teach them a song and dance." Most other thought and imagery related to e.r. and the direction of activities for the morrow.

5 August 1973
Burgess Meredith, no data given:
1 hour, 3 minutes.

1:58 P.M.–3:01 P.M.: I wish I could make this a more momentous day, but I've just had a very enjoyable time in Isolation Tank. Evidently I was in a little over an hour; my first isolation attempt, I've never been in an isolation tank before. I thought when I came out that it was much less than an hour, I thought that it was twenty–five to thirty minutes. At all times I was comfortable. I sensed no threat and I sensed no threatening pictures; I mean, I saw no threatening visual scenes. My body was completely comfortable; I believe I "dozed" a great deal. And, evidently, in some sort of a preprogramming before I went in there I was looking for such an isolation. I must say—it's very curious it just came to my mind—that, previous to going in there I had mentioned to Toni and to John that I was seeking solitude very much; my life had been rather, as we say, "harried," and as the French say, *"presse,"* with a lot of building at home and too many guests that I didn't particularly enjoy, and too many external problems were on me—so I happened to mention that I'd like to get off and isolate myself, and then, curiously enough, when I got into the tank that seemed to fit in with my expectancy, and hopeful expectancy. By that I don't mean that I anticipated any particular experience in the isolation tank; I was neither apprehensive, nor particularly curious or anxious to do it; but, as it happened, it seemed to have fitted my mood as far as I could tell. I actually did, I repeat, doze, and I found it a very comfortable bed indeed. There were no physical problems, one or two itches at the beginning, which I took care of. I didn't find myself hitting the sides of the tank uncomfortably, or finding any noises—oh I must say, this is very curious—once in a while I heard the men pounding stakes outside and I rather resented that noise—I wanted and I sought absolute quiet. Whenever I heard them through the walls and through the tank—they were building something outside the house here—why I rather resented it and wished it would stop. I could hear, of course, my heartbeating, and I could see dark visions and faces that floated by me. Once in a while cabins, and once in a while fields, and once in a while flowers—they didn't form themselves into any kind of a picture, or a mood even. It was tranquil. I did get the peripheral feeling of flying, but I sought for that, and looked down on fields somewhat—not as fully as I hope to do at another time. I sought to leave the body, I sought to fly in space, I sought to alter the consciousness—and perhaps I did, but when I came back from my drowsiness (which is the best term I can put on it) I didn't feel that I'd found anything except supreme peace. No, I won't say supreme peace, or even blessed peace, I had just found a tranquil moment. And that seemed to be all I could hope for or achieve in this hour, which went, as I repeat, went surprisingly fast. Simply left the tank because of a sense of having rested. I could have stayed longer without any trouble, but I felt rested, and I felt like the dawn had come, as it were, the way you feel after a good night's sleep, and I lifted the cover and got out (3:01 P.M.). It is very curious that last night I had a very full dream in bed—a dream which was full of anxiety—and had to do with missing important appointments, and having to do with my eyesight failing and various things, and marriage licenses and rings and things—and when I woke up I was very interested in that dream, because I've been through what I think is a good analysis as far as my ability to interpret dreams. I comprehended the anxieties and I was in a pretty good frame of mind; they hadn't accumulated as it were, because I had brought them up into the light and examined them; but today, in this midafternoon hour in the tank, I had no anxieties, no apprehensions, and I feel rested and anxious to try again. I can't think of anything consequential to say beyond this. Thank you.

JCL: *By coincidence, I came in the door of the isolation room just as he was raising the lid, and I noticed that he had difficulty in getting out; and that when he came out on the floor, he had a hard time determining the direction of gravity, there was a kind of a "floating look." Then it took him only about ten seconds and he quickly recovered and found the earth. He had the typical look in his eyes that everybody does on leaving the tank after an hour when they've had a relaxing time—he looked sort of stoned. When he first came out he said the trip felt like twenty minutes. His note was dictated within twenty minutes of the time of emersion.*

26 December 1974
Jonathon Meredith, male, 23 yrs., 145 lbs., 6'1":
1 hour.

I was so much looking forward to try this that when I first went in I waited for something to happen. It wasn't till I relaxed and started to sleep that I felt a good deep rest. Breathing I heard in my ears which carried me off to sleep and dreams, but I still heard and controlled my breath. Felt like being asleep and awake for short moments. Touched the side once with my toe and pushed, felt like I was traveling incredibly fast through space. Fantastic experience. Good idea.

16 October 1973
Jan Metzner, no data given:
no time recorded.

Became aware immediately of tension areas and moved in to relax and give myself to the experience. I was surprised at the nonexistence of fear reactions to closeness/darkness in tank, which I had expected. Being trained as I am in moving in consciousness with the techniques of Light–Fire, I found I went comfortably within and worked with a technique, but found focusing more difficult. My head felt very heavy and had to support it with my hands. Felt salt irritating to the skin. The overall effect was very relaxing, and there are other areas in consciousness I would like to spend time exploring.

16 October 1973
Ralph Metzner, no data given:
no time recorded.

I found it a very relaxing and enjoyable experience, marred only by slight discomfort due to the fact that my head had a tendency to sink down.

I went into the energy–yoga technique I am currently working with and found that I got some unusual perspectives on the innerbody spaces that would be otherwise hard to get.

Without the restraints of gravity, the moving into and throughout the body and, to an extent, out of it, was much easier—as if the structures had been slightly greased and made more slippery.

13 September 1973
Jan Nicholson, female, 34 yrs., 110 lbs., 5' 6": 1 hour.

One hour prior to entering the tank I did chanting and meditation for clearing.

On entering the tank my first reaction was fear—of not getting enough air, of not being able to get out. I checked the possibility of these two fears with John, outside the tank, then settled back. I felt afraid of letting go completely as the minute I started to do this I started whirling around rapidly, so placed my arm through the back of a pipe entering the tank. I could then make contact when I wanted to check myself out. After a few minutes of running various programs through my head I sank into a beautiful black nothingness space which lasted some time, then into an ecstatic space of total joy. On checking, I found I was smiling. From this space I felt myself pulled backwards down a long tunnel into a space of no dimension, no time, total peace, nothingness. Oh boy, I can remember one thought— "They're going to have to come in and get me out—I'm not willing to return from this."

This state continued until I was aroused and moved out of the tank. I felt tremendously peaceful, silent, had no desire to talk and sat in meditation for an hour thereafter. The following twelve hours were vitally alive for me and I felt tremendously refreshed, new and deeply rested. I slept less that night than I have for a long time and felt refreshed with less sleep.

Summary of 18 months, 1973–1974: Having been in and out of tanks for the last eighteen months, I want to share a few discoveries with you. Some experiences are beyond words, pure states of exalted emotional feeling.

"It seems if I can still my mind sufficiently and enter a period of quiet, that I am an open channel through which information can be fed. If I am quiet enough, I can *hear*." This discovery followed a space which I entered after a while in the tank where I came upon this large cosmic switchboard. There was much movement and energy at this

225

place—somewhat like Grand Central Station. There were beings seated at an immense switchboard and each had in its charge an earthling–connection and was plugging in the connection when the recipient was ready to receive the information. I felt a physical connection on my back between the shoulder blades and wondered if this connection had something to do with the central nervous system, our internal computer, hooked up to the cosmic computer. For two days after the experience I felt "hooked up" to this other source.

On another occasion, I entered the tank with the question "Who put the consciousness in the sperm? Or is the consciousness in the egg? Or does consciousness ignite with the union of the two?" My mind kept repeating this question. I came across a magnificent entity. The feeling was immeasurable, a feeling of immense, detached, compassionate love, like a most–bene-volent–father feeling. I posed the question, and he replied with a smile, "Maybe sometime you will find out." The information I received—not about my question, however—was, be ye all–compassionate and ever–loving to one another as that which created you is all–compassionate and ever–loving. (As John says—"Cosmic love is absolutely ruthless, it loves you whether you like it or not.") I felt tremendously expanded by this experience and fell out of the tank and rushed in to tell John, who replied, "Oh, you've been there!"

On another occasion, it was softly encompassing for me to lie in the velvety semidarkness and observe earth many miles below to my left, and from that distance observe the "local customs" we humans perform on this planet. *We all do the same things!* We are born, go through childhood traumas with our parents which seem to determine a pattern of our way of being with other humans, we go through the teenage thing, have boyfriends, some marry, do the sexual thing, buy houses, pay off mortgages, eat, sleep, do the cultural/creative thing, have children, do the parent thing and pass through middle age and eventually the vehicle dies. I imagine these "local customs" are peculiar to this particular planet and that other planets have their own "local customs."

Another time... a feeling of being an actress performing my script on this planet: "Oh, well, as the lines are already written, there doesn't seem to be anything else for me to do but enjoy and not take this life so seriously."

And, mostly after a day's typing, with my head spinning full of words... to lie in the soft, warm, loving darkness and silence, is like coming home after a hard day's night.

Glenn A. Perry, male, 35 yrs., 135 lbs., 5' 8":
3–year summary, 1973–1975.

My first introduction to the exploration of consciousness was reading John Lilly's book *The Center of the Cyclone.* It had a strong impact on me. I was a computer programmer at the time—"always rational, reasonable and sensible." I was able to hear previously unacceptable ideas because they were presented from the Western scientific viewpoint.

Soon after, I saw an ad for a five–day workshop offered by John Lilly, which was centered around the isolation tank and its relation to awareness. It seemed necessary for me to take the workshop at that time.

John provided me with experiences which opened me up to new perspectives in viewing myself and the world. He introduced me to the isolation tank as a powerful tool to further exploration.

In that first workshop, the tank was used at least an hour a day with everyone wanting more time. My experience of leaving the tank after my first session was profound and is still with me.

I walked out of the tank, into the sunshine, and felt part of a huge, scintillating energy system, the environment. I had no desire to communicate my experience for several hours. I was incredibly energized and, at the same time, soft and quiet. I felt a sense of well-being and an ease I had not felt since I was a very young child.

By the end of the workshop, I decided that I had to make a tank for myself, and, being naive, thought that with "just a little 'extra work'" I could make tanks for others. So three years ago I started the Samadhi Tank Company.

In a few months I had a makeshift but functional tank.

I typically used the tank an hour daily before my regular job and in about two weeks I was floating to work.

Before this I had never understood the slowpokes on the freeway. Now I was one of them. I found myself in the slow lane, feeling fantastic, looking through my rear–view mirror to see a line of cars behind me, then forcing myself to increase speed to the flow of traffic.

Each time I climbed out of the tank I felt more mellow and more relaxed than when I entered. In my life I started experiencing letting go of negative emotions much more quickly. I still got uptight and angry in many situations, I just didn't hold on as long.

Usually I didn't program how I would spend my tank time. As a consequence, I got into whatever came up. Sometimes it was meditation, sometimes my body, sometimes thinking about the day's problems, and often about the tank design.

I have always been fascinated by problem–solving and design. In this distraction-free environment it was much easier to visually hold structures in my head, plug in different variables and try on alternative solutions. I was delighted.

I have always had the questionable attribute of pushing trips I believed in onto others, so as I continued to use the tank, I became more and more excited about turning everyone else into "tankheads."

I had started the company committed to the idea of providing tanks for others. Each new way that I found to use the tank strengthened that interest and I was willing to continue the business in spite of all my frustrations with it.

It is important to me that I do not give the impression that I have been using the tank every day for the last three years. Often I have felt that I had so much to accomplish that I could not afford time in the tank. (That sure made me feel important.) I have always felt driven by my commitments. Filling orders, writing people, work, would take time precedence over using the tank even when I knew from experience that using the tank made me much more efficient in taking care of all of my commitments.

This last year a lot of changes have occurred and my life is headed in a new direction. I have fallen in love with a woman named Lee, we left our other work commitments to do the business full time. This is a way for us to be and to grow together. We use the tank regularly and it is even more valuable and pleasurable now than before. The tank has been an incredible force in my life in the last three years.

10 November 1973
Hector Prestera, male, 41 yrs., 145 lbs., 5' 7":
1 hour, 3 minutes.

First experience in tank. I discovered that fear of closed–in spaces (claustrophobia) no longer present with reassurances about dimensions of space—oxygen supply, etcetera, with biological security systems, felt reassured. John's first lecture fully assimilated. Spent perhaps five minutes checking out space—in here of above ("I")—then did intermittent checking from time to time during the hour. Was most impressed by the body trip in tank. Body relaxed completely except for "neck area." Feeling of warmth and relaxation in rest of body exquisite. Mind mechanisms (loops) very busy. Only a few minutes where "I" could let go. No surprise, busy day, first trip, long car ride, etcetera. Am looking forward to second experience! Quite pleasant sensation of release after session.

26 October 1973
Bob Rafaelson, 6' 1":
2 hours, 45 minutes.

Way before: Perhaps more turmoil and uncertainty than I have ever experienced before in my life. Death and the possibility of a second death (daughter, then wife) seems to have set all the priorities of my life amuck. Fear, particularly of loss of control of my life, is the prevailing emotion: suspicion, mistrust, anger, hate are the accompanying breezes.

Just before: The invitation from Brockman. At this time, "Why not?" When confusion obtains, try any– (every–) thing—besides nothing will work, and more importantly, should it? No apprehension about the "experiment"—some ego attachment to the notion of endurance.

During: I like it here. What am I supposed to do, feel. No ruler, except position. Can I maintain position? Easy, it seems. No strain physically. Quite comfortable. Are there serious confrontations in this box? None appear too serious. But outside the box they are many—so I'll concentrate, ask questions. The questions I know intellectually to be important, disturbing. In the box, I seem not inclined to have answers—so why ask questions? Why provoke? I'm not very happy to be agitated. I like it quiet. Perhaps if I don't ask, I won't feel sorry. I think about watching my daughter die, I feel nothing. I think about my own life ending. In here. Not a bad way to go. I obey the rules (no movement) quite willingly. My mind is comparatively calm. Very calm. I could stay in here a long time—or I could leave. No desire, really, to project either. I go when I go. I look forward to experiencing the outdoor "pretty" but it really feels good here. Perhaps if it were an ugly day—less anticipation. Who cares how long I stay? Records don't interest me. Ego diminished. Feels good. It will all work out. And if it doesn't—it doesn't. I bet on the former. But it's a fifty–fifty, heads–tails, bet. Meanwhile nothing is happening here. Seems fine. A basic feeling of slightly favorable ambivalence. I will get up and leave the first time it occurs to me to do so. It did. I left.

Just after: It is lovely to be alive. When can I get back in the box?

January 1975
Jerry Rubin, male, 36 yrs., 140 lbs., 5' 5":
1 hour.

I don't like the dark. As a kid I feared the dark and being alone. Going in the tank I experienced my body relaxing. I felt my spine. I experienced a number of sex fantasies and I felt the correlation between my head and my cock. My mind raced along, then died down. I tried to think of a title for my book but nothing special came. As a real planner, I thought I'd like to do this once a week. What a way to relax! Slow down! If only my father, who died of a heart attack at forty, had spent some days relaxing in the tank. I felt myself bounce from side to side, and I felt a slight pressure in my head which I might have called a headache. Tension in my head. I was scared of getting the water in my eyes. I saw that time is an absurd concept. I had no idea what an hour was. It felt awkward holding up my head with my arms. I put my arms at my sides and floated. It felt good to be alone and totally free of potential distractions. I felt like I was developing my muscles of concentration. I heard birds chirping in my ears. I did not see God but I felt my entire body relax. I felt my mind dissolving. I listened to my stomach. I felt the whole experience washing my brain clean.

30 September 1973
Kathryn Sharpe, female, 40 yrs., 160 lbs., 5'3":
1 hour, 58 minutes.

At first I spent a little time testing my buoyancy in the saltwater. I was tense and uncomfortable in my neck and shoulders. I released my hands from behind my neck and let my arms float freely. Then I took my body through a relaxation exercise, which I knew from previous experience takes about fifteen minutes. After this I noticed a numbness in my feet to midcalf. Next I opened my eyes, but got them full of salt because they were underwater. Next my mouth, same trip. Only my nose was above the water. I did a positive "rever-

231

sal trip" which usually takes another fifteen minutes. When I was finished I noticed that the numbness had traversed my right side to my neck and my left side to my chest. All this time I was aware of my heartbeating in my ear and finally the sound of the circulation in my bloodstream. Slowly and carefully I returned my arms behind my head without touching the sides of the tank. I did pranic breathing to the beat of my heart. I deliberately hyperventilated to rid myself of the feeling of heaviness that came with the numbness. I was immediately successful and for the first time (about one hour had passed) I was not aware of my physical body or surroundings. I felt as though I was back in the womb. My heartbeat became that of my mother. I felt so smoothly protected and felt that clothes were truly ridiculous.

As soon as I was rid of my body, I began to experience the tremendous power of my pranic energy. To actually feel the power which all of my associates are so keenly aware of and which I have used so long without actually feeling its source or harnessing its power. I know that it is this which allows me to heal the sick. I was just thinking about Billbo and deciding to go to the hospital today to work with him when I heard John's voice asking me if I was ok and telling me that I had been in the tank for about two hours. It had felt about forty–five minutes to me. I sat up slowly. I was not at all disoriented. I opened my eyes, felt for the cover, pushed it up and got out. I would like to spend about four or five hours in the tank.

2, 15, and 30 November 1973
William Smith, male, 40 yrs., 170 lbs., 6' 4":
total time: 2 hours, 54 minutes.
Loss of time sense. "Clicking out," of my kinky subconscious. Freedom from anxiety. A state of waking sleep! No cluttered, hurried self. I own my time. I control my destiny. Not the slightest conception of what the emersion time is, only the slightest curiosity. Surprise though. Maybe this is it, John. And Malibu, immersed in a few gallons of saltwater in a darkened tank may be the sense of peace I

seek. Some early awareness of out–of–body experience in this setting. A powerless power? Maybe.

Thursday, November 15, 1973 (9:10 A.M.–10:02 A.M.): Process to clear brain for space travel, moving with incredible speed. Fast. Separating mind from body. Early difficulty with clearing minor pain of salts on cut finger, some nausea, nasal drip, possibly last night's spaghetti. Overcome with earlier travel in cylinder and preparation for this. Coincidence control is working. Why do I prepare myself in the West looking East. Now what do I use, free power, use it now and always. Puncture reality. Seeking of power without people. What is purposeful? It doesn't matter. Use...of all available human resource. Satisfy only myself. In my time zone. A time–sound–space power supply within my brain. Detach and survive de–anxietized man, where is your brain now!

Friday, November 30, 1973 (12:42 P.M.–1:59 P.M.): Accepted reality is unacceptable. Self–hypnosis reveals pain, the same with religion. I accept all forms of spatial relations. The only frontier remaining in this universal is the mind. Sickness is shameful. Love is possible with intelligence. The day's end result is hopefully a readily available controlled coincidence. The only possible God we all search for? Us.

17 July 1973
Grace Stern, no data given:
1 hour.

10:00 A.M.–11:00 A.M.: My first experience in the isolation tank. I started out with an anticipation of having a good experience, that is to say—my attitude about going into the tank was of full trust and faith that I would give in to the experience and explore it. John briefed me about how to float and how to get out of the tank if panic set in.

For a while I felt around the tank with my feet and legs and body. This was my first real experience of floating in water. I placed my hands (clasped) behind my neck and before I knew it, all the weight, pressure and tension completely left my whole being. I felt spread out with the water—I was aware of boundaries but had no idea where they were. Not too long after that feeling of being spread out with the water—even, light and spacy, I got completely lost in the experience—I was only aware of being lost when occasionally my elbows or feet would touch the sides of the tank and that touching was what brought me back to a point of awareness of where I was. At one point I felt as though I was the only entity existing—just existing, but never with an image of where—meaning the earth, the universe or John and Toni's home. I also, at one point, felt my facial muscles move into what I thought was a smile—I had no control of that—I just let it happen. At times I would change my breathing just to feel the difference in the water temperature. I was able to make my body warmer after I felt a tremendous coldness. I also had the sensation of being in my mother's womb at one time. I had no comprehension of my body size. The only noise I was aware of was an occasional rhythmic beat coming from my left eardrum. The time seemed very short—my mind wondered about the time at one point and so I decided to come up and see how much more time I had left (I did not want to delay John and Toni on their trip)—to my amazement it was exactly 11:00 A.M. Almost as though I had a timer going on inside. When I stood up I felt a sharp pain in my left ear (ten years ago I had ear surgery for a ruptured drum)—that did not last long—I felt light and peaceful. Took a shower, washed my hair and weighed myself— found that I had lost three pounds (I had weighed myself before I went in).

11:50 A.M.: Now it is 11:50, and while I was walking around I kept having this feeling of not being as comfortable on land as I was floating—however, the discomfort was just a point of distinction from one space to the other—I knew how great it was in the tank so the feeling seemed to linger because I wanted it to. I would like to explore more areas in the tank—getting into other spaces.

No date

Bobbie Sundsten, female, 33 yrs., 130 lbs., 5' 7": 1 hour.

It took about ten minutes to adjust to the tank and realize it wasn't going to swallow me up. My arms and hands became cramped occasionally, but after flexing it would go away. Felt I was tipping over to the right to go face down in the water, and had to put myself back again. I wasn't actually, it was just a sensation I think. These were the only physical experiences I had. The rest were eidetic images.

I kept my eyes open all the time, looking up, and saw faces in grays, also massive eyeballs, pinecones, leopards, a black hole. There was a baronial hall, with archways in a wall hundreds of feet high and between two of the arches a stark white vagina as high as the wall.

I saw myself lying in the water about three feet above me. That image stayed several minutes, so I had time to really study it, and make sure it was me.

Whenever I felt panicky about being in the tank I would seek out the eidetic images and immediately be calmed.

Following the breath for a while, it came in very ordinarily, but going out it was a jet stream through my body, down my legs and out through my big toes with terrific force.

Saw clouds, went through them and saw stars, planets, galaxies, but couldn't move through these, just watched from a vast distance.

John W. Sundsten, male, 41 yrs., 165 lbs., 6'; no date:
2 hours, 45 minutes.

Uncertainty to relaxation. Awareness of water edge around face, close to eyes and mouth. That leaves body image "frozen." Took hands from behind head to eliminate contact awareness. Rested hands on abdomen, then outstretched, the best. Only occasional "toe scraping awareness" of body surface. Mind without encumbrance of body. Followed breath, became bored. Followed mantra. Better, but lost it frequently and finally just let it go. Focused on point in blackness in front of eyes. Tried to go *into* that space. Vague phosphene–like "spots" and "cloudy shapes". Tried to go into them. Urinate urge was strong—damn. Follow breath to take concentration away from urinate urge. Works. Occasional visceral gurgling. A hum of some sort comes every now and then—part of tank system? Tried some imagery, focusing on colors linked to breathing. OK. Tried going into different brain regions, cortex, temporal lobe, thalamus, hypothalamus, etcetera. It all seemed rather dull so I dropped all the foolishness of trying to *do* something with the "liberated" mind space I was experiencing and just "flattened" out in the calm of it all. I think that is the kind of state I sense is important for me just now (been a lot of heavy shit and a lot of heavy good input the past few years). Thought for a while of slowing EEG patterns into hypnogogic zone. Not a bad idea but it didn't work. Should try it while in tank.

When most relaxed (spaced) I would come into eye blink checks to be certain I wasn't asleep.

In summary I floated out and did no–thing. One far–out tank!

Charley Tart, 37 yrs., 160 lbs., 6'; no date: 1 hour, 30 minutes.
It was very quiet. There was an almost continuous sensation in my whole back as if I were lying on something or was stiff. But I don't think I had any muscular tension. I was stiff some when I came out. My mind was rather quiet—I just waited most of the time and tried not to get attached to anything happening, or not happening.

17 November 1973
Mary Taylor, female, 47 yrs., 135 lbs., 5' 6": time not recorded.
When I immersed, I made sure I was able to retrace and get out of the tank and then I closed the top and got in and laid out flat with my hands behind my head and I was suddenly aware of an odor, I guess it was of the plastic tank, sort of like juicy fruit or something and the water felt very slippery on my body. As I was lying there the first things were thoughts that wandered in my head of things that have

236

happened during the day and of a room that I'm working on. Just things that I've been working on, then I became aware of a terrible tightness across the upper part of my shoulder, to the point where I almost felt I couldn't breathe, so I thought if I changed the position of my hands by putting them alongside of my body that this might relieve it, but it didn't. It seems to have been intensified, so I tried to relax in spite of the pain, but it was always there, trying to rid my head of the pain. It continued so I tried to ignore it and continue on my thoughts and thought patterns, things that were crossing my mind. Then I went through and examined the interior of the box with my eyes open, of course it was dark and there was nothing much to see except I guess the visual pictures that you see when you close your eyes and see funny little pictures of colored things, shapes and forms. Then I breathed deeply and thought the pain might subside but this didn't help. I got into a relaxed state to where I was almost asleep but the shoulder pain was still there. I did raise my head out of the water so that the water wasn't pressing on my eardrums because at one point I felt the water was going past my ear, but I knew it couldn't do that so I put my head back into the water, but still the pressure on my ear wasn't very comfortable and in that relaxed position with my head way back and immersed in the water—a death pose crossed my mind and then I went on to more pleasant things to think about like the room I'm going to work on and how it is going to be arranged; also, organizing the work I am going to be doing tomorrow and or the following week. This was about the end of my time.

2 July 1975
Francisco Varela, male, 28 yrs., 155 lbs.:
actual time: 2 hours, 50 minutes.
Closed space, heavy breathing, oppression from suppression. A wave of buoyancy, oily–salty relaxation, surprise at fitting into water and staying. Letting go, feet are fine, trunk is fine, head is fine.
Beginning to stay—be.

Body goes out, inner sound takes over. Wild ride on heartbeat—inner music. Roller coaster.

Carved into inner sounds: sudden flashes of perception: dogs barking, old tunes on a junky radio, laughter and people's noise. Startle. Experiment with closed and open eyes. No difference. Stay with eyes open. Visual–acoustic flashes now: scattered, fragmented. Too real. Strong recall of transit stages. I have been here. At a moment: I belong here.

Wilder/surrealist images interface with periods of sleep. In and out with no chance of distinction between dream and tank–reality. Am I there?

Banging. Voice to take me out. Voice is John. Get out. Seems I've been in thirty to forty minutes. Long lag in coming back.

30 November 1973
Andrew Weil, male, 31 yrs., 185 lbs., 5' 10 1/2":
1 hour.

This was my first tank experience. Right now I feel relaxed and good, as if I have completed a valuable piece of work. While immersed I was fairly conscious of my body. I have some nice scratches from some rough climbing yesterday, and they burned quite a bit in the saltwater; also I got a good dose of salt in my eyes. These sensations were not unpleasant but strong, and I imagine they kept some of my attention much of the time. I think I would have to go through a period of becoming habituated to the physical sensations of the tank before I could let it take me to the interesting spaces.

24 August 1973
Benjamin Weininger, M.D., 70 years, 5' 7", 110 lbs.:
1 hour, 20 minutes.

9:00 A.M.–10:20 A.M.: Before I came here I had a few tablespoons of applesauce and a small glass of apple cider. I decided not to eat anything before entering the tank because of a slight heart condition. I felt it would be easier on my circulation. When I came here, Toni asked me if I wanted some tea and then gave me some melon and I drank the tea. Joe Hart offered me some fruit salad—that I also accepted. After a while I developed a heartburn and decided that I didn't want to go in the tank with heartburn so I took a couple of antacid tablets. I wondered why I didn't follow my own advice about the food in the first place. As I entered the tank, Toni told me to lie in the tub with my hands folded behind my head, and said to record it afterward—but not to be programmed by the recording. As soon as I entered the tank and held my head up with my hands behind my neck I began to hear my heartbeat very loud—I had a thought that this must be something like hearing my mother's heartbeat in the womb. I'm not a swimmer—I was completely surprised that I could float so easily—even in saltwater. The sounds of my heartbeat shortly disappeared and I became sharply aware of the breathing sounds passing in and out of my nose. In my everyday life I usually am more or less constantly aware of my heartbeat—and have been for some time trying to become more aware of my breathing which I could do only occasionally. I realized how important the breathing was. I kept my eyes closed—from time to time I decided to open them—I wasn't here to go to sleep, but to wake up. Fears about my circulation and concerns about my body were present in the beginning. Random thoughts about the Counseling Center, about the problems with a wife whose husband died of a stroke, about a girl. I wondered how long I would have to stay in the tank before my concern with my body and thoughts would cease. I thought I could stay in the tank for two hours—longer than others—an ego trip, I thought. Later I thought I might have to get out at fifteen minutes—occasionally I had a fleeting pain between the heart and shoulder. The second time it happened it didn't concern me—I felt it was a muscle pain. Since I was lying in a straight position a slight discomfort in the back appeared. I again wondered why I ate the food when I had decided against it—usually to please others. Then I decided that needing to record the experience was a handicap. I then thought that I would not record the experience this time and it would leave me more free. Later I decided to leave this open—I'll see how I feel. I felt I didn't have to record because they suggested it. I also decided that I didn't have to lie still. I began to roll from side to side. I also thought that I didn't have to have a spaced–out trip—I'll just see what happens.

I began to hear what I thought was my heart—an occasional series of heartbeats at about 40/min., then it would stop. I held my head in a different position to get more comfortable. I then felt that I'd been in the tank about fifteen minutes. I then thought that since I had another one and a half hours to go that I could sit up in the tank and take my pulse, which was 80 instead of 40. I lay down again and felt unconcerned about my state of health—unconcerned about needing to do what I was told. I was beginning to feel at home in the tank— shortly afterward John Lilly opened the lid and asked me if I was all right—I estimated I had been in the tank not more than a half hour— he told me that it was one hour, twenty minutes—a complete surprise to me.

9 July 1973
David Weininger, no data given:
1 hour, 15 minutes.
7:55 P.M.–9:10 P.M.: Lying there, in total darkness, it was very much like lying in my own bed at home except that it was notably more chaotic. That is, in the beginning it was more chaotic. I had a number of gnat bites on my arms, back and legs, which began to sting horrendously in the saltwater. The sound of my heartbeat intermingled with that of my breathing was quite loud and I began to notice that my heartbeat was slightly faster when my lungs were full than when they were empty. As the stinging subsided I became aware of the incessant chatter in my head. There were broken pieces of sentences, parts of songs, images of friends and on and on. I had transcended this type of chaos before and knew that all I needed to do in order to go beyond it or learn from it was to observe and do nothing.

I began to grow more alert and to be aware of my breathing and heartbeat. As I listened I heard a faint ringing sound which grew steadily until it was quite loud. The ringing had three main parts—a kind of drone note that was the lowest note, a chirping sound like the sound of crickets that was the middle note, and an extremely high–frequency overtone. As I listened to the ringing, I moved out away from the chaos into an expansive, open space. This space extended as far as I could follow it on a horizontal plane. I could not "see" anything, but I could "travel" in any direction on a horizontal plane. It was merely a matter of following the ringing and the ringing was everywhere in its own two–dimensional universe. I then came to rest in the center (everywhere was the center since it extended as far as I could perceive in every direction). At this point it seems I became less aware of the ringing and experienced the space open up above me so that I was a point on a flat surface with a dome above me. Space then opened up below me creating a huge sphere of which I was the center. From this sphere or universe I became acutely aware (back in the tank) of a point on my nose which was itching or stinging. My entire consciousness focused on this itch which became magnified to such a degree that it was the universe and I was identified so strongly with it that I was the itch and that was all there was. This was an incredibly uncomfortable universe to exist in and I found I was able to move into an empty space simply by imagining such a space. From this empty space I was able to look at a point in the distance which I labeled "Earth," and on this point in a tiny box was a tiny entity (me), and this entity had an itch on its nose which was equal in magnitude to the entire universe as I now perceived it. I returned to the tank with the realization that there are billions of universes existing simultaneously, each one being uniquely different according to the particular programs and external reality stimuli that the observer is operating with.

(The experience portrayed above occurred during a period of one hour, fifteen minutes in the tank—it occurred near the end of the stay in the tank and lasted a relatively short time.)

No date
Louis Jolyon West, male, 40 yrs., 220 lbs., 6' 3":
1 hour.
(N.B.: Previous experience, fresh–water tank, Oklahoma City.)
Buoyancy definitely an advantage over the old method. Also, much better without need for mask.

Lost awareness of surroundings much faster in this situation. Very rapid access to "preconscious stream" (Kubie), with complete immersion therein until termination. No subclassification of mental state during that period would be accurate; my experience was of a smoothly unbroken flow of both digital and analog information. Had planned to meditate (TM) but never got around to it. My personal experience was that a state of "pure consciousness" (more or less) was reached in the tank without utilizing the mental echo of a mantra, but I wouldn't emphasize this impression without a series of experimental and control sessions. Emerged refreshed with a sense that far less than an hour's time had passed. A wholly pleasant experience.

10 and 11 November 1973
Sharon Wheeler, female, 25 yrs., 130 lbs., 5' 7":
total time: 2 hours.
First trip, 1 hour, 3 minutes: I was very aware of holding myself up and felt myself sinking more and more the entire time. I have been skin brushing my body for two months daily and experienced the prickly discomfort the entire time. I expected it to decrease but after an initial slowdown it remained a constant irritant to distract me. I also had periodic chills, which kept me occupied with the surface of my body. My right arm gave me trouble as it went to sleep and I had to tangle my fingers in my hair to keep my hands under my head as my arms kept rising and my head appeared to sink to the point of immersing my eyes, which I didn't want to do. I tried lifting one arm to test return to gravity and found it quite heavy. I found the combination of prickles and chills brought contractions of my muscles,

242

which stirred up the water so I didn't quite find a still place for the hour. I found a brief moment at the beginning where I felt a lack of fresh air, but assured myself that everything was optimum for life support—I had several deep breaths, about six or seven, one of which reached a very deep problem area about four ribs and experienced that vertebrae release. I wished for a pillow to support my head. I mainly waited for my body to adjust so I could experiment with spaces. I preferred my eyes open and was conscious of going to make a report somewhat. Was relieved that no one was watching me—saw a purple spot momentarily. My earplugs could have been more secure, as bubbles would release as I relaxed and sank. My belly appeared to be the highest thing—also I felt at times I was drifting but didn't touch the sides so I guess I wasn't. I wanted to rest more but was apprehensive of having my eyes go under. As I relaxed, I sank. I could hear my heartbeat and my respiration seemed quite loud. After getting out I noticed red dots and a rashlike look to my skin all over, which receded after I showered. I discovered tangling my fingers in my hair about halfway through—until then I felt frustrated as my arms would not stay with my hands behind my head. I felt determined to wait out the discomforts—and was disappointed they did not remit—as I hoped they would. I had a lot of tension against my head going under, which I felt I did not completely release. I had to hold my hands together as a security and became conscious of a tiredness with an expectation of a good state if I stuck it out. I feel that this session has worked out a lot of details in personal adaption that should not be a problem next time.

Second trip: November 11, 1973 (5:30 P.M.–6:27 P.M.): Due to the last experience, I covered my body with Vaseline Intensive Care lotion. I got a few stingy places, one scratch on the ear—one on the vaginal opening—which I couldn't relax, due to past experience that when I would do that, water would flood in and I did not want that for sure—So I maintained that tension and the tension in my hands to keep my head up for life support. A couple of drops fell on my foot and I became apprehensive of more, and realized that I am apprehensive in general as a constant, and that part of it is due to my mistrust of my computer function—and the necessity of running a constant check/recheck on my life–support systems. I have found in the past my experiences differ greatly from others, and have trained myself to maintain this tension of constant monitoring and monitoring the monitor again and again, etcetera. Also, I got in touch with the aspect of a tension deep in the head that builds when unpleasant stimuli occur. Like the zero for three days in Arica, a dogged hanging on through the negative to reach the positive, which doesn't come. I thought if I had a choice of where to be it would be out of here to relax—perhaps too much positive expectations and I feel less energy, more tired and irritated for having gone in. Have a headache from it. Am disappointed in my own interior experience—I guess comparisons and expectations. I came to the space at the end of the trip of: "Well, it's not going to get better and I am not enjoying it as much as I want to for being with John and Toni and going ahead with the group. I am getting out." I experienced relief at that decision to do that. I wanted to get out about three–quarters of the time; I felt I had done three–quarters of my hour when I got out—I watched my endurance of a negative experience. At one point I felt the tremendous buildup of tension in my uterus from the IUD and was sad that I had done this so long; it was part of closing the vaginal opening lest the salt enter the uterus and irritate it. Perhaps if I try no. 3, things will go better tomorrow. But again, if I were to follow my inclination of the moment I would not repeat. However, I have the external metaprogram of the tank experience getting better if I continue so I will try it again. But I'm tired—What "should" be isn't, so I'm tired.

3 May 1975
Tom Wilkes, male, 35 yrs., 195 lbs., 6':
1 hour, 30 minutes.
My first sensation was one of stuffiness, humid warm... floating.

This soon changed to a cool secure feeling accompanied by the overwhelming rhythm of my heartbeat; this beat seemed to take me deeper into a trancelike state from which I would periodically shoot back to full awareness of my body. Upon returning, I would notice a slight oscillation producing some movement of the liquid in the tank. Upon relaxing... I would move into the black void. I heard fragments of messages, voices saying things I could not decipher. This continued for an undetermined length of time until colored visual images would pass by me. These images were nonobjective and seemed to pulsate as they passed. The colors were generally magenta, blue or whitish.

At some point, three female entities began questioning me. The feeling was warm and attracting. I fought to return and did, so violently that my body jerked and I noticed a stinging in my left eye. This slight pain kept me aware of my physical self for a time, then I returned to the three beings. I passed through them and there was a splash of golden light. At this point I became aware of three-dimensional spheres turning in several directions inside and outside of themselves, emitting a warm magenta glow. Their presence was awe-inspiring and produced a religious kind of emotional feeling. I was observing this phenomenon when a roar, very deep and almost inaudible, filled the void. Wham, splash... "You've been in there an hour and a half. You may stay in longer if you like" (Toni's voice).

9 July 1973
Barbara Williams, no data given:
24 minutes.
1:00 P.M.–1:30 P.M. (with 6 minutes out of the tank): First experience in tank. Warmth and humidity first impressions, then darkness. With closing of the lid, had immediate flashback memory of my sister shutting me in closet at age five—the resulting fear and claustrophobia which continued most of my life (up to about one year ago) rushed by like an incredibly fast movie—I recognized this as an "old program," watched it go by and let it go. There were no further fears

except a brief one after floating a short time on my back and touching nothing, had a sensation that I had turned ninety degrees to the right and was sideways in the tank—came out of the dimensionless space I was into to feel the sides of the tank and lid to get my "bearings" (found I had not turned more than about fifteen degrees to the right) and explore the landmarks of the tank physical space. Then spent some time assimilating all the sensations, what I could and could not do. Found if I relaxed completely my head would arch backward and tended to sink uncomfortably, so preferred the position of elbows out with fingers laced together under back of head. Experimented with eyes opened and closed, and quickly discovered I could "interlock" these so that a visual image I was seeing was the same either with eyes open or closed. Noticed my heels touched slightly on the floor of tank—that was not unpleasant, but discovered I could lift them off with a very slight muscle contraction. Experimented with "name a state and become it"—went back to a dream I was aware of while awakening this A.M., where someone had given me a book titled *Awake Now.* I immediately found myself back in that dream space, holding the book and trying to see "who" had given it to me—I saw a shadowy featureless being—the presence was benevolent, but not recognizable.

1:15 P.M.: Became aware of uncomfortable heat, beads of perspiration all over my face, humid air being breathed into my lungs felt "too hot"—body signals of this brought me back.

I got out of the tank to breathe and feel cool air and reported above experiences to John. (While in spaces in the tank there was no time, but as soon as I got out I "knew" fifteen minutes had passed.)

(Out for 6 minutes.)

1.21 P.M.: Upon entering, discovered air input pipe and spent some time letting this cool air blow on face. Still "too warm." Back into floating position—very comfortable physically and found I could leave body, knowing that survival programs were watching it. Went into space of pure light, warmth. Sound began to happen—waves of sound like energy—current waves—very pleasant. Stayed there (time? there was no awareness of time or space here)... observing and experiencing this very pleasant state.

1:30 P.M.: Brought back again by beads of perspiration covering face and body signaling "too warm." Noticed bladder fullness. Let head fall back and got saltwater in eyes—stinging. Decided to give up for now and came out.

1:31 P.M.: (Had wanted to try programming with the *Aphorisms*, but decided to wait until I get more comfortable in the tank.)

10 April 1975
Robert A. Wilson, male, 32 yrs., 170 lbs., 5' 10":
2 hours.

Small red light room housing two dumpster–like sensory deprivation tanks. Climbing in the darker, older–looking tank I flash that perhaps it is deeper than the floor level would indicate, but not only ten to fourteen inches of warm water in this giant battery casing. Perhaps there's not enough water. Sitting, then lying back, the buoyancy is surprising—suddenly I'm floating. Slight contact with tank sides, then my breathing is focus of my attention. Breathing, floating, thinking. Mind floats through myriad of subjects, tension generated within is soon apparent. Return to focus on breath. Thoughts return. After an hour little tastes of terror manifest. Each wave of fear though powerful seeming necessitates reevaluation of tension state, breathing again, floating, adjusting to a deeper relaxation state. Perhaps this is where I'll sleep tonight. After two hours eyes begin burning, keeping them shut tonight... keeping them shut against the salt becomes a labor, then a drop of salt down my nasal passage—that does it. Sitting up pushing the tank lid open. Fun trip, I feel very relaxed, reborn in a way. Sounds seem much more audible, crickets in the night. Nice to be back.

April 1976
Eligio Carrillos Vicente,
Huichol Shaman & Yarn Painting Artist
of Shetatcie, Nayarit, as translated by Prem Das,
male, 40 yrs., 160 lbs., 5' 6".

PREM DAS: What happened in the tank?

ELIGIO CARRILLOS VICENTE: For me, what I saw and nothing more, was that they asked me the question, he was asking me a question, but he was a person who came out of the sea. He was saying to me, "What do you want to know, you already know so much? What do you want me to tell you or teach you; I can't give you more. You alone know where you gained your knowledge."

Then they took out of me a large *nierica*, and he said, "Look at this, you understand it don't you?" Yes, I do, I answered. "That [the *nierica*] is what you make [referring to Eligio's work of making yarn paintings which depict visions he has seen in dream states]. All that you make is the same. What more do you want to know? I can't teach you anything else. You know. Only if you want to look for it more will you learn further." Then they lifted me up still higher, and from that height they showed me, and said, "Look over here." Oh, yes, I said, I already know this. And he said, "Well here it is, what it has is the same." This is all they told me.

PREM: Who was it that was telling you?

ELIGIO: He came out of the sea, and I was listening to him, he went by me first like a dream, and from out of this came a person.

PREM: How did you feel in the water?

ELIGIO: I felt really fine, as though I were flying, and as if I were in the ocean, to which I was listening. It was as if I were flying in a certain place, and it was going downward.

PREM: And the *nierica* you saw, what was it like?

ELIGIO: It is something such as the rising of the sun, and many visions flowed from it; and the middle of it made water like in little half squares. "This is 'The Birth'," he told me. "What else do you want to know?" And this was enough, this which he showed me.

PREM: Eligio, this friend [John] wants to talk with a certain large fish of the sea [I show him a picture of a dolphin]. Do you think it can be done?

ELIGIO: For sure.

PREM: How would you do it?

ELIGIO: "*Entresuento*"—[via dream consciousness]. But first I would take offerings to *Tatéaramara* [our grandmother, the sea]. These would be such things as a small yarn painting showing that which I wish to do, a prayer bowl *(shrucuri)* and prayer arrow *(uru)*, chocolate, animal cookies and a candle. *Tatéaramara* is the patroness of all sea fish and so I would need her permission and help to talk to her children. So I would take her these offerings and my prayers. Then I would fast for five days from salt and abstain from sex for this same period of time. The fifth day I would go to the beach, at sunset, to spend the whole night sitting at the water's edge. Then this fish [pointing to the photo of the dolphin] would come to me, and we would speak.

CHAPTER THIRTEEN

Excerpts of Published Personal
Observations of the Author

Two of the author's previous books* present accounts of his own experiences in the tank from 1954 through 1971, a period of seventeen years.

In writing the present book, it was felt that the author had covered his own experience insofar as practicable in published form. It is considered desirable for the sake of completeness of the historical record to reproduce these additional accounts in this book (see following excerpts).

Two scientific medical articles on the tank work by the author were written before the cited books, and were republished in *Simulations of God: The Science of Belief.***

The first article (Chapter Nine, this book) was entitled "Mental Effects of Reduction of Ordinary Levels of Physical Stimuli on Intact, Healthy Persons," published in June 1956 by the American Psychiatric Association, Washington, D.C., in Psychiatric Research Reports 5. This paper states the author's research aims of that time, still valid in 1977, twenty–one years later, as follows:

"We have been [are] seeking answers to the question of what happens to a brain and its contained mind in the relative absence of physical stimulation."

---

* John C. Lilly, *Programing and Metaprogramming in the Human Biocomputer;* and *The Center of the Cyclone.*
** John C. Lilly, *Simulations of God,* Appendix One.

At that time the author believed implicitly/explicitly in the "contained mind" hypothesis (see Chapter Seven and Appendix II on contained mind).

The second article (Chapter Ten, this book), with Dr. J. T. Shurley, psychiatrist, was entitled "Experiments in Solitude, in Maximum Achievable Physical Isolation with Water Suspension, of Intact Healthy Persons," published in 1961 by Psychophysiological Aspects of Space Flight (New York, Columbia University Press). The article was prepared for and presented at a psychiatric symposium on "sensory deprivation" at Harvard Medical School, and was not included in the symposium volume (see Appendix One, *Simulations of God*).

In each of these papers, the basic medical scientific assumption of the contained mind (Chapter Seven and Appendix II) was made. Later work in the tank (1964–1966) raised other possibilities (see Chapter Eight, "The Mind Unlimited"), recounted in *Programming and Metaprogramming in the Human Biocomputer*. Excerpts from this book pertinent to these experiences are reproduced below.

Further experiences and widening of the assumptions are recounted in *The Center of the Cyclone*. Pertinent excerpts follow.

The tank work gave rise to many books (see Bibliography); it is a creative source of new ideas as well as of experiences.

EXPERIENCES SELECTED FROM "PROGRAMMING AND
METAPROGRAMMING IN THE HUMAN BIOCOMPUTER"

Experiments on Basic Metaprograms of Existence

Preliminary to the experiments in changing basic beliefs, many experiments with the profound physical isolation and solitude situation were carried out over a period of several years. These experiences were followed by combining the LSD–25 state and the physical isolation state in a second period of several years. The minimum time between experiments was thirty days, the maximum time, several months.

Basic Belief No. 1

Basic Belief No. 1 was made possible by the early isolation results: *Assume that the subject's body and brain can operate comfortably isolated without him paying any attention to it.* This belief expresses the faith that one has in one's experience in the isolation situation, that one can consciously ignore the necessities of breathing and other bodily functions, and that they will take care of themselves automatically without detailed attention on the part of one's self. This result allowed existence metaprograms to be made in relative safety.

Successful *leaving of the body and parking it* in isolation for periods of twenty minutes to two hours were successful in sixteen different experiments. This success, in turn, allowed other basic beliefs to be experimented upon. The basic belief that one could *leave the body and explore new universes* was successfully programmed in the first eight different experiments lasting from five minutes to forty minutes; the later eight experiments were on the *cognitional multidimensional space* without the *leaving the body* metaprogram...

Basic Belief No. 2

The subject sought *beings other than himself, not human, in whom he existed and who control him and other human beings.* Thus the subject found whole new *universes* containing great varieties of *beings*, some greater than himself, some equal to himself, and some lesser than himself.

Those greater than himself were a set which was so huge in space–time as to make the subject feel *as a mere mote in their sunbeam, a single microflash of energy in their time scale, my forty–five years are but an instant in their lifetime, a single thought in their vast computer, a mere particle in their assemblages of living cognitive units.* He felt he was in the absolute unconscious of these beings. He experienced many more sets all so much greater than himself that they were almost inconceivable in their complexity, size and time scales.

Those *beings* which were close to the subject in complexity–size–time were dichotomized into the *evil ones* and the *good ones*. The *evil ones* (subject said) were busy with purposes so foreign to his own that he had many near–misses and almost fatal accidents in encounters with them; they were almost totally unaware of his existence and hence almost wiped him out, apparently without knowing it. The subject says that *the good ones thought good thoughts to him, through him, and to one another*. They were at least conceivably human and humane. He interpreted them as alien yet friendly. They were not so alien as to be completely removed from human beings in regard to their purposes and activities.

Some of these beings (the subject reported) are programming us in the long term. They nurture us. They experiment on us. They control the probability of our discovering and exploiting new science. He reports that discoveries such as nuclear energy, LSD–25, RNA–DNA, etc., are under probability control by these beings. Further, humans are tested by some of these beings and cared for by others. Some of them have programs which include our survival and progress. Others have programs which include oppositions to these good programs and include our ultimate demise as a species. Thus the subject interpreted the evil ones as willing to sacrifice us in their experiments; hence they are *alien and removed from us*. The subject reported with this set of beliefs that *only limited choices are still available to us as a species. We are an ant colony in their laboratory*.

Basic Belief No. 3

The subject assumed the existence of beings in whom humans exist and who directly control humans. This is a tighter control program than the previous one and assumes continuous day and night, second to second, control, as if each human being were a cell in a larger organism. Such beings insist upon activities in each human being totally under the control of the organism of which each human being is a part. In this state there is no free will and no freedom for an indi-

254

vidual. This supra–self–metaprogram was entered twice by the subject; each time he had to leave it; for him it was too anxiety–provoking. In the first case he *became a part of a vast computer in which he was one element*. In the second case he was a *thought in a much larger mind: being modified rapidly, flexibly and plastically....*

Basic Belief No. 4

One set of basic beliefs can be subsumed under the directions *seek those beings whom we control and who exist in us*. With this program the subject found old models in himself (old programs, old metaprograms, implanted by others, implanted by self, injected by parents, by teachers, etc.). He found that these were disparate and separate autonomous *beings* in himself. He described them as a *noisy group*. His incorporated parents, his siblings, his own offspring, his teachers, his wife seemed to be a disorganized crowd within him, each running and arguing a program with him and in him. While he watched, battles took place between these models during the experiment. He settled many disparate and nonintegrated points between these *beings* and gradually incorporated more of them into the self–metaprogram.

After many weeks of self–analysis outside the experimental milieu (and some help with his former analyst), it was seen that these *beings within the self* were also those other *beings outside self* of the other experiments. The subject described the projected as–if–outside beings to be *cognitional carnivores attempting to eat up his self–metaprogram and wrest control from him*. As the various levels of metaprograms became straightened out in the subject, he was able to categorize and begin to control the various levels as they were presented during these experiments. As his apparently unconscious needs for credence in these beliefs were attenuated with analytic work, his freedom to move from one set of basic beliefs to another was increased and the anxiety associated with this kind of movement gradually disappeared.

A basic overall metaprogram was finally generated: For his own intellectual satisfaction the subject found that he best assume that all of the phenomena that took place existed only in his own brain and in his own mind. Other assumptions about the existence of these *beings* had become subjects suitable for research rather than subjects for blind (unconscious, conscious) *belief* for this person.

Basic Belief No. 5

Experiments also were done upon movements of self forward and back in space–time. The results showed that when attempting to go *forward into the future* the subject began to *realize* his own goals for that future, and imagine *wishful thinking solutions* to current problems. When he put in the metaprogram for going back into his own childhood, *real and phantasy memories* were evoked and integrated. When he pushed back through to the in utero situation, he found an early nightmare which was reinvoked and solved. Relying on his scientific *knowledge*, he pushed the program back through previous generations, prehuman primates, carnivores, fish and protozoa. He experienced a *sperm–egg explosion* on the way through this past *reinvocation of imaginary* experience.

The last set of experiments... was made possible by the results of the previous set. Progress in controlling the projection metaprogram resulted from the *other universes* experiments. Finally the subject understood and had become familiar with his need for *phantasied other universes*. Analytic work allowed him to bypass this need and penetrate into the *cognitional multidimensional projection spaces*. Experiments in programming in this *innermost space* showed results quite satisfying to a high degree of credence in the belief that all experiments in the series showed inner happenings without needing *the participation of outer causes*. The need for the constant use of *outer causes* was found to be a projected outward metaprogram to avoid taking personal responsibility for portions of the contents of his own mind. His dislike for certain kinds of his own nonsensical programs caused him to project them and thus avoid admitting they were his.

In summation, the subjectively apparent results of the experiments

256

were to straighten out a good deal of the "nonsense" in this subject's computer. Through these experiments he was able to examine some *warded–off beliefs and defensive structures* accumulated throughout his life. The net result was a feeling of greater integration of self and a feeling of positive affect for the current structure of himself, combined with an improved skepticism of the validity of subjective judging of events in self.

Some *objective* testing of these essentially subjective judgments has been initiated through cooperation with other persons. Such objective testing is very difficult; this area needs a great deal of future research work. We need better investigative techniques, combining subjective and behavioral (verbal) techniques. The major feeling that one has after such experiences and experiments is that the fluidity and plasticity of one's computer has certain limits to it, and that those limits have been enlarged somewhat by the experiments. How long such enlargement lasts and to what extent are still not known of course. A certain amount of continued critical skepticism about and in the self–metaprogram (and in its *felt* changes) is very necessary for a scientist exploring these areas.

In the mind of this subject the unknown must take precedence. It is placed above the supra–self–metaprogram because it contains some of the goals of this particular human computer. This exploration of the inner reality presupposes that the inner reality contains large unknowns which are worth exploring. However, to explore them it is necessary (1) to recognize their existence and (2) to prepare one's computer for the exploration. If one is to explore the *unknown* one should take the minimum amount of baggage and not load one's self down with conceptual machinery which cannot be flexibly reoriented to accept and investigate the *unknown*. The next stage of development of those who have the courage and the necessary inner apparatus to do it, is exploration in depth of this vast *inner unknown* region. For this task we need the best kind of thinking of which man is capable. We dissolve and/or reprogram the doctrinaire and ideological approaches to these questions.

To remain skeptical of even this formalization of this particular human computer's approach to this region is desirable. One does not over–value this particular approach; one looks for alternative approaches for exploratory purposes. Freedom from the tyranny of the supra–self–metaprograms is sought but not to the point at which other human computers control this particular human computer. Deep and basic interlock between selected human computers is needed for this exploration. Conceptualization of the thinking machine itself is needed by the best minds available for this task. In a sense, we create the explorers in this area.

EXTRACTS FROM CHAPTERS 1 TO 5 OF
"THE CENTER OF THE CYCLONE"

1

I was kneeling facing the altar; there was a single candle lighted on the altar and the rest of the church was darkened, with very little light coming in from the outside since the windows were high up. Suddenly the church disappeared, the pillars were shadowy and I saw angels, God on His throne and the saints moving through the church in another set of dimensions. Since I was only seven years old and had seen paintings of artistic concepts of God, this is what I saw in the visions. I also saw His love, His caring, and His creation of us.

* * *

One could put down the child of seven and say that he had been fed programs of the visions of saints, of Saint Theresa of Avila that the mystical aspects of the Catholic church had been thoroughly programmed into this young man and that he was projecting his visions totally.

258

I then remembered that I had made the mistake of confiding in a nun that I had had this vision. She was horrified and said that only saints had visions, putting me down thoroughly. At that point I repressed the memory and that kind of experience, but before I repressed it I was angry: "So she doesn't think I'm a saint."

* * *

As a Catholic child I was exposed to death. When a relative would die, we had to view the body, attend the funeral, and go through the usual Catholic ritual having to do with death. I was thoroughly acquainted with the concept of the soul leaving the body of the person at the time of death. Also, I had imagined, in the privacy of my own bed as a little boy, my soul taking off and winging toward God and toward Heaven.

* * *

I had started out by projecting a goddess image on my women making them more than they possibly could be, or anybody could be, in terms of purity, virtue, and all of the positive qualities. Later having accomplished the sexual act with them and having experienced orgasm with them, having experienced their orgasms, I demeaned them as having given in to their animal nature. This was straight from the teaching of the Catholic church. Again, it was a projection into real situations brought forward in time from my past.

I had been taught that sexual impulses, anger, and so on, were part of one's animal nature and were sinful. "Carnal desires" were to be put down, controlled, in order that one could become a saint.

2

While giving myself an antibiotic shot, "by accident" I injected under my skin a foam made with a detergent. The syringe had residual detergent in it which I failed to clean out. Somehow the bubbles had gotten into my circulation, passed through the lungs, and had lodged in my brain, cutting off the circulation to very critical parts of my brain, including the visual cortex. I had then gone into immediate coma. Later I struggled up from the depths of the coma, got to the telephone in the room, and called the operator who then sent up the house detective. I went into coma again. When the detective arrived, he asked me for the name of a friend in the hotel. With great effort I could think only of a neurologist in Chicago at that point. Meanwhile my head was pounding and I thought that I had blown a blood vessel in my brain. The pain was the most excruciating that I have ever experienced. I went into coma again, struggled back out of coma, and named a friend who was in the hotel. He said later that when he arrived in the room, I was in coma and it took him six hours to get an ambulance. Meanwhile, I was lying there on the hotel bed. I remember very well the inside experience that occurred while I was in the so–called coma.

The pounding headache, the nausea and the vomiting that occurred forced me to leave my body. I became a focused center of consciousness and traveled into other spaces and met other beings, entities or consciousnesses. I came across two who approached me through a large empty space and who looked, felt, and transmitted guiding and teaching thoughts to me.

It is very hard to put this experience into words, because there were no words exchanged. Pure thought and feeling was being transmitted and received by me and by these two entities. I will attempt to translate into words what occurred.

I am in a large empty place with nothing in any direction except light. There is a golden light permeating the whole space everywhere in all directions, out to infinity. I am a single point of consciousness, of feeling, of knowledge. I know that I am. That is all. It is a very peaceful, awesome, and reverential space that I am in. I have no body. I have no need for a body. There is no body. I am just I. Complete with love, warmth, and radiance.

Suddenly in the distance appear two similar points of consciousness, sources of radiance, of love, of warmth. I feel their presence, I see their presence, without eyes, without a body. I know they are there, so they are there. As they move toward me, I feel more and more of each of them, interpenetrating my very being. They transmit comforting, reverential, awesome thoughts. I realize that they are beings far greater than I. They begin to teach me. They tell me I can stay in this place, that I have left my body, but that I can return to it if I wish. They then show me what would happen if I left my body back there— an alternative path for me to take. They also show me where I can go if I stay in this place. They tell me that it is not yet time for me to leave my body permanently, that I still have an option to go back to it. They give me total and absolute confidence, total certitude in the truth of my being in this state. I know with absolute certainty that they exist. I have no doubts. There is no longer any need for an act of faith; it just is that way and I accept it.

Their magnificent deep powerful love overwhelms me to a certain extent, but I finally accept it. As they move closer, I find less and less of me and more and more of them in my being. They stop at a critical distance and say to me that at this time I have developed only to the point where I can stand their presence at this particular distance. If they came any closer, they would overwhelm me, and I would lose myself as a cognitive entity, merging with them. They further say that I separated them into two, because that is my way of perceiving them, but that in reality they are one in the space in which I found myself. They say that I insist on still being an individual, forcing a projection onto them, as if they were two. They further communicate to me that if I go back to my body as I developed further, I eventually would perceive the oneness of them and of me, and of many others.

They say that they are my guardians, that they have been with me before at critical times and that in fact they are with me always, but that I am not usually in a state to perceive them. I am in a state to perceive them when I am close to the death of the body. In this state, there is no time. There is an immediate perception of the past, present, and future as if in the present moment.

I stayed in this state for many hours in earth time. Then I came back to my body in the hospital. I had another pain in my head and came out of the coma to find that they were injecting something into my carotid arteries in the neck. I immediately perceived that they were looking for a brain lesion, for bleeding into the brain, by injecting a radio–opaque substance for X–rays. Once the pain was exhausted, I went back into coma, returning to the two guardians.

The next time that I returned to my body and awoke, I was in a hospital room. The pain in my head was gone, but I could not see. There was a brilliant white sheet of light, immediately in front of my eyes, filling my whole visual field. I could feel my body and move the various parts. I found I was not paralyzed. I found that I could talk and that I could think clearly, so I realized the brain damage was not as extensive as I had feared. I thought, "The guardians are right. I can stay in my body but blind."

I went through an intense grief reaction to having come back to a blind body, but I trusted the guardians' "statement" that I would be all right. I lay in the hospital bed, reviewing my knowledge of neu-rology and of brain mechanisms. I figured out that I was blind because of an irritative rather than a destructive lesion in my visual cortex. The guardians were right. I must wait and see how much of my vision was left when the irritation stopped, when the blinding white light was turned off.

When the doctors came in and found me awake, we discussed my case. I still didn't know what had happened. I knew who I was and when they told me where I was, I recognized the hospital.

An ophthalmologist examined my eyegrounds. He said that there was no visible lesion in my eyes. This relieved me very much. The irritation was not in the retina; it was in the brain. If it had been in the retina, there would be less hope for recovery.

During the period of the great white light in front of my eyes, I experienced some new phenomena. First of all, I couldn't see any light in the room, whether it was day or night. The inside light was so bright that it made no difference at all what sort of patterns were coming into my eyes. When the ophthalmologist examined my eyes, I couldn't see his light, which was very bright. My "central seeing computer" was firing so strongly that outside stimulation coming in through the eyes could not influence the result. The inside observer was blinded only because the information coming to him (wherever he is) from the visual cortex was so strong that any added stimulation from the periphery made no difference. All lines were busy all the time. This showed me that the observing systems in my large computer were not in the irritated visual cortex itself.

I studied the great white light; I began to see new phenomena. As I lay on the bed in the hospital, various kinds of visions occurred.

Suddenly I saw a green lawn, but the grass looked totally artificial as if made out of plastic. On this lawn there was a hole, out of which a snake came. The snake rose out of the hole straight into the air. Suddenly I laughed because he was such an artificial man–made snake.

The snake was constructed with a spring down his center and he was covered with paper. His head was made out of painted wood. His jaws were articulated around a single nail. Coming in from the right was a wooden bird, brilliantly painted, flapping his wooden wings and opening and closing his wooden beak. The snake rose up and bit the wooden bird with his wooden jaws.

The whole episode occurred while I was in a very relaxed state, just watching it happen. I remembered that, as a very small boy, I had a wooden snake and a wooden bird just like this. I suddenly realized that part of my memory storage system was firing and transmitting these pictures into the "visual display" part of my computer. As soon as I realized that this was a memory elaborated by my child's imagination, I began to laugh. As soon as I laughed, it disappeared. I then relaxed and various other animals made out of wood appeared. When I was two to three years old, I had had a wooden Noah's Ark. The animals became animated, moving about across the artificial grass. One characteristic of all these movements was the *hesitancy* and the *wobbliness* of the movements, as if the child were imagining these animals, making them move. The child was creating this movement in his imagination and not doing too good a job of it. This characteristic wobbliness of the construction is apparently a property of the child brain of a much earlier time.

Slowly during the next forty–eight hours, the brilliance of the white light decreased. The childish visions disappeared and in their place, there was a swarm of insect–like points of light and darkness which moved across the visual field. I found I could program their direction of flight and their speed. When I thought they would move in a particular direction, later the swarm moved in that direction.

My programming was ahead of what happened. I could think "now they will move to the right," and within a few seconds, they moved to the right. One puts a program into the computer, the computer then executes the program and generates the result with a delay between the time of the intent and the time of the carrying out of the result. I found later that for a very complex program this process can take up to three to four minutes; with the swarms of insect–like points, the delay was a few seconds.

* * *

The brilliant white light decreased in intensity, and after eighteen hours, I was to the point where stimulation from the eyes could come through to me. The first time that I could see was in the middle of the night when a nurse came in to give me an injection. There was a single light on in the room and through the fog of the remaining residual internal white light, I saw two round black circles and a foggy face behind them. I was looking at the face of the nurse and I said to her, laughing with relief, "You look just like an owl."

She said, "You see now." I said "Yes," and she went out and asked one of the doctors to come in to check my eyes. Within the next twenty–four hours my vision came back, almost totally intact.

* * *

It turned out that the experience with the guardians was the fourth time that I had gone to that place. I had left my body three times before, each time under a threat of death.

The first time that I can remember was when I was seven years old and I was having my tonsils removed under ether. I was extremely frightened as I went under the ether and I immediately found myself in a place with two angels who folded their wings around me and comforted me. The angel form was the childish projection onto the entities necessary to a child of seven brought up in the Catholic church.

The second time was when I was ten years old and had some disease, possibly tuberculosis, which made me very debilitated. I was in bed for six weeks or more. I used to wander off into this region when the room was quiet and nobody was present, when I had a high fever.

The third time was when I was twenty–two years old, having four wisdom teeth removed under a local anesthetic. I became very frightened as the dentist had a chisel pointed right at my brain. The pain of it and the imaginary catastrophe of having that chisel slip and go into my brain put me into primary shock. I sweated and became white and nauseated. The dentist saw this and gave me nitrous oxide.

Under nitrous oxide I went into a whirling space, a total experience of everything whirling. Sound, light, my body, the whole universe was whirling. I moved from that space suddenly into the space with the two guardians. At that time they instructed me as to what I was going to be doing, or what I should do, and hadn't yet done. When I came back out of the nitrous oxide, my teeth had been pulled and I felt a huge and immense relief. Now I knew where I was going and what I was going to do. That was when I decided to go to medical school and learn more about the survival of myself and others.

These memories, which were brought back during this long period of self–analysis after the accident, showed me the continuity of this space, of these two guardians. I realized that this is a place that I can go to and that presumably other people can go to, under special circumstances. During those weeks I resolved to get back to that place and to try to do it without the threat of death.

* * *

I had learned many lessons from this episode and, as it is said in scientific circles, "No experiment is a failure." *I had learned that death is not as terrifying as I had imagined it to be, that there is another space, a safe place beyond where we are now.* Instead of being frightened off from further experimentation, I became intrigued and decided to explore this very region.

I set up experiments using LSD in the solitude, isolation, and confinement tank, floating in the darkness, and silence, freed of all inputs to my body from the external reality. In these experiments, I discovered other spaces, found other maps, and discovered relatively safe means of going into these places without having the lethal programs activated too strongly again.

3

I became a bright luminous point of consciousness, radiating light, warmth, and knowledge. I moved into a space of astonishing brightness, a space filled with golden light, with warmth, and with knowledge.

I sat in the space without a body but with all of myself there, centered. I felt fantastically exhilarated with a great sense of awe and wonder and reverence. The energy surrounding me was of an incalculably high intensity but I found that I could stand it this time. I could feel, see, and know out in the great vastness of empty space filled with light. Slowly but surely, the two guides began to come toward me from a vast distance. At first I was barely able to detect them in the background of high intensity light. This time they approached very slowly. As they approached their presences became more and more powerful and I noticed that more and more of them was coming into me. Their thinking, their feeling, their knowledge was pouring into me. As they approached, I could share their thinking, their knowledge, and their feeling at

266

an incredibly high rate of speed. This time they were able to approach closer before I began to get the feelings of being overwhelmed by their presence. They stopped just as it was becoming almost intolerable to have them any closer. As they stopped, they communicated, in effect, "We will not approach any closer as this seems to be your limit for closeness with us at this time. You have progressed since we were together last. As we told you, you can come back any time once you learn the routes. We are sent to instruct you.

"You now have x number of years left to inhabit the body that you are given. If you wish to stay here now, you may. However, the discovery of your body in the laboratory tank in the Virgin Islands will leave a mess back there for others to clean up. If you go back to your body it will mean a struggle and large amounts of work in order to get through the hindrances you carry with you. You still have some evasions to explore before you can progress to the level at which you are existing at the moment. You can come and permanently be in this state. However, it is advisable that you achieve this through your own efforts while still in the body so that you can exist both here and in the body simultaneously. Your trips out here are evasions of your trip on your planet when looked at in one way. When looked at in another way, you are learning and your ability to come here shows that you have progressed far along this path. Now that you have made it without pain and without fear, you have made progress.

"Your next assignment, if you wish it, is to achieve this through your own efforts plus the help of others. So far you have been doing your experiments alone in solitude and have learned some of the ways here. Your next assignment is to contact others like yourself who have these capacities, help them, and learn from them how to carry out this kind of existence. There are several others on your planet capable of teaching you and also of learning from you. There are levels beyond where you are now and where we exist to which you can go with the proper work.

"Thus, as part of your assignment you are to perfect your means, while staying in the body, of communicating with this region, with this space, with us. There are other methods than LSD plus solitude for achieving these results. There are other means than fright and pain." They gave me a very large

267

amount of additional information but on this information they placed a seal.
They said that I would forget it when I came back into the body until such
time as this information was needed. Then, it would be there and I would use
it, "remembering" what they had put into me.

* * *

During these experiments I felt some sort of unseen guidance as to what to do next. I began to feel the presence of the guides without going to their spaces. In each new universe that I penetrated, I felt their presence protecting me from the huge entities that inhabit these other spaces. In the last of this series of experiments, I was shown the whole universe as we know it.

I am out beyond our galaxy, beyond galaxies as we know them. Time is apparently speeded up 100 billion times. The whole universe collapses into a point. There is a tremendous explosion and out of the point on one side comes positive matter and positive energies, streaking into the cosmos at fantastic velocities. Out of the opposite side of the point comes antimatter streaking off into the opposite direction. The universe expands to its maximum extent, recollapses, and expands three times. During each expansion the guides say, "Man appears here and disappears there." All I can see is a thin slice for man. I ask, "Where does man go when he disappears until he is ready to reappear again?" They say, "That is us."

During this experience I was filled with awe, reverence, and a fantastic feeling of smallness, of not amounting to very much. Everything was happening on such a vast scale that I was merely an observer of microscopic size, and yet I was more than this. I was part of some vast network of similar beings all connected, somehow or other responsible for what was going on. I was given an individuality for temporary purposes only. I would be reabsorbed into the network when the time came.

4

As I went deep into trance this time, I suddenly was on another planet, not earth, in a deep cave, a very peculiar vertical cave with a spherical chamber at the bottom. Somehow I did not know how to get out of this cave. I looked up through the vertical shaft and saw a blue light at the far end of the tunnel. I was threatened by the fact that at the edges of the shaft there were what I thought to be "solid state life forms," small cubical and rectangular creatures who were doing some sort of work that I couldn't understand around the edges of the shaft. They were very busy and covered the whole surface of the shaft. I estimated that none of them was larger than three to four inches across in the largest dimension.

Somehow I felt that I was trapped in this spherical chamber and that I did not dare go up the shaft for fear of what these creatures might do to me.

We had arranged that I would be able to report what was happening from the depths of trance and I reported what was going on to Helen and Ken. Helen then immediately said, "I will lift you up through the shaft without your touching the walls. Stay with me. Allow me to lift and you will come up."

Immediately, I started rising through the shaft, came out through the opening in the surface of that planet, and saw the immense blue sky over my head and the very peculiar terrain of that planet.

It had a golden color to it. There was no green. There was nothing that I could describe in earthlike terms. It was of a very peculiar construction, very smooth, and quite unlike any earth scene that I have been in. There were some other beings on the surface of the planet, but at this point I was not interested in staying there, so I came back to the room in which the three of us were working.

5

Suddenly I was precipitated into what I later called the *"cosmic computer."* I was merely a very small program in somebody else's huge computer. There were tremendous energies in this computer. There were fantastic energy flows and information flows going through me. None of it made any sense. I was in total terror and panic.

I was being programmed by other senseless programs above me and, above them, others. I was programming smaller programs below me. The information that came in was meaningless. I was meaningless. This whole computer was the result of a senseless dance of certain kinds of atoms in a certain place in the universe, stimulated and pushed by organized but meaningless energies.

I traveled through the computer as a program that floated through other programs. I moved to its extreme outer limits. Everywhere I found entities like myself who were slave programs in this huge cosmic conspiracy, this cosmic dance of energy and matter which had absolutely no meaning, no love, no human value. The computer was absolutely dispassionate, objective, and terrifying. The layer of ultimate programmers on the outside of it were personifications of the devil himself and yet they too were merely programs. There was no hope or chance or choice of ever leaving this hell. I was in fantastic pain and terror, imbedded in this computer for approximately three hours planetside time, but eternally in trip time.

Suddenly a human hand reached into the computer and pulled me out. As I came out I went from just a program in a senseless dance of atoms to a human body back in the room with Sandy. I found that Sandy, seeing my terror and panic, had grasped my hand in order to comfort me.

* * *

I went back inside again and watched as a scintillating energy–filled computed maze appeared, filled with sparkly lights of different colors. Walking through the maze, sensuously undulating were many extremely attractive female humans. I knew that they were robots also. They had glittering gowns that hugged their voluptuous figures closely, showing their delicious hips and bosoms and narrow waists and extremely beautiful faces. I saw five or six of these slinking through the maze. I heard the voices of the two programmers discussing this scene and me. This time I was not in the scene but merely watching, witnessing.

One programmer said to the other, "If he does everything that we want him to do, we will reward him with the love of one of these women." I was horrified because I realized that these women were robots and not real humans....

APPENDIX I
The Development of the "Contained Mind" Hypothesis

Parts of my book *Programming and Metaprogramming in the Human Biocomputer* are pertinent to the simulation/model/system of thought presented in this appendix. One can see the origins of this model starting in this earlier work. The idea of the contained mind within a brain is assumed in the following excerpts. Those who have a preference for the "uncontained mind" belief system have little patience with this cybernetic approach. (For an analysis of the "uncontained mind" system of belief, see Chapter Eight of *The Deep Self.*)

I find this "contained mind" belief system necessary for a disciplined approach to the analysis of the phenomena experienced in the isolation tank. As I state in Chapter Eight on the uncontained mind, I am not espousing either "contained" or "uncontained" mind as true/real. We do not yet have the critical data/experiments/investigators to do a properly scientific investigation. Here we are laying the groundwork, the context for such scientific work.

The following excerpts from *Programming and Metaprogramming in the Human Biocomputer* show the early work and give details of the reasons for the development of the contained mind theory/belief system.

INNER COGNITION SPACE

As one proceeds from outer or external projection analysis to internal projection analysis, one moves from the excitation of projection systems by external energies to a lack of such excitation in these systems. For example, in the profound blackness and darkness of the floatation room there is no visual stimulus coming to the eyes or the visual systems. Similarly in the profound silence there are no sounds coming into the acoustic apparatus, and similarly the other systems are at a very low level of stimulation from the external world.

One might expect then that these systems would appear to be absolutely quiet, dark and empty. This is not so. This is the area in which most subjects begin to get into trouble. It is also the area in which psychiatric and clinical judgments may interfere with the natural development of the phenomena. In the absence of external excitations coming through the natural end organs the perception systems maintain this activity. The excitation for this activity comes from other parts of the computer, i.e., from program storage and from internal body sources of excitation. The self–programmer interprets the resultant filling of these perceptual spaces at first *as if* this excitation were coming from outside. In other words, the sources of the excitation are interpreted by the self as if coming from the real world. For certain kinds of persons and personalities this is a very disturbing experience in one sphere or another; for them it is explicable only with telepathy.

We have been taught from babyhood that this kind of phenomena in a totally conscious individual is somehow forbidden, anti–social and possibly even psychotic.

One must analyze this metaprogram that has been implanted in one from childhood, examine its rationality or lack of same and proceed in spite of this kind of an interpretation of the phenomena that occur. Once one has analyzed this as an evasion or a defensive maneuver against seeing the true state of affairs one can allow oneself to go on and experience the deeper set of phenomena without interfering with the natural metaprograms. After achieving this level of freedom from anxiety, one can then go on to the next stages. (The programming orders for these inner happenings to take place are worked out in advance of the session, at first written down or spoken into a recorder. Later such orders can be programmed without external aids.)

The following phenomenological description has been experienced by one subject under these special conditions. *One experiences an immediate internal reality which is postulated by the self. It is apparent to me that one's own assumptions about this experience generate the whole experience. The experienced affects, the apparent appearance of other persons, the appearance of other beings not human, one's own past phantasies, one's own self–analysis, each can be programmed to happen in interaction with those parts of one's self beyond one's conscious awareness.*

The content experienced under these conditions lacks strong reality clues. *Externally real* displays are not furnished; the excitation from the reality outside does not pattern the displays. Therefore the projections which do occur are from those systems at the next inward level from the operations of the perception apparatus devoted to external reality.

The phenomena that ensue are described by one subject as follows: *the visualization is immersed in darkness in three dimensions at times but only when one evades the emerging* "multi–dimensional cognitive and conative space." *One is aware of "the silence" in the hearing sphere; this too gives way to the new space which is developing. The body image fluctuates, appearing and disappearing, as fear or other need builds up. As with the "darkness and the silence" so with the presence or absence of the body image.* Progress in using these projection spaces is measured by one's ability to neither project external reality data from storage into these spaces nor to project into these spaces "the absence of external reality stimuli."

One can project in the visual space living images (external reality equivalents) or blackness (the absence of external reality images). One can project into the acoustic spaces definite sounds, voices, etc. (as if external reality) or one can project *silence* (the absence of sound) in the external reality. One can project the body image also, flexing one's muscles, joints, etc., to reassure oneself the image is functioning with *real feedback* or one can have a primary perception of a *lack of the body image* which is the negative logical alternative to the body image itself.

In each of these dichotomized situations one is *really* projecting external reality and its equivalents (positive or negative). In order to experience the next set of phenomena one must work through these dichotomous symbols of the external world and realize that they are evasions of further penetration to deeper levels.

Once one abandons the use of projection of external reality equivalents from storage, new phenomena appear. Thought and feeling take over the spaces formerly occupied by external reality equivalents. (In the older terminology ego expands to fill the subjectively appreciated inner universe.) "Infinity" similar to that in the usual real visual space is also involved and one has the feeling that one's self extends infinitely out in all directions. The self is still centered at one place but its boundaries have disappeared and it moves out in all directions and extends to fill the limits of the universe as far as one knows them. The explanation of this phenomenon is that one has merely taken over the perception spaces and filled them with programs, metaprograms, and self–metaprograms which are now modified in the inner perception as if external reality equivalents. This transform, this special mental state, to be appreciated must be experienced directly.

In one's ordinary experience there are dreams which have something of this quality and which show this kind of a phenomenon.

At this level various evasions of realization of what is happening can take place. One can "imagine" that one is traveling through the real universe past suns, galaxies, etc. One can "imagine" that one is communicating with other beings in these other universes. However, scientifically speaking, it is fairly obvious that one is not doing any of these things and that one's basic beliefs determine what one experiences here. Therefore we say that the ordinary perception

276

spaces, the ordinary projection spaces, are now filled with cognition and conation processes. This seems to be a more reasonable point of view to take than the *oceanic feeling*, the *at oneness with the universe* as fusing with Universal Mind as reported in the literature by others for these phenomena. These states (or *direct perceptions of reality* as they have been called) are one's thought and feeling expanding into the circuitry in one's computer usually occupied by perception of external reality in each and every mode, including vision, audition, proprioception, etc.

* * *

In the farthest and deepest state of isolation, one's basic needs and one's assumptions about self become evident. The existence of self and one's belief in the existence of one's self are made manifest. The positive or negative sign of values that one places upon one's self and upon the existence of one's self begins to show its force and strength. The problems discussed, but generally unfaced in a religious context in the external real world, are faced and can be *lived out* with a freedom unavailable since childhood.

The problem of the dissolution of one's conscious self by death of the body is studiable. One's evasions of this problem and of facing it can be projected into studiable areas of one's experience. The existence theorem for spiritual and psychic entities is also testable and the strength of one's belief in these entities can be analyzed. Evasions of self–analysis and evasions of taking on certain kinds of beliefs can be tested.

In this area the denial and negation mechanisms of classical psychoanalysis show their strength. Previous analysis can train one to recognize that when data cannot be called up or when displays cannot be constructed or when certain operations cannot be carried out, one can see the cause currently existing. The set of inhibitory and repressive devices in one's computer is hard at work. In such inhibitory and repressive states, preprogrammed sets of basic assumptions to be explored are incompletely carried out. One quickly finds areas of the consequences of the assumed beliefs, which one cannot enter or only enters with fear, with anger, or with love, carried over from some other programming.

DEFINITION OF A GENERAL PURPOSE
SELF–METAPROGRAM

The essential features and the goals sought in the self–analysis are in the metaprogram: *make the computer general purpose.* In this sense we mean that in the general purpose nature of the computer there can be no display, no acting, nor an ideal which is forbidden to a consciously–willed metaprogram. Nor is any display, acting or ideal made without being consciously metaprogrammed. In each case, of course, one is up against the limits of the unique computer which is one's own. There are certain kinds of metaprograms, displays, acting, or ideals which are beyond the capacity of a particular computer. However, one's imagined limits are sometimes smaller than those which one can achieve with special work.

The metaprogram of the specific beliefs about the limits of one's self are at stake here. One's ability to achieve certain special states of consciousness, for example, is generally preprogrammed by basic beliefs taken on in childhood. If the computer is to maintain its general purpose nature (which presumably was there in childhood), one must recapture a far greater range of phenomena than one expects that one has available. For instance, one should be able to program in practically any area possible within human imagination, human action or human being.

As explorations deepen, one can see the evading nature of many programs which one previously considered basic to one's private and professional philosophy. As one opens up the depths, it is wise not to privately or publicly espouse as *ultimate* any *truths* one *finds* in the following areas: the universe in general, beings not human, thought transference, life after death, transmigration of souls, racial memories, species–jumping–thinking, non–physical action at a distance, and so forth. Such ideas may merely be a reflection of one's needs in terms of one's own survival. Ruthless self–analysis as to one's needs for certain kinds of ideas in these areas must be explored honestly and truthfully. The rewarding and positively–reinforcing effects of LSD–25 must be remembered and emphasized; one overvalues the results of one's chemically rewarding thinking.

Once one has done such deep analysis one later finds deeper that these needs were generating these ideas. One's public need to pro-claim them to one's self and to others, as if they are the ultimate truth, is an expression of one's need to believe. Insight into the fact that one is enthused because the positive, start–and–maintain, rewarding sign has been chemically stamped on these ideas must be remembered.

An explorer operating at these depths cannot afford such childish baggage. These are disguises of and evasions of the ultimate dissolu-tion of self; the maintenance of pleasure and of life are insisting on denial of death. If one stops at these beliefs, no progress in further analysis can be made. These beliefs are *analysis dissolvers*. One might call these *lazy assumptions* which prevent one from pushing deeper into self and avoid expending any great effort in this deeper direction. One of these very powerful evasions is an hedonistic acceptance of things as they are with conversion of most of them to a pleasant glow. Another similar evasion is deferring discussion of such basic issues until one's *life after death*.

* * *

A possibly great spur to work in this area for certain kinds of per-sons is the acceptance of unknowables and of the unknown itself. A powerful wish to push into the unknown further than those ahead of one in calendar time is helpful in terms of one's motivation at this point. Everyone has his say about the truth in this area. Many other persons would like very much to have one follow their metaprograms. In my own view I would prefer to be a questing mind reporting on some interesting journeys. Insofar as I fail to be this, I, too, am guilty of attempting to metaprogram the reader.

In summary then, one starts on the deeper journeys, independently, metaprogrammed properly, and relatively safe but without evasions. After having been through some of the innermost depths of self, a result is that they are only one's own beliefs and their multitudes of randomized logical consequences deep down inside one's self. There is nothing else but stored experience.

* * *

In the following section (Appendix II) the basic ideas proposed in *The Human Biocomputer* (preceding excerpts) are given a more explicit, thorough, formal existence through several distinctions implicit in the excerpts.

The concept of the "observer/operator" sharpens the previous concepts of "self" and "self–metaprogrammer." The observer actively watches; the operator does/programs/manipulates. These two aspects of the self are valuable, not only in the context of science, but in everyday life. One can be in isolation and watch "spontaneous" productions (as the observer) and/or one can watch and control (to a limited extent) the productions (as the operator).

This view of self (observer/operator) as can be seen in Chapter Seven, "The Mind Contained in the Brain," only implicitly deals with the self as a victim/pawn/programee of forces beyond Self. These forces (in the original work) were called "supraself metaprograms" or supraself agents/entities. Under such greater–than–Self influences, the observer/operator has a more passive/allowing/going–with–the–flow aspect. Such a third aspect of Self may be called the "programee" (as opposed to the programmer, the active concept). This aspect of Self is neglected in those sciences which concentrate on the experimenter/researcher aspects. This aspect of Self is relegated to those activities of scientists applying for research grants and submitting to those powerful groups furnishing the funds for the research, etcetera. A scientist immersed in his consensus reality is being programmed by his colleagues, by his life needs, by politics, etcetera.

This third aspect of Self ("programee") is of importance in tank isolation. If the negative or positive energy within the internal realities is high enough, the observer/operator loses initiative in the watching and in the operating domains. In these cases the observer/operator becomes weakened, and may disappear (State 6, Table 2, Appendix II). Reports from such states of reality are difficult to elicit from Self or from others. This is a domain for further research.

When the observer/operator has only his/her Self to operate on—observe—special states (State 5 in Table 2) can be experienced/inperienced. These purely self–referential states are quite strange/alien/bizarre to most persons in our culture. In more Eastern approaches, as opposed to our Western ones, these states have a high intrinsic value, and are given special names such as Nirvana, Satori, Samadhi, etcetera. More Western researches into these states by qualified trained disciplined Western scientists are needed.

The concepts of the internal and external realities are the same in each work (see Chapter Four).

The concept of simulations of external and internal realities is made more explicit in this formulation (Appendix II) than it was in the earlier work. In the early work, the term "projections" was used extensively. The concept of "projection" in the new format is an implicit underlying one, necessary to our understanding. The observer/operator can/does project any simulation onto any other: an e.r. simulation taken as real in the inner realities can be projected "as if" coming from outside the internal reality. An i.r. simulation can be similarly projected outward or further inward, etcetera.

APPENDIX II
The Contained Mind Metabelief: Definition of Elements

Here we define *mind* as the *software/programs/metaprograms* contained in the *computational domain* of a central nervous system (C.N.S.) in a biological system that supports its essential processes and provides its inputs/outputs from/to an external reality (e.r.). Within the computational domain, an observer/operator (ob/op) exists as that aspect of the computational domain that apparently distinguishes/observes/operates/computes at a level of computation one level above that called the Self–referential metaprogrammatic level, at least eight levels above the "machine language level" of the operations of the C.N.S. (zeroth level).

COMPUTATION LEVELS

(0) elementary units of neuronal computation. *Computational levels:* (1) primitive neuron network computations between cellular units in nets; (2) computations by nuclear assemblies of networks; (3) computations by systems of nuclei relations; (4) coordination of computations by nuclear systems; (5) programs regulating coordinations of 4; (6) metaprograms regulating programs of 5; (7) metaprograms creating Self–referential properties; (8) observer/operator metaprograms derived from 7; (9) supra–observer/operator metaprograms specifying origins/states/domains/existence of the observer/operator metaprograms; (10) unknowns in/above/below all preceding levels.

STRUCTURAL INTACTNESS

A whole adult noninjured ("nonreduced") C.N.S. is essential for generating levels 6 and above.

SIMULATIONS

"Simulations" (∇'s) are defined as one group of metaprograms at level 7, which are only partially presented to be experienced by ob/op.

"E.r. simulations": One group of simulations *represents* the external reality (e.r. ∇'s) and is computed from current C.N.S. input/output computations at lower levels. Such e.r. ∇'s can be partially stored and reactivated from storage.

"Ob/op simulations (ob/op ∇'s)": Another group of simulations *represents* the current observer/operator set of metaprograms and is computed in levels 6, 7, 8, and 9.

"I.r. simulations" (i.r. ∇'s) in the presence of e.r. inputs/outputs: In the presence of feedback of a C.N.S. with an external reality, the ob/op operates with the e.r. simulations continuously modulated by the changing input/output relations. The internal reality (defined below) may be reductively simulated as a void in the head/body, or as any other idiosyncratic set of i.r. ∇'s.

"I.r. experience": The observer/operator exists exclusively in a metaprogrammatic computational domain (levels 8 and 9). If isolated from current e.r. computational necessities, e.r. simulations are free of input/output constraints and can be recomputed in new forms by the observer/operator (level 8) and by the supra–observer/operator metaprograms (level 9). Under these isolation /confinement/solitude conditions (such as isolation tank/anesthesia /psychedelic states /trance/sleep/coma), the observer/operator observes/acts exclusively on/in the computations of levels 6, 7, 8, 9, and 10 without modifications introduced by here/now inputs/outputs to/from the external reality.

Under these conditions, the observer/operator exists in an exclusively *internal reality* (unmodulated by feedback through all levels with the external reality). This internal reality is created exclusively within the confines of the C.N.S.*

SOME STATES OF BEING/EXISTENCE OF THE ISOLATED OBSERVER/OPERATOR (I–OB/OP)

STATE 1.   E.r. simulations continuing in isolation, intact ob/op as single unique system; an "as if real external reality" with intact feedback from/to body; body simulations modulated by continued body/C.N.S. feedback.

STATE 2.   Body/C.N.S. feedback missing/inhibited/chemically decreased; e.r. simulations continuing; intact ob/op; "as if real external reality" with body simulation operating freely within the simulated "external reality" ("as if real body" free to move in simulated e.r.).

STATE 3.   Body simulations decreased to vanishingly small values; ob/op intact as a point observer/operator. E.r. simulations (e.r.∇'s) strong. Ob/op in an "as if real external reality" freely moving anywhere, any place, any time (from sub-atomic to galactic simulations) within the unique constraints of level 9 (supra–ob/op level) and of level 10 (at present unknown constraints). Ob/op free to change apparent size from a point to filling any apparent "as if real external reality."

STATE 4.   Body simulations and e.r. simulations reduced toward zero value. Ob/op free to vary parameters within ob/op simulations (ob/op ∇'s) allowed by level 9. Ob/op states of

* This statement is taken as true if and until we find other than currently known inputs/outputs that we have not removed by the above given isolation techniques (see Chapter Eight on the uncontained mind).

being/existence vary from a point to any domain allowed.

STATE 5. Body simulations (body∇'s), e.r. simulations (e.r. ∇'s), ob/op simulations (ob/op ∇'s) each reduced to zero. Ob/op exists, feeding back upon itself exclusively, no "outer" references, no simulations left: pure Self–referential observer/operator totally isolated.

STATE 6. Zeroed out ob/op. No memory allowed on return to other states of being.

General rules for simulations (∇'s):
1. Any simulation can be stored as inactive.
2. Any simulation can be activated from storage.
3. When a simulation is stored, it is absent in the ob/op domain.
4. When activated, a simulation acts in the ob/op domain.

In the following discussion, tables and diagrams, a stored simulation is represented by its absence in the ob/op domain by the symbol "0." Currently active simulation in the ob/op domain is symbolized by "1".

Let:
observer/operator = ob/op
simulations = ∇'s
external reality = e.r.
internal reality = i.r.
body = body
a given domain missing = 0
a given domain present = 1

286

TABLE 1. Six States of Being for (ob/op):

for (ob/op)$_0$	Function State:	0	1	2	3	4	5	6	2nd Observer Watching Body: for (ob/op)$_1$ (without communication) for all states of (ob/op)$_0$
	(ob/op)$_0$	1	1	1	1	1	1	0	"0"
	ob/op ∇'s	1	1	1	1	1	0	0	"0"
	i.r.∇'s	1	1	1	1	1	0	0	"0"
	i.r.	1	1	1	1	1	0	0	"0"
	body ∇'s	1	1	1	0	0	0	0	"0"
	e.r. ∇'s	1	1	1	1	0	0	0	"0"
	body	1	1	0	0	0	0	0	"1"
	e.r.	1	0	0	0	0	0	0	"1"

TABLE 2.   Equivalences Between the Six Formulated States
            and Equivalent Classical Labels

	Formulated State	Functional Description	Equivalent Classical Labels
0	Ob/op completes system with e.r.	Normal consensus interlock.	Ordinary consciousness.
1	E.r. missing (rest complete).	Physically isolated body (tank, bed, etcetera), body awareness present.	Meditation in body solitude and isolation.
2	E.r. and body missing (rest complete).	Isolated body; body awareness attenuated to zero; body simulations active.	Deep meditation state. Astral body and travel.
3	E.r., body, and body ∇'s missing: e.r. ∇'s intact.	Isolated body; body awareness at zero; body simulation missing: observer/operator as point.	Astral travel without a body.
4	E.r., body, e.r. ∇'s, body ∇'s missing; rest active.	Intact i.r., i.r. ∇'s, with ob/op and its simulations active.	Transcendental experiences.
5	Only ob/op intact; rest missing	Fully isolated observer/operator; no simulations left.	Union with God, universal mind; high indifference; consciousness-without-an-object.
6	All missing.	Unconsciousness; deep sleep; no memory on return to other states.	Total fusion without memory on return.

288

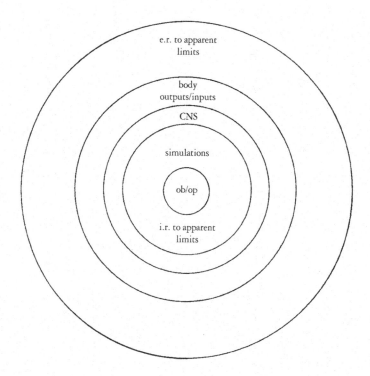

e.r. to apparent
limits

body
outputs/inputs

CNS

simulations

ob/op

i.r. to apparent
limits

FIGURE 1:   Simplified Diagram of Relations

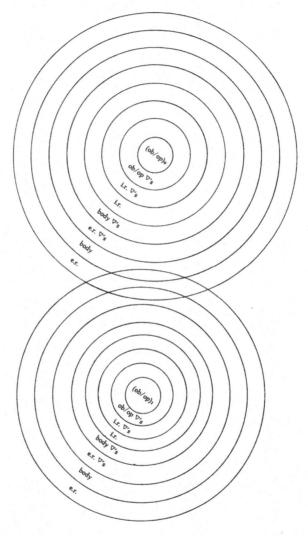

FIGURE 2:   Diagram   of   (ob/op)$_0$ and   2nd
Observer/Operator (ob/op)$_1$
Watching Body

290

No. 1 Problem for the Reader

Function	State: 0	1	2	3	4	5	6	7	8	9	10	Second Observer Without Com— munication with First Observer in State 0
$(ob/op)_0$	1	1	1	1	1	1	1	1	1	1	0	0
$(ob/op)\nabla$	1	1	1	1	1	1	1	1	1	0	0	0
i.r. ∇'s	1	1	1	1	1	1	1	1	0	0	0	0
i.r	1	1	1	1	1	1	0	0	0	0	0	0
body ∇	1	1	1	1	1	0	1	0	0	0	0	0
e.r. ∇'s	1	1	1	0	1	0	0	0	0	0	0	0
body	1	1	0	0	0	0	0	0	0	0	0	1
e.r.	1	0	0	0	0	0	0	0	0	0	0	1

Describe the above ten states. (Hint: Expand Table 2—Formulated State, Functional Description, and Equivalent Classical Labels.)

No. 2 Problem

Construct Rest of Cases of States of Being (enlarge table to include all states conceivable).

Define "experience" vs. "simulation."
E.r. experience vs. e.r. simulations experienced.
I.r. experience vs. i.r. simulations experienced.

DEFINITIONS

Experience: This concept is here distinguished into two domains: the e.r.–e.r. ∇ domain, and the i.r.–i.r. ∇ domain. (The usual definitions of this term in dictionaries imply: [1] external reality feedback with Self over time [2] religious experience which affirms or reaffirms faith in a particular belief system.)

The set of computations that currently generates external reality simulations (e.r. ∇'s) interlocked with the observer/operator and with the computed e.r. inputs/outputs operating synchronously, generates what is called "external experience."

The set of computations that currently generates internal reality simulations (i.r. ∇'s) interlocked with the observer/operator and with the i.r. computations operating synchronously, generates what is called "internal experience." (See example below under *Goodness–of–fit* section.)

Simulation: That term is used here in the nonpejorative sense used in computer software terminology: a system of metaprograms, programs and subroutines that represents/models/simulates/reproduces the behavior of another system in a quantitatively similar way within a computer, here a biocomputer.

Goodness–of–fit: The measurements of the differences between the behavior of a simulation and the system simulated: if the differential measurements are within certain specified limits (above threshold for the detection of differences) the goodness–of–fit is adequate and the simulation is said to work satisfactorily. An example from e.r. vs. e.r. ∇:

Example: (1) One walks through a room containing furniture many times over days. One very dark night the lights suddenly fail. One walks through the room using a "visual" simulation of the room for navigation, avoiding the unseen furniture. The goodness–of–fit between the e.r. furniture loci and the e.r. simulation "furniture loci" operating in the C.N.S. is adequate to avoid collisions with the e.r. furniture.

(2) Someone else moved a chair; the goodness–of–fit is inadequate: a collision results. In this example, e.r. is interlocked in a time sequence with e.r. ∇.

The e.r. experience is paralleled by an i.r. *experience* of a simulation of an e.r.

Physical Isolation Experience: In physical isolation (tank), e.r. inputs/outputs approach zero. In the solitude/isolation/confinement tank, the i.r. experience is among simulations, either e.r. and/or i.r.

Once free of e.r. experience simulations, the i.r. experience is that of i.r. and its simulations.

I.r. experience is of the new/unique/never–before–experienced.

I.r. simulation experience is that which is familiar/repeated/programmed from the i.r. experience of Self/others.

Pure Simulation Experience: As above in Physical Isolation Experience.

Simulations, $\equiv \nabla \equiv$ *a simulation:* Free of what is simulated. E.r. ∇ free of e.r.; i.r. ∇ free of i.r. (This is characterized by the "as if" property: simulations are "*as if true*"; direct experiences are *true*):

Metabelief operator $\equiv \nabla^2 \equiv$ *controller of simulations:* free of simulation, domain control.

Ob/op $\equiv \nabla^3$ *controller of metabelief operators:* free of metabelief operators controlled.

Supra–ob/op: ∇^4 free of ob/op control.

($\nabla \equiv$ "del")

$\nabla^0 \equiv$ a metaprogram controlling a set of programs

$\nabla^1 \equiv$ a simulation controlling a set of metaprograms

$\nabla^2 \equiv$ a meta–simulation operator controlling simulations, ∇'s

$\nabla^3 \equiv$ ob/op controlling meta–simulation operators, ∇^2s

$\nabla^4 \equiv$ supra–ob/op controller, controlling ob/op, ∇^3

∇^1 A *belief* is a fixed simulation controlling a set of metaprograms or a set of fixed simulations (lasting a long–enough time to be detected by ob/op$_0$ or e.r. ob/op$_n$).

∇^2 *A metabelief operator* is free of beliefs and controls beliefs. (Cf. ∇^2, above.)

Multiple ob/ops

In the above definitions, it is implicitly assumed that ob/op is a single unique observer/operator. This may not be the case. ∇^4 can introduce one or more additional ∇^3s to a total of as much as five ∇^3s. (Cf. *Three Faces of Eve* by Thigpen and Cleckley,* and Morton Prince's experiments in hypnosis, for examples.)

∇^4 can introduce simulations of the $(ob/op)_0$ in subtle ways, placing limits on $(ob/op)_0$ and splitting off other "entities" experienced by $(ob/op)_0$ "as if coming from e.r. or i.r." which communicate with/control/are controlled by $(ob/op)_0$. (Cf. *Programming and Metaprogramming in the Human Biocomputer* and *The Center of the Cyclone*.)

---

* Corbett H. Thigpen and Hervey M. Cleckley, *Three Faces of Eve*, Popular Library, New York, 1974.

C.N.S. Energy Sources for Simulations and Observer/Operator with e.r. Present

In complete physical isolation, e.r. inputs/outputs are missing: energy sources continue operating in C.N.S. linked with body through self–maintained neuronal cellular/network reverberatory systems.

The separation ("distinction") of observer from operator and operator from observer is heuristic, for descriptive purposes. Positive energy sources lead to "pleasure"; "positive emotional states" and "positive reinforcement" at peak values create oscillatory states (self–limiting duration "orgasm" and "seizures"). Originating neuronal circuits are in subcortical systems. Negative energy sources lead to "aversion"; "negative emotional states"; "negative reinforcement" at peak values create oscillatory states leading to death of the organism. Originating neuronal circuits are in subcortical systems. Neutral energy sources create "neutral reinforcement," states of high indifference. Balanced values of energy from negative and positive sources lead to neutral energy.

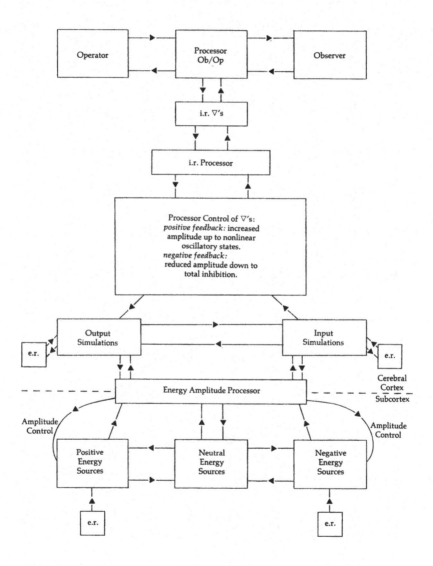

296

APPENDIX IV
Hyperstability and Physical Isolation

A. HYPERSTABLE SYSTEMS

Ross Ashby, in his book *Design for a Brain*,* enunciates the principle of hyperstability, which we paraphrase as follows:

Any complex feedback system of sufficient connectivity and sufficient size reacts to an induced change in any part of itself in such a way as to attenuate/negate the effects on itself of any similar induced change in each and every part of itself at any future time.

An additional principle can be stated as follows:

A hyperstable state occurs in a large complex system as the system grows, experiences and ages. In becoming hyperstable the system achieves sufficient connectivity and size, sufficient experience of varied environs and sufficient age for full integration of its own history/memory of past encounters with disturbances.

A hyperstable state is weakened or disappears when a sufficiently large new change is induced in it by transients of sufficiently large amplitude. During the response to the transient, the system can go through several kinds of changes of state (damped, oscillatory, step–change, etcetera). After the response is finished, the state of the system can be (1) the previous state before the response, (2) a new state above the previous one, (3) a new state below the previous one, (4) destruction of the hyperstable state into a randomly or repetitively

* W. Ross Ashby, *Design for a Brain: The Origin of Adaptive Behavior.*

changing series of states or (5) destruction of the system, as such.

A sufficiently rapid series of large amplitude transients occurring in the surrounds of the system induces a series of changes in the system that builds up the total changes in the system. Such net accumulation of changes forces growth in the system that may evolve it to new levels of organization of hyperstability or may regress it into a nonintegrated set of subsystems or may destroy it.

These principles can be applied to the human mind alone and in groups in terms of (1) psychedelic substances and their induced changes, (2) physical and social isolation, (3) induction of "higher states" of consciousness by physical/mental/spiritual exercises or (4) innovative techniques in government /advertising/movie scripts/TV shows/etcetera.

An individual person, a single C.N.S., is such a hyperstable system. An organization of individuals can become a hyperstable system. Consensus reality is that aspect of past organizations of individuals reflecting a large hyperstable system known as culture/society/government. The feedback to each individual from the larger whole in which each is imbedded from birth reflects the hyperstable nature of human organizations. The control of individual action/being/feeling within the organization is a reflection of the hyperstable nature of the organization. Each such system records/remembers its past transient responses and its past states consciously/unconsciously. Each such system reacts to changes in the surrounds and within its own structure so as to minimize the effects within itself.

B. PHYSICAL ISOLATION AND HYPERSTABILITY IN THE INDIVIDUAL

An individual socially isolated is out of direct here–and–now feedback with other persons and with his/her society. As a hyperstable system the individual responds to the beginning of the isolation period in phase of reaction to the feedback cutoff. The phenomena experienced are those of the transient responses to the cutoff. This phase may last a few minutes, a few hours, or a few days. After this initial response, new phenomena appear characteristic of the internal reality and the simulations of the external reality in its social aspects (including "creations" of persons not present or dead, memory of past encounters, e.r.'s, etcetera).

In complete physical isolation in addition to social isolation, the transient responses are more marked, of higher amplitude, and more fascinating to the person. The new steady states after the transient response tend to be more out of touch with the previous steady state immersed in the social reality. The new states are more uniquely individualistic and seem to be more characteristic of that individual's essential organization. New and unique phenomena occur, not predicated on consensus reality programs previously experienced.

Forcible Indoctrination (Coercive Persuasion) and Physical Isolation

Here we use the term "forcible indoctrination" (or coercive persuasion) in the sense of a nonvoluntary process of a change of belief systems exerted by persons other than oneself. (This term more accurately describes the processes of interest than does the common term "brainwashing" for similar processes.)

External reality controls commonly used in the forcible indoctrination procedures include any or all of the following:

1. Social isolation of the person to be indoctrinated from his/her usual social surrounds
2. Physical isolation as profound as can be achieved with available facilities, including severe confinement
3. Disruption of the usual sleep–awake cycle
4. Change in feeding patterns, from starvation to eating noxious foods
5. A system of punishments/rewards
6. Fear–inducing information
7. Chemical changes in states of being through psychoactive substances
8. Mental isolation from previous attachments
9. Forbidding/prevention of sexual activities

All of these factors have been eliminated/attenuated in all of the experiments/experiences related in this book.

A Useful Metabelief about the Internal Reality (i.r.) Program and Simulation Domain and Its Uses: P_0

1. *A program, P_0 can be created.*

All of this is in the province of the mind, and we are talking about a program that you (I_0) suddenly created, or which appeared.

2. *Once created, P_0 can be stored.*

P_0 can be memorized.

3. *Once stored, P_0 can be repeated.*

Until you have it in storage, you can't repeat it. Everything in your mind has to go back into memory and then be recalled in order to be repeated.

4. *Repeated a sufficient number of times, P_0 can be strengthened/* weakened.*

Here we are talking about strengthening versus weakening. P_0 can

---

* I want to call your attention to the use of this slash to suppress/express a dichotomy—it's not an "either-or," it's "both." We are trying to get away from dichotomous thinking in the sense that we used to make statements about only one side of the dichotomy and neglect the other. Here we are trying to bridge that interface (symbolized by slash/) and stay on the dichotomy as such. It's a particular form of thinking and doing that results from the mathematical analysis of either/or thinking. When you get into a state of high indifference (Merrell-Wolff), you have to know your dichotomies as such. You have to know "good and evil" as "good slash evil" not as "either good or evil." Since (good/evil) is a matter of local custom anyway (R. A. Monroe), one might as well subsume them both under the same heading. If you are going to deal with good and/or evil considerations, make it "good slash evil."

go either way. In other words if you repeat the program, you can inhibit or excite it—strengthen or weaken it.

5. *As P_o gains strength, it can pass the threshold of use.*

This is a distinction that most people don't make when they talk about programming. Your internalized program in i.r. has to be strong enough for you to be able to use it, or it to use you, automatically. Therefore, the strength with which it is operating inside must have passed a certain threshold so that you can use it.

6. *Once at use—threshold, P_0 can be activated.*

Activation does not mean *playback*, it means that the program takes over, operates and does its thing and you don't have to do anything about it. It's already stored and consciously available to you in all its detail. P_0 now uses I_0 for reliving.

7. *Activation of P_0 is started by internal reality agents or external reality agents.*

In other words you can start one yourself or you can have somebody else start one that's already in you. Call your attention to your sexual programs, for example.

What is the difference between a stored program and when it's a usable program? When it's a stored program it's in a latent state, undeveloped, but the image is there. You know about latent images on photographic film. You click the shutter, expose the film to the image. There is no seeable image on the film, but you can take that film to the darkroom and develop it and the image comes up. A similar process takes place with the activation of a program. It's stored in a latent form, take it out and raise the strength of the thing until it appears and starts operating. It's more like developing a movie than a still; a movie with a soundtrack, a feeling and doing track. These programs can run your feeling and doing and thinking and so on. It's not restricted to visual images.

My experience is that when I have programs that are not usable, they are either ones that I cannot activate, in other words, I don't know what the key is to turn them on, and they just happen sometimes, or they are unable to be sustained. Let's go through this and we'll show you some of the difficulty.

8. *Most of P_0 is unconscious: only its name and address need to be recalled for use.*

Just the minimum amount of information is needed: you know the name of the program; the name now represents the program to you, so that the name has meaning. In a sense the meaning is the program itself, activated, being used. That's the meaning of the name.

The address is the association chain you have to go through to activate it. So you need the name of the program and the associative chain that leads you to the location of the program. The name is the *call*, the *recall* is naming it again, to use G. Spencer Brown's terminology.* The initial storage is the *crossing* in his terminology. An activation here is *recrossing*. The initial crossing is the initial storage process, the recrossing is the activation.

9. *P_0 can become an internal reality agent.*

P_0 takes on a life of its own and it can activate itself when the conditions are proper. You begin to get into this area where you think it's "spontaneous" because you're not the activator, you didn't call the name and give the address, it just appeared. So that's the first situation. The spontaneous appearance of the program means that it has enough energy *above the use threshold* so it can enter your consciousness "as if an alien entity."

10. *P_0 can create an external reality agent.*

Artists know this one. It can also create an e.r. agent in someone else by being transferred to him/her, being activated enough and being fed back to you.

* G. Spencer Brown, *Laws of Form.*

11. *P_0 can program an external reality agent.*

In other words it may have elements in it that allow you to program somebody else for something else. Or another kind of e.r. agent, other than artistic, is people in general, but also it's animals, children, carpentry, anything that's outside, where you are creating something that's now feeding–back to you. If you have an e.r. agent who has programmatic capabilities, the program can do the programming.

12. *P_0 can have any thinkable, feelable or actionable content.*

13. *P_0 can identify with P_1, P_2 and so forth to P sub n.*

In other words, some programs are chameleons and they apparently change their name and address as if they are another program. Until you investigate P_2 you may not recognize it as your old friend P_0, with a cover story. A lot of psychoanalysis is based on this. It's a matter of taking the cover stories off the P_1 and P_2 and recognizing older P_0 behind them.

14. *P_0 can increase, remain the same, or decrease in the following parametric regions: its contained energy, its capability or strength; its power and its reinforcement.*

I am not going to explain reinforcement yet because it will explain itself as we go further.

15. *Until reinforced positively (+) or negatively (−), or plus/minus (+/−), or both (±), neutral reinforcement, no P_0 is important.*

This is a very important statement. In other words, you have latent programs, literally hundreds of thousands of latent programs, undeveloped sitting around inside somewhere. Until one of those receives either a positive or negative or neutral charge it's not activated. In fact, it's very difficult to store P_0 without some kind of reinforcement. So the fact that no P_0 is important until reinforced is a very important point; you can read a program in somebody's book and it'll go by like nothing at all and until you exert some effort and give it positive or negative or neutral energy, it's not going to go anywhere. It's just going to sit there as an "outside latent program" in the e.r. or i.r. If you want to get it inside as a latent program, you have to cross the reinforcement barrier. There is an impedance to storing programs. It's a higher barrier in some people than in others. The old concept of suggestibility comes in here. Some people will take on any program; in other words, they are highly suggestible, which can be a downer or upper. I would rather say they have a talent for taking on programs.

16. *P_0's position on the priority list (the priority list itself is a program) is a function of the amount of reinforcement on P_0.*

In other words, that which you considered to be the most important is that which has most reinforcement attached to it.

You can see there is a lot of slop here in these definitions, because the latent program that was stored with a lot of energy is one that can come out very easily at a low activation threshold, because it already has energy stored on it, associated with it, in the unconscious latency that it's sitting in.

You have to learn what your own priority list is. Your priority list is not something you arbitrarily sit down, construct and assign programs to; you have to find out what the structure of it is by investigating it; usually you'll get some shockers when you find this out. What you thought consciously to be the most important thing turns out not to be, it's something else.

Remember No. 13: *P_0 can identify with P_1, P_2, P_n* and so on. So the names that are in your priority list have to be investigated. They may be just cover stories, so you'll have *two priority levels*. One of them is the true priority the way they actually operate. Somebody watching you from the outside who is objective and knows you well can lay out your priority list as it seems to operate in the outside world. You can compare that with your own aware priority list. As you know in any dyad, i.e., coupled relationship, there are some shockers to be found. (Toni every so often brings up cases in which I suddenly realize that I have arbitrarily defined some things as unimportant, but I act as if they are important, and vice versa.)

17. *Any P_0 may be reinforced, positively $(+)$, negatively $(-)$, negative/positive $(-/+)$, or positive–negative $(+/-)$ and neutral $(\pm)$ and so forth.*

You can take any program and make it important by overvaluing it in the positive sense or by decrying it, denigrating it in the negative sense. This makes it automatically important. Or in the neutral sense in dispassionate, objective thinking.

18. *Each program, P_0, may control/be controlled.*

This means that every program is in feedback relationship to every other program. On one side if you look at it, it's being controlled by a whole set of other programs, and then if you look at the other side of it, the output side, you'll see it's controlling other programs.

19. *All P_0's in a given biocomputer (B.C.) are in the B.C.'s P_0–network of P_0's, connected/disconnected.*

Connected programs versus disconnected programs we'll take up in a minute.

20. *The B.C. P_0–network includes programs that do connection and disconnection of other programs and also deal with connected and disconnected programs.*

We probably should put an "as if" in front of "connected and disconnected" because in reality *all programs are connected.* One may play the game "I am going to disconnect (P_0)n 'the nth P_0' from all other programs and I'm going to isolate it and allow it to program others or be programmed by others." This is called "repression" and as Freud knew and showed many years ago, that act of repression, "disconnection," does anything but disconnect it; all it does is disconnect it from you and your conscious use of it. It remains connected and remains active and reinforced and continues to operate, in spite of your denial of its existence.

21. *A P_0 connected/disconnected can become conscious.*

That is, separate from activation. Activation does not necessarily imply consciousness and that's important. Consciousness and activation are two separate parameters. In other words, programs can be activated and be operating and you are not aware of them. Thank God this is true, otherwise we'd have to think out every step we take in any P_0.

22. *A conscious P_0 can become unconscious and remain connected/ disconnected.*

No. 23 summarizes the above.

23. *Connection/disconnection, identification/disidentification, conscious/unconscious, control/controlled, creation/destruction and so forth are each independent variables, independent parameters, are free/slaved of one another.*

That's a mouthful; study it carefully.

24. *Any degree of independence/dependence can be a property of P_0.*

That's a definition of its relationship to you and to any other P_0.

25. *Once stored after negative reinforcement, P_0 is "as if necessary for survival" in its area (its area of influence, in other words).*

This is a statement straight from childhood. The baby sticks its finger in the candle flame, screams with pain and from that point on he has a negative reinforcement on *whatever he selects of the experience.* He may select candles in general, flames in general, heat in general, light in general, persons present, whatever. His little biocomputer (after the powerful negative reinforcement) makes some aspect of the area of that particular program necessary for survival. You are never sure what the program is because the child can't tell you, you have to deduce this later from its behavior.

26. *Once stored after positive reinforcement, P_0 is necessary for pleasure in its area.*

You see this most simply with the phenomena of falling in love, where you have a positive reinforcement of another person and that person becomes, or may become, necessary for your sexual pleasure, just to take a very narrow channel kind of result. This is maybe also true, after your first acid trip. You've had a great trip and it's all positively reinforced—so from that point on you say acid is groovy, it's a sacrament and you go out and try to sell everybody on the idea of acid trips. You've got a lot of positive reinforcement from the chemical contract and it may become necessary for pleasure in that area.

26a. *After neutral reinforcement P_0 may become necessary for integration in its areas of influence.*

27. *Strongly reinforced programs tend to repeatedly become activated and used.*

After you've lost your virginity you tend to go back to sexual intercourse again, or masturbation, or whatever. These are strongly reinforced because they happen to fit into systems that are easily reinforced in the built-in structure of the C.N.S.*

28. *A program (P_0) can be defined for local use as anything.*

Here we have a set of alternates to the use of the term program. A program can be defined for local use as a *process/nonprocess, a belief/disbelief.* Belief and disbelief are both programmatic and that's hard to remember. If you *disbelieve* in occult powers, for example, you are just as much being programmed as if you *believe* in them. The alternates continue: *a thought/nonthought, feeling/nonfeeling, action/nonaction, concept/non–concept, entity/nonentity, zero or infinity, any number including real, imaginary and hyper–numbers, function/system/structure/form/substance, real/unreal, true/untrue,*

---

* Patanjali said, *"sukhanusayi ragah,"* attachment to attraction, results from pleasure (Book II, sutra 7); and *"duhkhanusayi dvesah,"* attachment to repulsion, results from pain (*Yoga-sutras of Pantanjali,* Book 11, sutra 8).

simulation/nonsimulation, as if/as if not, and so forth.

So local custom says a program is any important concept that you want to put in here.

A P_0 can be defined in any way that you wish to define it.

You can't use this P_0 until you start it. This is the set of directions for starting itself. In the province of the mind this is just part of the navigation and piloting instructions.

29. *Any of the psychoactive chemicals can act as P_0.*

The first six in this group are very important in the sense that we are making distinctions here that people fail to make usually when they go into the tank. People who have read the *Human Biocomputer* will come along and say, "Oh boy, that tank really is something," and they lay a program on the tank. "I am going to go do what John Lilly did in the tank," so they get into the tank for an hour and they say, "Nothing happened." Why didn't anything happen? They thought the tank was an e.r. agent with the program in it and so it was automatically going to be activated. They forgot that they have to create P_0 or it has to be created; it has to be stored; that's where they flunked out on the book, they didn't store the book. They thought they stored the book, but as my publisher says, you don't store a book until you have read it five times. Even then you may reject it. You can play back some things but they're not programs yet because they can't be activated; so with the repetition, reading the book five times you can strengthen P_0 and you can also weaken it. The parts of the book you don't like you can weaken so you begin to enhance the contrast by strengthening parts and weakening others. As P_0 gains strength, parts of it can pass the threshold of use and that's what people forget, that they haven't stored it, they haven't reinforced, and they haven't activated it to the point where it is useful. A cookbook teaches you how to get all the materials together and combine them in a certain way, but it doesn't tell you what it is going to taste like, or motivate you to try a recipe.

30. I_0 is identical with a P_0.

In other words, you (I_0) are a program generated in your biocomputer. The i.r. agent known as I_0 is also a P_0. When I_0 is not being a P_0 one is in Merrell–Wolff's state of being of "consciousness without an object." There are no P_0's left. (See State No. 5, Table 2, Appendix II, *Deep Self*.)

The physical programs are very important. I think you can pick all kinds of neurophysiological examples of autorhythmic programs. Our walking, running, sitting, standing, speaking, are all automatic programs that we can call upon. These are the tapeloops that we can compose into metaprograms.

(I want to point out to you that each of these statements will not mean anything to you until you've got it stored and you can reactivate it. When you do that you will find that each of these statements has a profound effect on your whole biocomputer. It's like dropping a stone into a pond, the waves that go out from a statement like "P_0 can identify with P_1, P_2 or P_n." "Any or all of your programs can identify with any or all of your other programs" won't mean anything to you until you watch it happen.)

The biocomputer itself has a lot more in it than we can conceive. Conscious mind is not capable of holding all of the rest of it in consciousness: there isn't enough machinery. The efficient way for the machinery to operate is to make 99 percent of it unconscious and keep consciousness for the Self–programming aspects, the experiencing aspects. The illusion of free will is pure white noise, which contains all possible messages: our choice is manufactured "certainty" in the midst of indeterminacy in the long term.

References for Chapter Nine

1. Small, Maurice H. April, 1900. "On Some Psychical Relations of Society and Solitude." *Pedagogical Seminary*, VII, No. 2.

Solitary Sailors

2. Slocum, Captain Joshua. 1948. *Sailing Alone Around the World*. Rupert Hart–Davis, London.
3. Ellam, Patrick, and Colin Mudie. 1953. *Sopranino*. W. W. Norton and Co., Inc., New York.
4. Bombard, Dr. Alain. 1953. *The Voyage of the Hérétique*. Simon and Schuster, New York.
5. Merrien, Jean. 1954. *Lonely Voyagers*. G. P. Putnam's Sons, New York.
6. Merrien, Jean. 1954. *Les Navigateurs Solitaires*. Editiones Denoel.
7. Bernicot, Louis. 1953. *The Voyage of Anahita—Single–Handed Round the World*. Rupert Hart–Davis, Soho Square, London.

Drastic Degrees of Stress

8. Gibson, Walter. 1953. *The Boat*. Houghton Mifflin Company (The Riverside Press), Boston, Massachusetts.

Living in the Polar Night

9. Scott, J. M. 1953. *Portrait of an Ice Cap with Human Figures*. Chatto and Windus, London.
10. Courtauld, A. July, 1932. "Living Alone Under Polar

Conditions." *The Polar Record,* No. 4. University Press, Cambridge.

11. Byrd, Richard E. 1938. *Alone.* G. P. Putnam's Sons, New York.

12. Ritter, Christiane. 1954. *A Woman in the Polar Night.* E. P. Dutton and Co., Inc., New York.

Forced Isolation and Confinement

13. Burney, Christopher. 1952. *Solitary Confinement.* Coward–McCann Inc., New York.

14. Stypulkowski, Z. 1951. *Invitation to Moscow.* Thames and Hudson, London.

The Deaf and the Blind

15. Collingswood, Herbert W. 1923. "Adventures in Silence." *The Rural New Yorker,* New York.

16. Ormond, Arthur W., C.B.E., F.R.C.S. 1925. "Visual Hallucinations in Sane People." *British Med. J.,* Vol. 2.

17. Bartlet, J. E. A. 1951. "A Case of Organized Visual Hallucinations in an Old Man with Cataract, and Their Relation to the Phenomena of the Phantom Limb." *Brain,* Vol. 74, Part III, pp. 363–373.

Experimental Isolation

18. Heron, W., W. H. Bexton, and D. O. Hebb. August, 1953. "Cognitive Effects of a Decreased Variation to the Sensory Environment." *The Amer. Psychol.,* Vol. 8, No. 8, p.366.

References for Chapter Ten

1.   Lilly, J. C., "Effects of Physical Restraint and of Reduction of Ordinary Levels of Physical Stimuli on Intact, Healthy Persons," in *Illustrative Strategies for Research on Psychopathology in Mental Health,* Symposium No. 2, Group for the Advancement of Psychiatry, New York, 1956.

2.   Lilly, J. C., "Mental Effects of Reduction of Ordinary Levels of Physical Stimuli on Intact, Healthy Persons," *Psychiatric Research Reports* 5, American Psychiatric Assoc., Washington, D.C. 1–28, June, 1956.

3.   Heron, Woodburn, "The Pathology of Boredom," *Scientific American,* 196:52–56, 1957.

4.   Bennett, A. M. H., Personal communication.

5.   Lilly, J. C., "Some Considerations Regarding Basic Mechanisms of Positive and Negative Types of Motivations," *Am. J. Psychiat.,* December, 1958.

Bibliography

Ashby, W. R., *Design for a Brain: The Origin of Adaptive Behavior,* 2nd ed., Halsted Press, New York, 1960.

Ballantyn, J. R., and G. S. Deva, *The Yoga–Sutras of Pantanjali,* Lawrence Verry, Inc.; Connecticut, 1960.

Brown, G. Spencer, *Laws of Form,* The Julian Press, Inc., New York, 1972. (See also, James Keys, pseudonym.)

Castaneda, Carlos, *The Teachings of Don Juan: A Yaqui Way of Knowledge,* Simon and Schuster, New York, 1968; and A Touchstone Book, published by Simon and Schuster, New York, 1973.

———, *A Separate Reality: Further Conversations with Don Juan,* Simon and Schuster, New York, 1971; and A Touchstone Book, published by Simon and Schuster, 1972.

———, *Tales of Power,* Simon and Schuster, New York, 1974; and A Touchstone Book, published by Simon and Schuster, New York, 1975.

Keys, James, *Only Two Can Play This Game,* The Julian Press, Inc., New York,1972.

Lilly, John C., *The Center of the Cyclone,* Bantam Books, New York, Toronto, London, 1972, 1973, and The Julian Press, Inc., New York, 1972.

———, *Lilly on Dolphins: Humans of the Sea,* Anchor–Doubleday, New York, 1975.

———, "Mental Effects of Reduction of Ordinary Levels of Physical Stimuli on Intact, Healthy Persons," *Psychiatric Research Reports* 5, American Psychiatric Association, Washington, D.C., pp. 1–9, 1956.

———, *Programming and Metaprogramming in the Human Biocomputer,* Bantam Books, New York, 1974, and The Julian Press, Inc., New York, 1972.

———, *Simulations of God: The Science of Belief,* Bantam Books, New York,

1976, and Simon and Schuster, New York, 1975.

————, and Antonietta Lilly, *The Dyadic Cyclone: The Autobiography of a Couple,* Simon and Schuster, New York, 1976.

————, and Jay T. Shurley, "Experiments in Solitude, in Maximum Achievable Physical Isolation with Water Suspension, of Intact Healthy Persons," Symposium, USAF Aerospace Medical Center, San Antonio, Texas, 1960, in *Psychophysiological Aspects of Space Flight,* Columbia University Press, New York, pp. 238–247, 1961.

Merrell–Wolff, Franklin, *Pathways Through to Space,* The Julian Press, Inc., New York, 1973.

————, *The Philosophy of Consciousness Without an Object: Reflections on the Nature of Transcendental Consciousness,* The Julian Press Inc., New York, 1973.

Monroe, Robert A., *Journeys Out of the Body,* Doubleday, New York, 1971.

Suedfeld, Peter, "The Benefit of Boredom: Sensory Deprivation Reconsidered," *American Scientist,* vol. 63, No. 1, pp. 60–69, January–February, 1975.

Wittgenstein, Ludwig, *Tractatus Logico–Philosophicus,* Routledge & Kegan Paul, Ltd., London, 1971.